RUSCH
TO GLORY

RUSCH
TO GLORY

ADVENTURE, RISK & TRIUMPH
ON THE PATH LESS TRAVELED

REBECCA RUSCH
with Selene Yeager

Boulder, Colorado

3002 Sterling Circle, Suite 100
Boulder, Colorado 80301-2338 USA
(303) 440-0601 · Fax (303) 444-6788 · E-mail velopress@competitorgroup.com

Distributed in the United States and Canada by Ingram Publisher Services

Library of Congress Control Number: 2014946296
IBSN: 978-1-937715-25-0

For information on purchasing VeloPress books, please
call (800) 811-4210, ext. 2138, or visit www.velopress.com.

This paper meets the requirements of ANSI/NISO Z39.48-1992
(Permanence of Paper).

Interior design and composition by Heidi Carcella
Photo retouching by Paula Gillen

Text set in Warnock Pro

14   15   16 / 10   9   8   7   6   5   4   3   2   1

For everyone who's ever thought, *That looks amazing, but I could never . . .* these stories are for you. I believe you can. I'm living proof of that. And I hope you enjoy the trying as much as I have.

CONTENTS

FOREWORD

My most memorable impression of Rebecca Rusch came in Morocco, during the 1998 Eco-Challenge. In the competition, we asked that four-person teams race through the rugged Atlas Mountains, carrying all their own food and water, and often sleeping just an hour a night. As you can imagine, competitors were forced to push their mental, physical, and emotional limits in order to succeed. Many racers later told me that they found the Eco-Challenge to be a true judge of their character, simply because in the face of such severe hardship they found out what they were truly made of. Several of my later television programs, such as *Survivor* and even *The Apprentice*, put competitors in similar situations, but nowhere did this play out more radically than in Eco-Challenge.

Night was falling at Checkpoint 11 during that 1998 Eco. It was the last stop before a long and dangerous rappel into a gorge near the town of Tinghir. But there was a problem: One team was lost and had not been seen or heard from for more than 12 hours. Team Rubicon had somehow misread its maps and could have been anywhere within the steep crags and canyons. I was personally leading the search party by helicopter. As the hours passed and darkness would soon require that we suspend the search, I became more and more frustrated. But just when all seemed lost, the men and women of Team Rubicon limped into the checkpoint, safe and sound.

With most teams, that would have been the end of it. After marching off course for more than 12 hours, they would either quit the race or sleep until morning before attempting something so daring as a thousand-foot rappel down a sheer cliff face in the dark. Once it became clear that Rubicon had no intention of quitting, I demanded that they halt for the night. Clearly, there were severe safety issues at stake. Each and every member of the team was exhausted. You could see it in their body language and in their eyes—pure, utter, bone-deep fatigue.

I expected that Team Rubicon would welcome my decision. In fact, each member of the team was obviously relieved that I demanded they sleep before pushing on.

Every member except one.

Rebecca Rusch took charge, insisting that she and her teammates be allowed to choose their own competitive path. By resting for the night, she argued, they would fall even farther behind the competition.

I argued back. As the television cameras caught the moment so vividly, I told her that she was being foolish and perhaps risking her life. And at what cost? It was clear that Team Rubicon would not win the race. Why press on when the most sane thing to do would be to sleep and wake up to start fresh?

But that's what makes Rebecca Rusch such a special individual. Many of us pay lip service to the concept of pushing our mental, physical, and emotional limits, but that notion is more than just a mere concept to Rebecca. In a world that all too often settles for mediocrity and conformity, Rebecca knows that the secret to success is being your best in all you do. And once you establish that baseline, you push through it.

Again, and again, and again. Never settling. Never resting on her laurels. Never once striving to be anything but her best.

Within these pages you will learn how Rebecca does this, and how you can do it too. You will read these words and be inspired. What you do next is up to you. Perhaps it is enough right now that you hold this very special book in your hands, knowing that a great adventure is about to unfold—one that will at the very least make for a very entertaining read, and at the very most may change your life for the better.

I relented that night in Morocco. Team Rubicon was allowed to bash on into the fading light. But I sent a team of mountain guides to follow behind, just to ensure that they were in capable hands.

They were, thanks to Rebecca. And now, so are you.

Mark Burnett
Los Angeles, California
July 2014

PREFACE

For years, my friends and colleagues told me I should write a book. I was flattered and intrigued, but reluctant. I felt that I didn't have the skill, an acclaimed name, or anything relevant to say, and that writing about my accomplishments would come off as egotistic. Also, I figured I'd likely never have the fortitude to make a project this big happen. But when VeloPress approached me with the same suggestion, I sheepishly admitted that I had turned over the idea in my head a few times: I *do* have some really good stories, after all.

A willing publisher and support from fellow racer and writer Selene Yeager was the invitation I needed to nudge me to finally dive in. All I had to do was say yes and they would guide me through the process. My career has been a long, hard push to pitch, sell, and convince sponsors, partners, and teammates that I was worth the risk and that my unusual path was a worthy one. But here was this next challenge coming to me on a silver platter. I was not accustomed to this kind of presentation, but I knew it would be foolish to pass it up.

My original intent for this book was to use my experiences to create a tool kit people could use to go beyond their own perceived limits, as athletes and as people. Through the difficult process of researching and mulling over life's lessons, the book took an unexpected change in course. I came to realize that simply relating my personal stories and experiences was the best way for me to expose my struggles alongside my triumphs. This book chronicles my strengths and weaknesses, my highs and lows in the context of my own adventures as a professional athlete. During this tough writing journey, I realized that we're all wired to learn and grow through experience, and experience connects us to the world and the people around us. I sincerely hope there's something in my story that will resonate with you and give you a nudge to chase your own dreams.

Writing this book has been one of the biggest, scariest, most intimidating challenges I've ever tackled. Over the course of this project I've had to trust, collaborate, and ask for more help than I imagined. I hope that many hands will thumb through these pages and many hearts will be touched and inspired by these stories. Even if that doesn't happen, I will remind myself that the biggest rewards in life come from hard work and commitment and are often not the payoff that was expected. I have a feeling this is one of those situations.

ACKNOWLEDGMENTS

This collection of stories would not have been possible without the cast of characters who helped shape me and were my partners in crime on this journey. There are so many of you who have inspired me, pushed me, laughed and cried with me, and even pissed me off, but it made me stronger, and I'm eternally grateful for your continued tutelage.

Patrick Harper, we are bonded for life as adventure racing teammates and friends. Thanks for letting me follow your compass around the world and for picking me up when no one else would.

Chris Kalous, thank you for getting my feet off—way off—the ground and showing me an entirely different view of the world.

Donna Forst, thank you for being my first, last, and only best friend.

Greg Springer, thank you for teaching me that power tools don't care and for assisting me in getting the wheels to my freedom truck rolling.

And to Mom and my sister, Sharon, thank you for never questioning my choices, at least not to my face, and for never pushing me to get a "real" job.

This book would still be a curious thought in my head if it weren't for the solid vote of confidence and kick in the ass to make it reality from Renee Jardine, Haley Berry, Faith Marcovecchio, and Dave Trendler at VeloPress. And Selene Yeager, I'm not sure how you did it, but you pulled things out of my head that I didn't know were there and made sense of my chaotic thoughts. Thank you all for your patience and for being devoted teammates on one of the toughest journeys I've taken. I'm so glad we're on the other side of it now!

To all of the professional writing friends who put up with my late-night, desperate e-mails and offered numerous pep talks, your expertise and understanding were a buoy for me to hold onto when I felt like I was drowning in words. You know who you are, Marty Dugard, Greg Fisher, Kathy Bedell, Shea Andersen, Biju Thomas, and Allen Lim.

Finally the biggest thanks of all to Greg Martin, who has cleaned snot off my face, taught me to ride a bike, put up with my insecurities, listened to my laments, and been there for me at all of the important finish lines in my life, including this one.

INTRODUCTION

The Wild Ride

Over the course of my career as a professional athlete, I've repeatedly had to reinvent myself in the face of fear and uncertainty. Never was that more true than in the fall of 2005. I was enjoying the golden years of a successful career in adventure racing, and though I was methodically completing my firefighter and EMT training during my downtime in my adopted hometown of Ketchum, Idaho, I wasn't quite ready to walk away from being a professional athlete. But when Montrail, my most prominent sponsor, called to say the company had been sold and their sponsorships would be shut down, it looked like I wasn't going to have the luxury of choosing my own exit.

Just like that, a 10-year span of world travel, team management, and expedition competition was over. When the dust settled, I had just one sponsor remaining. Instead of cutting me loose, the team at Red Bull said, "Find something amazing to do." It was in this big bang of opportunity that my professional mountain biking career took shape.

The average American changes jobs around 11 times in the course of his or her professional life. I certainly fit that statistic. I've worked as a marketing associate, aerobics instructor, limo driver, barista, outdoor guide, climbing-gym manager, motivational speaker, construction worker, firefighter, and professional athlete. These days most people know me as a professional cyclist and assume my world championships and Leadville wins were years in the making. But the truth is, I didn't become a professional mountain biker until I was 38 years old, and I didn't win the Leadville Trail 100 MTB—the most prestigious mountain bike race in the United States, if not the world—for the first time until I was 40.

Ironically, I will likely be most remembered for a sport I initially loathed. Long before members of the media christened me "the world's greatest female endurance cyclist," I hated racing a mountain bike. It was the bitter pill I had to swallow in order to participate in the sport I *did* enjoy: adventure racing. Even after racing on two wheels became my paycheck, I still didn't love it and honestly was not very good at it. Being on a mountain bike made me feel clumsy and outmatched. I crashed, chickened out, cried, and ran an awful lot in my first races, and even now, though I certainly have the fitness and endurance to compete and win, I still struggle with the technical aspects of the sport. It wasn't too long ago that I was so physically and mentally broken trying to navigate a river of rocks in a race in Pennsylvania that I picked up my bike and hurled it as far as I could while I shouted expletives into the woods. This was the very same bike I would pilot to a record-smashing victory at Leadville just three months later.

Time heals all wounds, and a bruised ego eventually recovers too. Along with skill and experience came a new appreciation for mountain biking and eventually a deep, lasting love. What was once my nemesis became my primary outlet for adventure and joy. The bike relaunched

my career and ultimately turned into my ticket to a steady paycheck—
or at least as steady as they come for a professional athlete.

I'd like to think that the millions of miles I've covered by foot,
boat, bike, and even by camel have earned me an honorary PhD in
how to get through life. When I found myself clinging to El Capitan,
more than 3,000 feet off the deck with nowhere to go but up, I learned
a little something about finishing what I started. Nursing a sick teammate back to health from heatstroke and dehydration in Vietnam as
one of the biggest races on earth slid from my grasp changed how I
think about patience and failure. After river-boarding the Grand Canyon unsupported in winter, standing on the other side of what seemed
an impossible challenge, I knew for certain that limits are much farther
in the distance than we imagine.

All of these adventures, journeys, challenges, and explorations
have allowed me to see the beauty and wonder of places I never knew
existed. I've been touched and enriched by the people who inhabit these
corners of the world. Through it all, I've come to a deeper understanding of who I am, what motivates me, and what I'm passionate about.
I've been able to step outside of my comfort zone to do some scary
stuff. I've failed and succeeded, but nearly every time, I've arrived at the
finish line a better person. My formula is simple: Say yes to opportunities, ask a lot of questions, and then dive in.

I never in a million years imagined I'd become a professional athlete. I thought athletes were born just how I saw them on TV: fit and
ambitious, somehow divinely destined to be standing there, hoisting
broken finish line tape and trophies over their heads. After all, they'd
been dealt a fistful of athletic aces in the game of life and they were
simply playing their hand. Having lived it, I can tell you that professional athletes are just regular people who've followed a passion with
intense determination. As in any career, a professional athlete must
do the hard work, endure setbacks, and make sacrifices. So while you

might look at my life now and think I'm just another pro who was groomed for glory, once you know the whole story, you'll realize that we have more in common than you might think.

Finding Myself at the Finish Line

I t all started with a tracksuit.

Being the typical younger sibling, all I wanted to do was hang out with my sister, Sharon, and her high school friends. Carol was my sister's best friend and our next-door neighbor. She was tall, thin, and energetic, and she had an awesome tracksuit with block lettering boldly proclaiming "Downers Grove North" across the chest. With a drawstring at the waist and elastic at the ankles, the thick cotton pants ballooned into a silhouette only MC Hammer or a paratrooper could love. It was the early 1980s, I was 14, and I had to have a tracksuit like Carol's. "Join the cross-country team," she told me. "They give you one for free, and if you're a runner, you'll never get fat." It was music to my ears. My own family tree was more oak than willow. Even though I tipped the scales at around 95 pounds, I figured if I didn't do something, I was destined to get fat, so I promptly enlisted in organized sports.

I was a tomboy at heart, but I had never thought about joining a team until Carol told me about cross-country. Growing up, I had

Barbies and other dolls, but I loved to play outside with the boys and come home dirty and scraped up. I lived for the camping and skiing trips Mom took us on a couple of times every year. Back at home, I'd find my own adventures camping in the backyard with my sister or racing around the block playing tag with the other neighborhood kids. I got a charge out of getting sweaty and out of breath, feeling my heart pounding after riding my Huffy up the hill on our street. But as a girl about to enter high school, the games and adventures I found exhilarating as a kid were replaced with social pressures of what to wear, how to fit in, and how you looked. So it wasn't the allure of camaraderie or crossing a glorious finish line that prompted me to enlist in organized sports upon entering high school—it was a cotton tracksuit and a blossoming weight complex.

WE LIVED ON A QUAINT brick street in the suburbs of Chicago. Normal as that might sound, I didn't exactly grow up in a traditional family. My father, a U.S. Air Force captain, was shot down in Laos in 1973. My parents were divorced by that point, and I was too young to fully comprehend his death or the factors that contributed to it. People often asked me about my dad, and I'd respond mechanically, "He was shot down in the Vietnam War," and that would quickly end the conversation. It never occurred to me that I was missing out on having a dad—I had no reference to make me feel sad about it.

My mom, Judy, made the arduous daily commute into Chicago. After graduating summa cum laude with a math degree, she landed a job in the computer industry, where she worked her way from programmer to the upper ranks of management. As a woman in a predominantly male profession in the 1970s and one of the only women at the top, she was a pioneer. She had to be tough and work more diligently than most of her male coworkers to prove her worth.

Mom didn't have to talk to us about hard work and dedication; she lived it. Whether it was riding the train 45 minutes each way to watch a track meet or staying up until 2 a.m. to bake cookies for my class, she continually stretched herself to meet traditional expectations while also being the breadwinner and disciplinarian. She was supportive, but she was also tough, never the doting mother. She was independent and efficient because she had to be, and my sister and I learned to be that way too.

With my mom working long, unpredictable hours, Sharon and I were left to our own devices in the afternoons and evenings. I was notorious for losing the house key, so Sharon would elect me to break in through the basement window. I'd shimmy through the tiny opening, hang from the sash by my fingers, drop a few feet onto the cement floor, and then claw through the cobwebs in the dark and dash up the stairs to turn on the lights. It was always tempting to wait a while before unlocking the front door for Sharon. Once we were in, we'd raid the fridge, concocting some pretty crazy after-school snacks. For those times when we weren't opting for a "sensible" dinner—frozen entrées or peanut butter and jelly sandwiches—we would simply eat ice cream or cheese and crackers for dinner.

Despite being a good student and having a loving, if irregular home life, I started to feel overwhelmed with anxiety about pretty much everything—my family, my mom's job, school, my body, what to wear, making friends—and I felt very alone. I didn't think it was something my mom or sister or any of my friends dealt with, so I bottled up the stress until it reached the point where I had to find an outlet: I'd stuff down a jar of peanut butter or whatever was in the house. The momentary satisfaction of eating was soon displaced by the guilt and disgust I felt toward myself, so I'd go to the bathroom and purge myself of whatever I'd eaten.

The vicious cycle continued on and off throughout much of high school and college until one night my mom heard me vomiting in the bathroom and confronted me. We were both really upset, and the words didn't come easily. I was embarrassed and ashamed. Mom was shocked, confused, and felt like she had failed as a parent. Once we calmed down a little, Mom said, "We have to sort this out, but it's bigger than me." She arranged some one-on-one and family counseling at our church. In one of the sessions, Mom admitted to worrying about a raise that hadn't gone through at work and the resulting financial strain of raising a family as a single parent. This was heavy stuff for me and my sister. Mom had worked so hard to take care of everything and shield us from the stress in her life. So much so that when I ran up against my own problems and insecurities, I felt confused and alone, with no one to turn to. When I was finally able to open up about the important issues in my life, it felt like throwing off a heavy blanket that had been suffocating me for years. Other people were sad, depressed, scared, and lost too. It was a revelation to find out that I was not alone in those emotions.

It was in the midst of all of this drama that running had entered my life. Looking back, I can say that running was essential in helping me break the cycle of bulimia. Sports became a healthy outlet for my stress and worries, and the team proved to be a supportive peer group. I knew that I needed to treat my body better. And it turned out I was pretty good at running. I was scrappy, didn't mind the hard work, and was extremely competitive with myself. The cross-country team led me to the track team, where I ran the 200, the 800, and the 1600, as well as 200 hurdles and the long jump. I excelled in the longer-distance events, but I dabbled in everything. The track team was a much bigger group of girls, so that meant fuller buses, bigger events, and an even larger group of friends. The variety was a blast, but it was cross-country running that really grabbed my soul. I liked the feel of the grass and leaves under my running cleats, and the fact that each course was different. I liked not knowing what was around the next turn. I was easily bored with the repetition of running in circles. I craved variety and a taste of adventure.

Sure, I liked the physical transformation as I flourished in running, but the psychological benefits were even better. I liked the discipline athletics was teaching me and the person it was helping me become. It was thrilling to discover how hard I could push myself. My bedroom was becoming littered with medals, trophies, and plaques—proof that I was good at something and publicly recognized for it.

I was also beginning to feel like a leader and developing lifelong bonds of friendship with my team. Though we ran individually, we were scored together. We cultivated a competitive energy that pushed us all to be better, and in the process we formed the unbreakable bond that accompanies a common goal and shared work.

Coach Ritter was a real father figure in my life—strict, yet gentle and reassuring. He didn't say much and didn't need to. He offered support and direction but also expected us to do the work and gave us the freedom to make a few mistakes on our own. Since I wasn't as experienced as a lot of the other runners, I'd often get frustrated with myself because my skill didn't match my desire. So he would spend extra time helping me with my technique and strategy, strengthening my work ethic along the way. He continually reminded me to not take myself too seriously, and he taught me how to win and lose with grace. It was the first glimpse of what I'd missed by not having a dad around.

Running was also where I learned about the bitter, lingering aftertaste of quitting. My senior year, I'd been sick during the week leading up to the regional cross-country meet, a qualifying event for the Illinois state championship. When the race was well under way, I found myself unable to keep up with the top girls and struggling mentally. There was nothing obviously wrong, but it was clear that I was not having a good race. Finally, I just stepped off the course, relieved to stop the pain. When the race ended and my teammates, mom, and coach all rushed over to see if I was okay, I had no answer for them—I'd simply given up, and in the process let everyone down. Without my points, the team's chances of qualifying for the state meet were in jeopardy. I was a quitter. Fortunately, other girls on my team had the races of their lives.

Going into the state meet two weeks later, I needed to get my head out of the way and run as I'd always run, but I didn't know how to go about it. The assistant coach sat me down and gave me a mantra to chant: *I can, I will, I won't be denied.* When the gun went off, I ran for the team and for myself, and I ran my heart out. I shook off my insecurities to earn individual all-state status, and we won the state title. I vowed to never quit a race again.

Three decades later, I still bear the scar from that day in Glenview, Illinois, when I stepped off the course. Should the notion of quitting ever enter my mind again, I would ask myself this: *Would you rather suffer now and finish this race, or quit—only to suffer through the process of explaining yourself to friends and family?* I've competed in a lot of races over the years, and the answer is almost always the same: The pain of quitting far outlasts the pain of pushing forward. I'd rather roll in dead last as volunteers are packing up the finish line (which happened to me in my first cross-country ski race) and have people think, *Look at that lady hanging in there. Good for her!* By lining up for a race, I'm making a commitment—to myself, my friends, my family, my teammates, my fans—to finish, no matter what place I'm in. I rise to the occasion when I remind myself that someone else is watching.

2

Running Away from Home

Unlike my sister, who'd known her career path since she was 10, I had absolutely no idea what I wanted to do with my life when it came time to go to college. The only thing I felt sure of was running. I thought I would choose a school with a good cross-country team. Regular training, goal setting, and the friendship and support of a team gave me real direction. When I was offered an academic scholarship to the University of Illinois at Urbana-Champaign, the seemingly life-changing decision became simple. U of I was a great school with a strong Big 10 running team. Even better, my education would be paid for. Choosing a major, on the other hand, was more difficult. Because the business school was well respected, I landed on business with a marketing focus since that came naturally and gave me the freedom to decide on anything more specific later.

I packed up and moved into the dorm with every intention of joining the track and cross-country teams as a walk-on athlete. Despite running varsity for four years in high school and ultimately ranking as an all-state athlete, I didn't for a moment expect to be a superstar on the college scene. I thought I could earn my spot if I worked hard. I knew I still needed guidance and support from a coach and a team to thrive. After all, the open arms and support I received in high school had brought out the best in me.

The coach let me join the team, but he proceeded to badger me to lose weight, telling me I was too heavy to be fast. Every Monday morning I had to provide a food diary for his scrutiny. He would take a highlighter and ceremoniously circle the things I had eaten that he deemed bad or excessive, such as pizza or a second bowl of cereal. But it wasn't just me; he used the same negative reinforcement to motivate the rest of the team too. As far as he was concerned, we were all overweight and slow. His domineering coaching style manifested an equally unproductive team dynamic; my teammates viewed each other not as supportive friends but as competition. Instead of providing the stability, focus, and confidence I was yearning for, running was tearing me down. Piled on top of my low self-esteem, a lingering eating disorder, and freshman-year homesickness, the situation was a recipe for disaster. I found myself wallowing in injury, dreading workouts, and not performing well. My psyche couldn't take the beating, and I quit the team during my freshman year.

So much for not quitting. It was a frustrating decision to walk away from a sport that was the best thing I'd ever known. I concentrated on my studies and dabbled in other sports in an attempt to stay active. I bought a road bike and tooled around alone in the cornfields surrounding the campus and beyond. But even with a big yellow Sony Walkman for company, cycling was too boring and solitary to be a replacement for running. It was a gloomy time.

At the start of my sophomore year, I knew I had to find something to fill the void and get me back on track. I went off campus in search of a free gym membership and a different, positive group dynamic. Even though it was a long shot, I applied for a job as an aerobics instructor. I lacked both experience and rhythm, but I followed instructions until I learned the moves and eventually loosened up a bit. Decked out in my neon body suit and tights, I cranked up the music and truly enjoyed motivating my class. We would all be sweating in unison to "Eye of the Tiger," doing moves like the grapevine and around the world. With the full-length mirrors and bright lights, it was a show as much as a work-out, and I was expected to have my hair properly poofed and my leg warmers coordinated with my leotard. My favorite part of the required uniform was the white high-top Reeboks with Velcro ankle closures. I proudly kept those shoes pristine and only wore them indoors with big, fluffy, colorful socks bunched over the tops. It was a surreal experience coming off my short-lived collegiate sports career, but it did provide a diversion and positive outlet, even if it didn't improve my musical taste. I respected the people who came into the gym day after day and worked hard to improve themselves—their discipline was contagious. My new team now consisted of gym rats, aerobics fanatics, and weight lifters.

AT THE END of my four years at U of I, I headed back to Chicago with a marketing degree in hand and no real plan. I loved athletics, and even thought I wasn't on a competitive team anymore, it was a social outlet and it inspired me to move. It was also how I fought off a negative body image and felt better about myself. High school running had saved me from an eating disorder and changed the trajectory of my life. I didn't want to go back to that insecure place. I knew sports would (and needed to) always play a role in my life, but I had no idea in what capacity. Becoming a pro athlete never entered my mind. I was just an average runner and aerobics instructor. I figured maybe I'd open a gym, become a sports promoter, or some combination of the two.

After scanning the job listings and sitting through my fair share of interviews, I took a position at a posh downtown health club. It was the sort of place where big-time executives and professional athletes worked out. The executives just seemed arrogant and rude, but I was a bit starstruck by the pro athletes, especially by their physical prowess and self-assured demeanor. I was in a whole new world, so I did my best to appear confident and do my job well, even if I was green and making things up as I went along. It was my first real job, and my manager was a bona fide chauvinist. Demanding, cocky, and cutthroat, he had me shaking in the stupid panty hose and skirt that I was required to wear. The staff walked on eggshells around him. Although I'd had very few male role models early in life, I'd also been somewhat insulated. In my naiveté, I'd fully believed chauvinistic men like my college track coach were far from common. My new manager set me straight on that fact, but I held my own, grew a bit more of a spine, and lasted much longer than the line of employees who came before me.

So there I was, working the desk at an exclusive health club, typing up member newsletters, putting flyers on the bulletin boards, signing in the likes of Michael Jordan, and gazing at the 100-foot indoor climbing wall that went right up the center of the eight-story facility. I'd never seen anything like it. All these hotshot climbers—mostly men—would come in, rope up, choose their routes and handholds, and propel themselves upward, Spider-Man style. You could stand on any of the levels and be eye-to-eye with the climbers as they labored and lunged for the next hold. Just beyond the wall, people were droning away on treadmills, going nowhere and working out just for the sake of working out, to avoid getting fat, or to fulfill a sense of obligation. I spent hours staring at that damn wall. In the middle of this concrete jungle, I witnessed people doing physical activity for the sheer love of the movement, and I wanted to rediscover that passion myself.

I began hanging out at the base of the wall with the climbers, who seemed more like my tribe than the treadmill or aerobics junkies. Because the gym was the only indoor climbing facility in Chicago at that time, these climbers scraped together their pennies for a membership and a chance to get their climbing fix in the big city. You could tell them apart from the rest of the membership by their baggy, faded Gramicci shorts and cotton tank tops. They had weathered backpacks instead of leather gym bags and wore Five Tens instead of Nikes, and they were just a little less polished and put together than the rest of the people who walked through the marble-tiled entryway. It was fitting that they hung out in the basement of the gym, away from all of the gym bunnies. But they liked it down there, and so did I. I felt more at home with that passionate climbing crowd than the super rich folks hanging out on the spa level.

My insecurity and intimidation were finally overshadowed by my desire to experience the thrill I saw in every climber's eyes when they were on the wall. I asked the guys down there for a lesson. Other than camping in the dirt as a kid, this was my first "outdoor" experience—on a giant, fiberglass indoor wall in Chicago. I only made it a short way up on my first attempt, but I was hooked. It was scary and exhilarating, and I loved every minute of it. The burn in my forearms seared, but as I stared upward, all I wanted to do was try to go higher. It was a gravitational pull in the opposite direction.

Dave, the climbing wall director, took me under his wing and introduced me to real outdoor rock climbing. Dave was a confident, good-looking climber who introduced me to the exhilaration of the outdoors. It's only natural that my enchantment with climbing was also rolled into an attraction toward him as well. We started dating, and they were the best dates ever: camping and climbing in Wisconsin, Michigan, and Illinois every weekend. We slept under the stars and spent our days on the rock face, far removed from the concrete canyons we returned to on Mondays.

Though I felt completely at home in the outdoors with dirt under my nails, I was not a natural rock climber by any stretch of imagination. Rock climbing was an unlikely sport for me, given that when I get nervous my hands sweat profusely and being off the ground petrified me. I counteracted this fear response by using a ton of chalk and continually trying to quiet my primal instincts with breathing and mental relaxation. Sometimes it worked, but more often it didn't, and the sweat and fear would take over.

I slowly made improvements and did my best to learn everything I could from my growing circle of climbing friends. The downside of surrounding yourself with skilled athletes is that you perpetually feel like you suck, even if you're not half bad. It wasn't so hard to learn the ropes (pun intended), but it took a while for me to feel confident taking the lead in rock climbing. I operated in the student role for a very long time because it was safe and easier. The transition from student to equal or student to teacher is complicated and a subtle, long-term shift. During my early climbing days, I didn't realize this evolution was happening as I meticulously gathered more experience and put in more time. I always felt like a rookie in comparison to the super-experienced climbers I hung out with, so it was a surprise to me when I realized I could stand on my own at the climbing crags without a mentor to hold my hand or the rope. It was exhilarating to make the transformation and finally plan my own climbing trip—choose the route, what gear I would take—and head out on the sharp end of the rope. When I made that transition, I wanted to take some women with me to perpetuate the cycle and share what I had discovered in this marvelous sport.

My first guinea pig was Donna Forst, an amazing, self-employed fashion stylist and New York City transplant who was living in a gigantic loft in a rough part of Chicago. She inhabited a world I knew little about, filled with fashion, art, photo shoots, music I'd never heard, and lots of black clothing. She would never have called herself athletic, but she wanted to stay healthy, so she'd joined the gym. Like mine, Donna's step aerobics days were doomed the moment she laid eyes on that indoor climbing wall. Donna really wanted to try climbing, but she just didn't want to put her "ass in a harness for all the club to see," as she put it. Admittedly, that was one of my hesitations early on too. Old insecurities die hard.

Eventually, Donna pushed past her anxiety and put her ass in that harness. She started hanging out at the base of wall with the climbing characters. There were very few women climbing, so she was spending a lot of time with Dave, and they became friends. Naturally, I thought she was angling for my boyfriend, so I responded in the typical, catty way by being less than friendly to her. One day, as we were both primping in the locker room mirror, she turned to me and said point-blank, "I'm not after your boyfriend. I have a tall, handsome boyfriend of my own who's an artist, so I'm not looking for another." She went on to tell me, "Someday, we'll definitely be good friends."

I was blindsided, and exhilarated. Here was a strong woman who spoke her mind and didn't want to compete with me. We were an unlikely pair, but we became fast friends and started climbing together. She wasn't a natural, but she loved the sense of freedom and the physical and cerebral challenge that climbing gave her. This was no step aerobics class.

Although I had put in plenty of time on rock faces with the guys, I never considered myself a true climber until I started taking Donna out with me. Over the course of many years, Donna and I would take on big adventures in Nevada, Wyoming, the Gunks in New York, and the big walls of Zion. It would be just the two of us on a great big cliff with all of our gear and a pink portaledge. (I've never loved pink, but gear is gear when it's on clearance.) We would often hear guys down below say, "Holy shit, I think it's two girls up there." We'd just laugh and exchange an amused glance.

As the more experienced of the two, I was responsible for us both. Donna was a very willing, hard-working student. She was used to being in charge, fearless in life; yet, she was quite timid on the rock. I was comfortable on a climb because I could see a path clearly laid out in front of me, but in life I was far less focused and confident in my direction. We pushed each other to be better and stronger by propping and building one another up. It was the beginning of a long friendship built on trust and support.

THE FURTHER I DELVED into climbing, the more I dreamed of staying longer at the cliffs. Weekend trips just weren't cutting it for me anymore. One afternoon as we were working at the wall, Dave asked what I thought about transferring to a new multimillion-dollar club that the company planned to open in California. As he turned away to help someone with a harness adjustment, I gave it some thought. I'd never had a deep attachment to Chicago or a sense of it as home. I'd always loved travel and exploration. If it didn't work out, I could always simply come back home. By the time he turned back around, I'd already made up my mind and said, "Let's do it."

We applied for and got the jobs in California. I would not be sorry to say goodbye to my boss at the Chicago club. Dave suggested we give our notice early and take three months off to travel across the country and climb along the way before starting our new lives out West. The prospect was positively thrilling. Of course we wouldn't be making any money, so there was some planning to do. We'd be camping and living out of my little red Acura Integra. I had squirreled away a little bit of money, so after some quick calculations, I once again said, "Hell yeah, let's do it." We set about planning our adventure, week by week, based on all the cool places we wanted to climb on the way to Southern California, including Utah, Yosemite, and even Idaho.

Those three months were a blur of driving, camping, and climbing. Maps, guidebooks and dirty gear littered the car. One morning, as I was making coffee and watching the sun rise over the towering red rock skyline and filter into the burnt-orange canyons of Moab, I had a revelation: People actually *live* here. You can do better than merely passing through or vacationing in magical places like this; you can stay forever. You can live anywhere, not just in a city or suburbs.

My nomadic fire was now fully stoked. Maybe I didn't want a traditional job after all. Maybe I could find a way to do this—travel, climb, see the world—and still make money. I carried that thought with me across the country. I was perfectly at home with only a few possessions, bathing in mountain streams, searching for the best camping spot or local coffee shop, wearing the same clothes every day, going to sleep with the stars overhead, and just living in the moment. I didn't want the trip to end.

I was greeted with another revelation when we got to California. I didn't have a job after all. As a result of some major miscommunication between the Chicago office and the California office, Dave had a job but the club had no idea who I was. Maybe it was my asshole boss getting in one final insult. It was devastating. This was not part of the plan. The hiring manager, feeling sorry for me, told me I could work in the laundry room. I suppose that was nice of him, but it really just freaked me out even more. I'm a Virgo: industrious, methodical, and efficient. While I felt drawn to the nomadic life, I had made a sustainable plan before we'd hit the road. What was I supposed to do without the security of a job?

I searched for work in the classifieds, found an apartment for the two of us, and got settled. My degree landed me a job as a barista at Starbucks in Laguna Beach. Aside from the obscenely early morning shifts and some exceptionally rude California commuters, it actually wasn't a bad gig. They offered health insurance to part-time employees, and it was a great place to meet people. It also didn't hurt that the shop was on the Pacific Coast Highway, so I could watch the waves crashing on the beach as I worked the counter. And I can still pull a mean espresso.

The Starbucks job was just a stopgap, and I soon set my sights on finding a job that fueled my passion. I decided to apply for an outdoor climbing instructor position with a local retailer and outfitter. As an indoor climber from the flatlands of the Midwest with less than two years of experience and no teaching background, I was an unlikely candidate. But what I *did* have was the passion and eagerness to learn. Against the odds, I was hired and became a real live outdoor climbing guide, which made me feel like maybe the whole gym debacle was a blessing in disguise. It was a dream job, and it would propel me even further into the counterculture of climbing. I was getting paid to sleep in the dirt, camp under the stars, and learn the tricks of the trade from some of the best climbers in the country.

This lifestyle fit me like a glove. Days and weeks were spent camping, climbing, and hanging out in Joshua Tree, Taquitz, and Yosemite. I adopted the uniform of Five Tens, Verve pants, baseball hat, and sunburn. My climbing gear was now getting that truly weathered look, and the pages of my California guidebooks were dog-eared and had check marks next to all of the routes I had ticked off. I fit into this community of dirt bags with ease. They were incredible athletes who were relaxed, welcoming, and loving life.

While I was thriving with my newfound freedom and sense of the unknown, Dave seemed to long for the routine and familiarity he'd left behind. Not long after we got settled, he decided to return to the Midwest. I knew I never would.

3

Facing My Fears

Although I had managed to find and create some opportunities back in Illinois that fueled my passion, arriving in Southern California felt like a rebirth. I mean, it was California, baby!—an endless summer vacation, where people bike everywhere, surf, climb, and wear shorts to work, sunglasses at night, and sundresses in winter. The sun, sea, and mountains create a gravitational pull, drawing people out of their houses and into the fresh air. SoCal had the same effect on me, though it was really the call of the massive rocks—places like Joshua Tree and Yosemite I'd only read about in books—that tugged at me. It was easy enough to escape the crowded city and head into the hills, where I could feel the dirt under my feet and smell the granite under my fingernails. For me, working as a rock climbing guide was like getting a corner office in a traditional line of work. My new job allowed me to immerse myself in a sport that I couldn't get enough of. Turns out, I was a pretty good teacher too: patient and understanding, but I also pushed students to challenge themselves just a little more than they thought they could. Witnessing the lights go on in their eyes as they reached the top of a climb was better than any monetary compensation I could receive. I could see myself doing this job for a very long time. As it turned out, guiding was a stepping stone to a new business venture that catapulted me into some of the most demanding and exhilarating moments of my life.

When presented with the opportunity to become part owner and manager of an innovative indoor climbing gym opening in California, I couldn't resist. This was nothing like the Chicago health club. Housed in a massive warehouse with 50-foot ceilings complete with cracks, overhangs, canyons, and interchangeable handholds, Rockreation was a climbers' paradise, built just when climbing was becoming more mainstream. I had saved some money and decided the $10,000 investment was a risk I wanted to take, so I made the first grown-up commitment of my life. I laid down all the money I had in the world, took my place at the helm of the Costa Mesa location, and got to work building the company.

In a start-up business you have to make tough choices every day. Sure, I had a boss, but for the first time in my young working career I was free to mold and shape a business as I saw fit. The responsibility and accountability pushed me, but I was thriving under the pressure. I hired and managed the staff, approved big purchases, and oversaw the budget, marketing, and day-to-day operations. To my disbelief I was actually using my business degree in a setting that I never envisioned possible. Sure, I still had to clean the toilets and stock the vending machine, but I was happy to do some of the dirty work because we were building something really cool. Rockreation was one of the country's first big indoor climbing gyms, a successful business model that grew to include three more facilities, and I was on the front end and a player in all of it.

Rockreation taught me the power of an introduction, and California had no shortage of amazing individuals to be introduced to. Bumping into movie stars, business tycoons, and famous artists was just another part of my new life. More important, I was meeting climbing royalty like Hans Florine, Peter Croft, John Long, and Lynn Hill. These luminaries expanded my athletic horizons beyond the walls of the gym. Trips to legendary locales such as Yosemite, Red Rocks, and Joshua Tree were fast becoming regular jaunts, and every trip further inspired my quest to climb bigger and better places.

On a trip to Rocky Mountain National Park in Colorado, I met another climbing connoisseur. Chris Kalous was a seasonal guide, and in the off-season he fully embraced the lifestyle of a climbing bum. He played guitar and wrote poetry, and his truck was his home, parked at the base of whatever crag inspired him. Chris relentlessly pursued his passions like no one I had ever met. Not just content to climb on the weekends or fit it in around his life, he instead made it his entire life. We immediately hit it off and hatched a plan to meet up for a multiday climbing trip on the sandstone cliffs just outside of Las Vegas. The month of waiting for the trip couldn't pass quickly enough. At Red Rocks, Chris ushered me up some of the biggest ascents I'd ever done and really opened my eyes to what was possible in both climbing and a relationship. I was completely smitten, and one passion fueled the other. I knew he had never climbed in California and was looking for more permanent work, so I dangled a carrot by offering him a job at Rockreation. His dynamic personality and world-class climbing skills would make him a stellar employee at the gym, but I'll be the first to admit I had ulterior motives. I wanted to open the door for our personal and climbing relationship to flourish.

In the years that followed, Chris took me on some of the most epic climbs of my life. The most memorable was our seven-day attempt to ascend Bermuda Dunes, a 27-pitch, 3,000-foot aid climb on the sheer face of Yosemite's El Capitan. This route is a pristine natural line up the tallest part of the southwest face of El Cap. Rated VI, 5.11c, A4, Bermuda Dunes saw its first ascent in 1984, but for whatever reason, it had not grabbed the attention of the summit chasers and had sat there unconquered for 20 years. If we were successful, we would grab the second ascent and I would nab the first female ascent.

I had grown into a really good climber at this point, good enough to be teaching people with enough cash how to climb, set up anchors, belay, and rappel, but I hadn't been climbing for all that long. I was a Midwestern girl, still wide-eyed with wonder over this new life, and I was especially green in the world of big-wall climbing. By attempting this route on El Cap, which is mecca for every accomplished big-wall climber, I would join the ranks of an elite group of climbers who graced the pages of the climbing magazines I pored over every month. Here I was, light-years out of my league, trying to make history and keep up with one of the best in the world, and Chris, in typical male fashion, was incredibly nonchalant and, as I saw it, overly confident about it. "C'mon let's just do it. Whatever happens, happens. I'll take the lead." I was scared to death to say yes, but I was also scared to say no. An opportunity like this might never come again. Would I regret it if I didn't go? I also didn't want to let him down. And I trusted him. I knew that whatever happened, he would take care of me and take control of the situation. No one I knew had more big-wall experience than he did, and I knew he cared about me as well.

Once our feet left the ground we toiled upward, lived, breathed, and slept on the wall for seven days and six nights. All of our equipment was either strapped to our bodies or stuffed into a gigantic, heavy haul bag that we called "the pig" and dragged up behind us. The contents of the pig included food, water, the sleeping ledge, clothing, climbing gear, a beer or two, and poetry that Chris would read to me. Once we got a day into our journey, we were 100 percent committed, since going down would have been just as arduous as going up. There was no turning back.

It was insanely frustrating and demoralizing at times. Normally on a big-wall climb you swap leads or at least try to take turns. But that only works if the climbers are of a similar skill level. We had selected this route because it was a good mix of really hard and easier pitches. Chris was taking all of the hard pitches, and I got all of the A1 pitches (the easiest rating for aid climbs). A1 was still my limit. When I did get out on lead, I kept getting stuck and having to shamefully come back down. Chris would take over and finish where I'd left off. Each time I had to back off a pitch, I was either in tears or on the verge of tears. I wanted to be better than I was. I wanted to do my part and pull my weight. I wanted Chris to be proud of me. I wanted to be proud of myself.

Chris was one of the first people to really understand my roller-coaster temperament. Having already faced his own fears while attempting first ascents alone, he could manage fear better, but he also understood the power of the emotion. He knew exactly what to say to be supportive. Even more important, he knew when to say nothing.

On Bermuda Dunes, I released my fair share of emotion and cuss words while trying to manage a deep, primal fear that kept bubbling to the surface. Even through the struggle, I did manage to complete some of the pitches on my own, and on Day 7, I stood on the top of that massive cliff. I could now say I climbed El Capitan. We claimed the second ascent, and I was the first female ascent. By the time I came down from that wall I looked like I'd been in a boxing ring. Bruises and cuts covered my entire body, but I had a new sense of strength.

As I stood naked in a Yosemite campground shower washing up before putting on clean clothes for the first time in a week, I caught a glimpse of my dirty, battered, dehydrated body in the mirror and smiled. The magnitude of my struggle was visible. That ascent was written all over me, and I liked what I saw. I was hooked on the adventure and commitment it took to be completely engrossed in a task with nothing but rock above my head and air beneath my feet. Chris and I worked as a team, literally tied together by rope, but individually I had to rise to the occasion too. In his stoic way, Chris pushed me to be better on El Cap, to try harder, to not give up. He was there to catch me if I fell, but he also wasn't going to put the net out unless it was absolutely necessary.

That climb bolstered my confidence to go on and do more big wall climbs, without Chris or anyone else. I climbed Skull Queen and Romulin Warbird in Yosemite and Moonlight Buttress and Prodigal Sun in Zion completely on my own. No safety net or expert to bail me out.

My relationship with Chris ultimately ended up on less solid footing. More and more, he felt he couldn't stay put in L.A. He was feeling the pull of the road while I was busy opening a second Rockreaction facility and embracing new opportunities—like paddling and adventure racing—as they came my way. Even though it seemed like the best thing for both of us, I was devastated to see him go. Our relationship had taught me a lot about myself—what I was capable of and what I really wanted.

LIKE ROCK CLIMBING, paddling wasn't an obvious sport for me. Honestly, I've always hated the water. My mother was shocked when I started paddling because as a kid, I didn't even want to swim in the community pool. She would drag me, kicking and screaming, toward the pool. Instead of jumping in and splashing around with the other kids, I'd sit there on the edge and dip my toes in the water, feeling left out and embarrassed. Water was terrifying to me, especially the notion of putting my head underneath it. I feel the same way about it today. I attribute some of that to my asthma issues, but I also think fears like this are something we're born with. But I was living in California, and the Pacific Ocean is right there and everyone is out playing in it, on it, and under it. It was only a matter of time before I joined them.

The Offshore Outrigger Canoe Club in Newport Beach has one of the most esteemed outrigger canoe teams in the world. This bunch of *haoles* (the Hawaiian term for white people) had been dominating the traditionally Polynesian sport for years. Because climbing had honed my lats, shoulders, and arms, I caught the attention of a few of the team members and was recruited to come out to a practice. When I strolled onto the beach, I was met by the biggest, baddest, most beautiful Amazons I had ever seen. They could move that huge outrigger canoe around with unbelievable force and finesse. More than half of the women on the team were also firefighters—I was seriously impressed. I also felt really short. I was a runt by comparison, but I wanted to become good enough to paddle with the best of them in the top boat. Perhaps some of their sexy strength and confidence would rub off on me in the process.

If you've never seen an outrigger canoe, it's not the typical canoe that threatens to tip every time you shift positions. These are giant, several-hundred-pound, six-person watercraft with a lateral support float (the outrigger) fastened to one side of the main hull. When you're in the thing you're not really submerged in the water, so you can just focus on paddling. The steerswoman has the stress of riding the swells and keeping the boat upright while the grunts in the middle just have to stay in rhythm and pull their paddles through the water as hard as possible. It all seemed really tame when I was admiring the canoes resting majestically on the beach in the calm harbor. What I didn't realize is that ancient traditional canoes are designed to travel great distances in the open ocean and take on monstrous waves without tipping over. The ocean races also ran a nine-person crew for the six-person boat. This meant rotating paddlers in and out of the seats by dropping them in the ocean to tread water while the big canoe came crashing toward the upstretched arms of the next paddler to be picked up. I would find that part out later. For now, this paddling thing seemed like a great upper body workout that could complement my rock climbing.

In the beginning, I kept my mouth shut so I could listen, learn, soak up as much knowledge as possible, and focus on working hard. After all, I was the rookie in terms of experience on the water, and those huge waves scared the crap me. With my climbing, the more strength training, route research, gear selection, and preparation I did, the better I stacked my odds to succeed. Focusing on the things I could control helped mitigate some of my fear of the things I couldn't control. With outrigger, I would again attempt to control my fear by being prepared. I wanted to prove to my teammates that despite my size and inexperience, I would not let them down. I hit the gym, did extra paddling workouts, and watched the best paddlers closely and emulated their movements.

It was the first time since my cross-country running days in high school that I was part of a team of athletic women working toward a common goal. I thrived on the competitive but cohesive spirit that a team of women brings to the table. There was no room in a huge ocean swell for pettiness, inflated egos, or excuses. Women who didn't fit the mold quickly weeded themselves out, while those of us who thrived on that cohesive spirit became bonded by hard work, exotic international travel, fear, and shared success and failure.

As I settled into the team, I started to realize that each individual person, including me, contributed something different to make the whole better than its individual parts. Because I was the rookie, I took practice really seriously. I was always on time, brought my A game to every workout, didn't complain, stayed late after practice to help clean up the boats, and did the hard physical work. I enjoyed my role as the new recruit, bringing motivation to the team, keeping the competitive spirit alive, and inspiring everyone to up their game a little too.

It wasn't long before I was sucked into the sport, and eventually I achieved what I had set out to do—I was good enough to be able to paddle with the big guns in the historic Molokai Hoe in Hawaii and in the Hamilton Cup off Australia's Gold Coast. Traveling to international events as part of the storied Offshore Canoe Club made my shoulders feel a little broader, and I wore my team-issued floral bathing suit with extreme pride.

Outrigger canoeing soon introduced me to some white-water paddlers, and I found myself burrowing even farther down the rabbit hole toward my nemesis: the water. Because I could move a beastly outrigger canoe, it was assumed I'd be a perfect match for the U.S. women's white-water rafting team. What a joke! These women were not inviting me to float a Styrofoam cooler of beer down a lazy river while working on my tan. They needed strong bodies to sit in the middle position of the raft and rip through Class V rapids and technical slalom courses in some of the biggest white water in the world. The task for the middle paddlers: Be a strong engine and whatever happens, do not fall out of the boat. White-water experience was less important to them than being a hard worker with a solid paddle stroke. I could paddle, but I didn't know if I had the courage to contend with the chaos of rapidly moving currents. What if I *did* fall out of the boat? While an outrigger canoe sits above the worst of the water's swells, a white-water raft dives right into the melee. The team wanted me to balance on the tubes of a giant rubber raft, hang my body over large drops, and paddle my heart out as we navigated waves as big as buses and skirted condo-sized rocks. The only thing holding me in the raft would be the rubber tubes I crammed my feet under.

It's an understatement to say I was hesitant. The idea of dropping over waterfalls was alarming. There had to be someone more qualified than me. After all, these were the best white-water women on the face of the earth: Julie Munger, Beth Rypins, Kelley Kalafatich, and Sue Norman. Their names graced river guidebooks, they were stuntwomen in Hollywood movies, and they were some of the first female guides in the industry, pioneers breaking barriers in the sport of white-water paddling. Once again, there I was in the company of really accomplished world-class athletes who were inviting me along for a rip-roaring ride in a sport I knew nothing about. Though it's harrowing to be thrown into this kind of talent pool as a newbie, what better teachers to have than the best in the world?

Before I committed to racing on the USA Raft Team, I asked the girls for some education on their home training ground, the American River in California. They were more than willing to scare the crap out of me by intentionally flipping us over in small rapids and making me climb in and out of the boat as I hyperventilated with fear and swallowed gallons of water. I knew my outrigger experience had honed my paddle stroke and that I could keep digging in and pulling as long as the race required. What I didn't know was how to read water, how to stay in the boat when it was bucking like a bronco, and how to survive if I fell out. They taught me all of that, and although I wasn't confident I was the right person for the job, they were. Due to lack of a better alternative, I was on the team. During those training trips on the American River, I realized that much of what I brought to this team was leadership, motivation, and training knowledge. I had fresh eyes and a strong work ethic, and I was often cheerleader and motivational coach all rolled into one. Although I was less helpful when it came to boat handling and tactics, I still had something to offer the team, and the girls were open to any ideas that made us better as a unit.

Success breeds confidence. We won the U.S. Whitewater Rafting National Championships in 2001 and 2002, and I had the opportunity to travel and compete (and be scared out of my mind) in some of the most amazing rivers in the world, like the Futaleufú River in Chile. I even went to raft guiding school and spent a couple of summers guiding rivers in Colorado.

IN 2001, I took the single most life-threatening, no-holds-barred, insane, challenging water adventure I could dream of—actually, I never would have dreamed of anything this extreme. But of course I had friends who dreamed big, and they invited me to join them. World-class river guide and white-water rafting pro Julie Munger, whom I had just raced with in Chile, called and explained her outrageous plan. She wanted to run the entire length of the Grand Canyon on river boards (picture a 4-foot boogie board with handles) in the dead of winter. That's some 300 miles of Class II (basic) to Class V (seriously advanced) rapids in 18 days. And she wanted to do it with me and our teammate, friend, and fledgling filmmaker Kelley Kalafatich. Not only that, but she also wanted to tackle the journey unsupported, which meant we'd have no safety measures and no raft following us as backup. We'd tow all of our gear and food on additional boards behind us. Nobody had ever done it or even attempted it before, let alone three women, self-supported.

I'll confess, this was one of the few times I agreed to do something when I actually didn't know what I was committing to. I'd never done anything remotely like this, nor did I understand the magnitude of what Julie was proposing. The three of us had never even done an overnight trip of this nature, let alone spend nearly three weeks river-boarding on high water in winter. But I trusted Julie. I'll always have an image etched in my brain from our white-water training days: Julie, standing alone on a rock in the middle of a rapid on the American River. The team had wedged our raft against that rock and we'd all climbed out to safety onshore while Julie braced herself against the angry river, an open knife clenched between her teeth, and single-handedly freed the bucking raft. She is the best in the business and a rock solid, self-reliant woman, which is why I agreed to the Grand Canyon adventure without the foggiest notion of what I was getting into.

We made camp at Lees Ferry, just above Grand Canyon proper. From the banks of the Colorado River, I stared at the vastness of the task before me, unable to process it. I was jumping into this big ditch in the earth without knowing anything about what was down there. All I had heard were horror stories from people warning me that the rapids are huge, contrasted with miles and miles of barely moving flat water where we would stall out and freeze in the icy cold river. Some called the Colorado River through Grand Canyon a liquid predator. And that was coming from people who'd made the trip on 18-foot rafts. We would be at eye level with this predator, flat on our bellies, immersed in her freezing black waters without the forgiving cushion of an inflatable raft to protect us.

The fact is, the National Park Service wasn't even going to let us do it. They likened paddling around on river boards to swimming, which is illegal in Grand Canyon. Not to be deterred, Julie launched a multi-year mission to fulfill her dream. She did loads of research and even presented her case to the head of the National Park Service. She was able to prove that the Carlson river boards we were using are considered U.S. Coast Guard–certified vessels. It worked. The NPS conceded that since we would be aboard "vessels" and not really swimming, they would grant us the permit. This was November 2001. I was pretty sure they granted the permit thinking no one in their right mind would actually commit to submerging themselves for more than two weeks in frigid 46-degree water. They underestimated Julie.

Coast Guard–certified vessel or not, as our departure drew near, I was having trouble finding the nerve to join Julie and Kelley on this crazy expedition. In truth, I was terrified. Julie was doing her very best to reassure me as we stood onshore and surveyed our starting point.

The banana seat, training wheels, and patent leather shoes are long gone, but my pigtails have stayed with me.

My dad, Capt. Stephen A. Rusch, exited my life much too soon. He was gone before I learned how to ride a bike, but I see my love for exploration and living passionately as his gift to me.

My mom fed my wanderlust by taking us on summer road trips and adventures. I thrived on the sense of the unknown, never wanting those journeys to end.

Our annual ski trip was my first taste of mountain living. We were that Midwestern family who didn't know how to ski, wore ridiculous matching ski outfits, and proudly sported our goggle tans on returning home.

My high school running coach, Bruce Ritter, always tried to get me to look forward and be confident in my abilities. I still race like I'm being chased.

I was proud to wear the orange and blue at the University of Illinois, but my experience there pushed me away from organized athletics for a long time.

The Downers Grove North Cross Country team was a force to be reckoned with. In the four years I ran with them we finished third, second, second, and first in the Illinois State Championships.

Donna Forst and I toured the West together, camping and summiting big walls. She was game for any route, even if it involved sleeping on ledges, eating out of a can, and not showering for days.

Heading up a big wall in Zion on my own was a rite of passage. The solitude, self-reliance, and sheer amount of work it required would open the door to many more solo adventures.

My sweaty hands and fear of falling worked against me on the rock. But the cerebral nature of climbing and the lure of the summit kept me coming back for more.

Bermuda Dunes offered a room with a view. Chris Kalous and I spent seven days and six nights on El Capitan in Yosemite dangling in space and living on a sea of stone.

In 2001, I received simple instructions heading into Class V rapids on Chile's Futaleufú River with the U.S. women's white-water rafting team: "Just stay in the boat and keep paddling as hard as you can."

Our self-supported river board expedition team set out to travel 300 miles to reach Lake Mead, the end of the Grand Canyon. Kelley Kalafatich and Julie Munger were my white-water heroes, and this trip cemented our friendship.

The Grand Canyon is known for white water, but over the course of so many miles there was plenty of flat water to provide the Buns of Steel workout. Decked out in neoprene, each of us had a board to ride, fins for propulsion, and an additional board loaded with supplies that we towed behind us.

"You just bob over stuff. You don't go underwater," she told me, explaining how she put true novices on these boards all the time with no problems. "So I'm not going to go underwater in the Grand Canyon?" I asked, completely disbelieving. "Well, in the rapids, yes," she said with a laugh. I was having a hard time keeping my sense of humor with this potentially life or death undertaking. I was also already freezing, and we hadn't even gotten in the water.

I came as close as I ever have to backing out on something, and I know Julie could sense it. I sat on the banks of the river the day before we were set to embark, called my friend Patrick, and started crying. He was one of my best friends, my adventure racing teammate (another new interest by that time), and an expert kayaker. I was hoping he could talk me off the ledge. Even after some assurances from him, a big part of me still wanted to bail; this felt like a colossal mistake. We had done a little test run, and it sucked. We were zipped into layer after layer of neoprene and latex—wet suits and insulation under dry suits—in a futile attempt to keep the freezing cold water out. We had giant flippers on our feet in an equally futile attempt to control where we'd be going. And it hurt pretty much everywhere. My neck ached from craning awkwardly, trying to see over the river. My back seized from arching against the board. My ankles and shins throbbed from pushing against massively strong water with my flippers. After just 15 miles of flat water, I was exhausted and sore all over. How would I make 300 more?

Although ever fiber in my body wanted to quit, I didn't back out. Scared or not, I couldn't bear to let Kelley and Julie down. I tried not to let my trepidation put a wet blanket over their enthusiasm and the celebratory launch. I would at least start the trip. I told myself that I would try to run all the rapids, but it was okay if I didn't and had to walk around. And if I had to bail and walk away from the expedition when we reached Phantom Ranch, the halfway point, I would.

On launch day, we dove into the ribbon of frigid blackness with the canyon walls looming above us. It was a strange sensation. I felt very small and insignificant, bobbing along like a piece of driftwood in this massive force of water, doing my best to stay out of trouble and and flowing in the path of least resistance. Within the first 20 miles I heard tremendous thundering, but there wasn't a cloud in the sky. It was Badger Creek Rapid, the first big challenge. Julie was ahead of me, whooping, laughing, and bobbing in and out of view. I stuck to her lines like my life depended on it—it did. We flushed out the bottom, and I was pumped full of adrenaline, giddy that I'd made it through my first big rapid on a river board. I was a little deflated to find out later that the difficulty rating on Badger Rapid really isn't all that impressive. It felt plenty big to scare the crap out of me, but the rapids would get bigger—much bigger.

We floated and kicked on, and I started to get the rhythm of this river-boarding thing. You can't go blindly into rapids and hope for the best. You need to scout them out, see how the water is flowing and find the obstacles you're trying to avoid. You're looking not only for big rocks but also for places where the water flows rapidly over the rocks or, worse, crashes over them and then recirculates to form a strong undercurrent. You look, evaluate, and then run it. When you kick out of the eddy, you can only think about where you're going and hold on with all your might. Ultimately the river calls the shots. You do your best to work with it instead of against it.

When I heard the deafening roar of House Rock Rapid on Day 3, I looked once again to Julie and Kelley for their sage advice. We were building trust and experience as we moved farther down the river. House Rock is a big drop where the river swings around a corner, and most of the current leads into a huge hole at the bottom. You need to keep to the right, but not *too* far right or you'll get bashed into the rocks along the river's edge. I looked, listened, and planned my approach like a dutiful student. Once again, I emerged unscathed and elated.

River doctrine says that 90 percent of all accidents happen on shore. To prove that point, on Day 4 in South Canyon, just as I was getting into the groove and feeling more confident, I had a nearly catastrophic accident while making dinner. I went to turn off the camp stove when the top somehow melted and the whole thing went up in flames, squirting fuel in the air and catching my down jacket on fire in the process. My entire right hand and the sleeve of my jacket were engulfed in flame. Kelley reacted quickly, extinguished the fire with sand, and dunked my hand in the cold river water. Julie snatched the first aid kit and sprinted over. Her face went white when she looked at my hand, which was puffy and blackened with soot. Her first thought was third-degree burns, which would have meant emergency evacuation and the end of our journey.

After the wound was cleaned, blisters started to form. Although it was clear that the situation wasn't good, the burn wasn't third-degree damage. As I sat there lancing big, puffy blisters with a needle, I was filled with a whole new fear. *Will I be able to complete the trip?* As hesitant as I'd been to embark on this expedition, now that we were in it, I didn't want to leave or become the weak member of the team. I already felt like Julie and Kelley were taking care of me, and now I had this injury to my right hand, so I was going to be even more limited in what I could do. We covered the burn in salve, bandaged it up, and I slipped on a rubber glove, hoping for the best. There wasn't much conversation around the campfire that evening.

Fortunately, it worked. I was able to hold onto the board well enough with my charred right hand and do most of my daily chores and heavy lifting with my left. By the time we reached the really big rapids, the burns were becoming a distant memory.

The days that followed were less dramatic but full of discovery. With no cell coverage, only a handful of encounters with other people, and nowhere to go but downriver, we began to become part of this magical, isolated place. There are few places you can go and completely unplug from the noise and distraction of life for even an hour, let alone 18 days. Never in my life have I had so little human interaction for such a long time. At first the solitude was extreme, but it began to seem like this was how life was meant to be lived.

There is a time in the middle of a big expedition when the mood changes and suddenly your body and mind are no longer fighting the process but instead fully embrace it, and you live in the moment. We got into a routine of waking with the sun to pack camp and dress in all of our gear, kick and float for a few hours, warm up for lunch by lying like lizards on the rocks or taking a hike in a side canyon, kick some more until dark, set up camp, eat, dry our clothes, review the river map for the next day, and repeat. I almost didn't want us to reach our take out at Pearce Ferry on Lake Mead, even though that was the ultimate goal. We continued making our way in this trance for days and days, negotiating scary rapids like Granite, constantly mending our leaking dry suits, burning more calories than we could consume, and reveling in the majesty of this place and the fact that Julie's insane dream was actually being played out between the canyon's walls.

The final test came on Day 16: Lava Falls, the most storied rapid on the entire length of the Colorado River. It's a big vertical drop with a lot of water compressed into a very narrow area. There is a gigantic breaking hole at the top that we had to shoot through, which would be followed by, as Julie said, "chaos and some really big waves." In a big raft there are more options, but lying on a river board, diving in head first, there's less room for error because the options are limited to navigating one very fine line that keeps you from running into obstacles or getting your ass kicked. It was time to put together all our skills and knowledge.

We scouted for an hour to memorize the line. The plan was for Julie to run Lava first, then come back and run it again as my escort.

Except when Julie launched, she immediately kicked too far to the right and was funneled down a massive corridor of crashing water. Kelley and I watched helplessly from the shore. Julie dropped into the first giant hole and the churning water pulled her under. Then she popped up and spun around a couple of times, was pulled back under, and got spit out backwards. She was repeatedly battered in the thunderous washing machine. By the time she was flushed out the bottom of the rapid, breathless, Julie decided she would not run Lava Falls again that day. She did not want to press her luck by challenging the river once more. Kelley was filming from a rock on the far shore. That meant I was on my own. My heart sank, and I felt physically sick to my stomach with fear.

I mulled over the decision to run Lava Falls for what seemed like hours. The easy and totally acceptable choice would have been to pass on this rapid. Much to Julie and Kelley's surprise, I instead slowly started zipping up my gear, grabbed my board, and made the long, slow walk to the top of the run. After a two-week crash course in river boarding, this was my final exam.

I had memorized my spot and my line, and I reviewed the plan again. But once I was eye level with the river, I couldn't find my landmarks. I craned my neck but couldn't see anything. From shore downriver Julie calmly pointed for me to go left. I was way too far to the right and heading straight for the middle of the ledge, precisely where I didn't want to go. Even from a distance, I could read the urgency in her eyes. The currents were accelerating, and I was quickly being sucked into the point of no return. Kicking furiously, I managed to eke out just enough momentum to push to the left, around the ledge hole. I got bucked and thrown. The river yanked the board out from one hand, but I snatched it back to my chest violently, determined to keep fighting. In between waves, I gasped for a mouthful of air before going under again. After what seemed like an eternity, I washed out into the calm eddy below, feeling like I'd done battle. Instantly the noise of the rapids, which sounded like a freight train bearing down on me, was replaced by my heart pounding in my ears and cheers from Julie and Kelley. All three of us knew that this was the virtual finish line. We had succeeded in doing something no one else had attempted. The remaining days on the river would be a victory lap during which we could reminisce about what we'd achieved and prepare ourselves for reentry into the real world.

I know the only reason I survived that trip was because I trusted and listened to my partners. I followed instructions and did exactly as I was told. Except for maybe when it came to operating the stove. Mentally, I broke the task down one day, one hour, one rapid at a time. I had a bailout plan, and I also had the unwavering support of some very good friends who made me laugh at myself when the fear got too overwhelming to bear.

The whole adventure was eventually made into a Durango Film Festival award-winning documentary narrated by Meryl Streep called *Three Women, Three Hundred Miles*. Watching it more than a decade later, I can still taste the metallic trace of fear in the back of my throat. The expedition was so far beyond my skill and comfort level that I still can't believe I made the 18-day journey. Nobody had done it before, and nobody has done it since.

A LOT OF PEOPLE live their lives in fear—they are fearful of what people think of them, fearful of the future, fearful of opening themselves up to new experiences, fearful of being vulnerable, fearful of letting go of the things they don't need or going after what they do, fearful of taking risks. Fear reduces life to an oppressive experience. My rock climbing and paddling days were representative of all of that. As a climber, you confront the natural human fear of heights, feel the vulnerability of exposure, and know the risk of falling. But every strength and weakness—physical, mental, and emotional—is visible when you're on a wall. You can't fake it up there, which means you have to face fear and deal with it head on in order to move forward. It's the same on the river, when you're fighting the current and every instinct in your body is focused on preserving your ability to breathe.

To everyone who has ever said to me, "You're just fearless," I say bullshit. I'm no daredevil. I still experience fear almost daily. Although I've lived some really big adventures, I could very well be the biggest wuss to ever call herself a professional athlete, a real-life scaredy-cat. The reaction is both emotional and physiological. My hands get sweaty just remembering trips where I was suspended high above the ground or engulfed in icy river water. Yes, I am brave enough to step out of my comfort zone and try new things. But these movements were all extremely calculated; I don't just throw caution to the wind and jump. Case in point, I couldn't force myself to bungee jump off a bridge in New Zealand. I just don't have it in me to blindly leap, literally or figuratively.

I *do* take well-planned, calculated risks. Sometimes it was a relationship, rooted in trust, that gave me the courage to try something outrageous, like climbing El Cap or navigating the Grand Canyon on a river board. Both times I was scared shitless. But going into those endeavors and others like them, I was surrounded by supportive, knowledgeable people. These friends, teammates, and climbing partners are my safety net. Oftentimes they are the ones who believe in me long before I do.

4

Vehicle for Change

When my outdoor lifestyle began blossoming in every direction and on every type of terrain, I quickly realized that my racy red Acura Integra was not going to cut it much longer. The hunt began for a new vehicle. I needed more space, more tire clearance, more gusto. I needed a truck, but I couldn't afford anything new or nice. When I stumbled upon a boxy 1975 Ford Bronco with four-wheel drive, it was love at first sight, even though it looked like a mail truck in a nice shade of baby-poo brown. As often happens with love at first sight, it was not the most logical relationship for me to get into. This truck hadn't moved in 10 years. It had been parked gathering rust and would need work inside and out, so I was taking on an intense fixer-upper. I wasn't exactly a car expert, either. I knew how to check my oil and change a flat tire, but that was it.

However, my boyfriend at the time, Greg, was a great mechanic who drove an International Scout and had a passion for fixing up old cars. He agreed to show me how to rebuild my Bronco, lent me tools, and pointed me in the right direction, but he informed me in no uncertain terms that I would be doing all the work myself. I plunked down $2,000, had the Bronco towed to Greg's shop, and spent the next year going through the painstaking process of completely rebuilding a truck, including its engine, transmission, and bodywork. I learned how to weld my own bumper, drop a transmission, change leaf springs, and use a cutting torch to remove rusty floorboards. I was completely out of my element but eager to learn. My grease-stained hands and bloody knuckles were badges of honor. I even invested in my own set of killer tools, and they started to feel natural in my hands. I spent every moment I wasn't working, climbing, or sleeping at the shop tinkering with the Bronco.

Though I have some great scars from climbing, mountain biking, and paddling, I got my favorite scar while rebuilding that truck. It's on the front of my left thigh, halfway between my knee and hip, a straight, thick line across the quad. On that day I was using a heavy handheld rotary grinder to prep the inside of the truck bed for painting. Filthy, sweaty, and holding a big power tool, I felt supercool. I turned the grinder off and stood back to admire my work. Funny thing about grinders—they continue to spin even after you turn them off. My proud moment was interrupted by the smell of burning flesh. The grinder had buzzed right through my Carhartts and seared the flesh of my thigh. The heat of the blade had cauterized the skin so it wasn't even bleeding, but I now had a big, deep burn on my quad. Greg casually looked up from his work, the corners of his mouth cracking a wry grin. "You've just learned an important lesson: Power tools don't care." He laughed and went back to work.

Rebuilding the Bronco was a lesson in patience and dealing with frustration, but it was also one of the most rewarding things I've ever done. So what if there were a few extra bolts left over that never found their rightful place back on the truck? By the time it was all put back together, I'd spent months toiling underneath that pile of metal. When I heard the engine roar to life for the first time, it made me giddy.

I christened the Bronco "Betty" and decided that she needed some feminine, homey touches; after all, I intended for this to be my camping and climbing adventure vehicle. I called my best friend, Donna, who's always had way better fashion sense than me, and she decided we needed to make some curtains for Betty. She found this cool vintage fabric that was straight out of the 1940s. It was cream-colored with big flowers on it—a perfect complement to Betty's bold, freshly painted orange and white exterior. Donna's boyfriend made a little table for the inside that I could slide crates of gear under for double-decker storage and as a makeshift platform for sleeping on. I clipped a few photos of friends and family to the sun visor and hung some strands of Buddhist prayer beads, a Barbie key chain, and my dad's steel MIA bracelet from the rearview mirror. I was ready for the open road and whatever I might find out there.

I have to confess that in my great enthusiasm to acquire and overhaul this magnificent off-road vehicle, I actually didn't know how to drive it. Back in Chicago, we just learn to dodge potholes and navigate icy roads. I mean, it's a car, right? You turn the ignition, put it in gear, and hit the gas. Well, it wasn't quite so easy with Betty. I needed a lesson in how to drive a manual transmission just to pull Betty off the lot, stalling and lurching all the way. Once I mastered the clutch, I was determined to tackle some truly technical terrain on a weekend trip with my friend and boss Jeff Cooper, an elite-level wilderness instructor.

Coop was dying to climb Valley of the Moon, this amazing stack of boulders and cliffs nestled between the San Diego County line and the Mexican border. It's riddled with huge granite outcroppings, mines, and caves and is one of the most adventurous and scenic sites in that area. It's also not easy to access the really good stuff. You need a true four-wheel drive with a short wheelbase and a good turning radius—just like Betty. Perfect! Coop and I planned our trip to the Moon. He agreed we could take my truck instead of his so I could initiate Betty and show off the fruits of my labor. Everything was going well, until we got to the off-road part.

Sure, I'd been on dirt roads, and so I locked the hubs for the four-wheel drive and set off. But this road was like nothing I'd ever seen before. It wasn't a road so much as a subtle suggestion of a route winding through house-sized boulders. In some places we drove straight over rocks as tall as the wheel wells, and it wasn't uncommon for all four tires to be on different planes. I had a death grip on the wheel, and sweat was dripping from my hands onto my knees. Honestly, it might have been faster to simply walk into the climbing area. Betty had a "three on the tree" transmission, meaning the three forward gears were operated by a shifter lever on the column behind the steering wheel. The four-wheel-drive shifter was on the floor. Even in the lowest gear in four-wheel drive, the truck still wasn't going slow enough to maneuver over the rocks and obstacles. I kept stalling out trying to go more slowly, but the gearing wouldn't let me.

After an embarrassing string of jerks, lurches, and stalls, Coop finally turned to me with a knowing grin on his face and said, "You don't know how to drive this thing, do you?"

"Well, not really, not off-road." Betty and I had spent the bulk of our outings on the dirt superhighway that led to the popular camping and climbing areas in Joshua Tree National Park.

There was a simple solution, but having to learn it from Coop was a humbling experience. As an eager, young guide with my first-ever truck I wanted to be in control and confident, but I'd missed the difference between 4WD low and 4WD high and how to move the transmission between the two.

We went on to have an amazing week of climbing in the Valley of the Moon. Even better, the trip opened my eyes to all the spots on the map I now had the power and the driving skill to explore. I would have to grind some gears in the process, but I was starting to see that stepping out of my comfort zone to see what was around the next corner was a worthwhile endeavor.

I NOW HAD TONS of outdoor experience under my belt and a vehicle that could take me anywhere. Inspired by the possibilities, I decided to celebrate my 30th birthday alone, on a roped solo climb of Spaceshot in Utah's stunning Zion National Park. It was time to take what I'd learned from mentors like Chris and Jeff and stand on my own two feet. No safety net, no hand-holding, just me and the wall.

Spaceshot is one of Zion's classic routes. I'd chosen it for the beauty, the appropriate difficulty rating, and its reputation for being a high-quality climb. The exposure is breathtaking as you work your way 1,200 feet above the valley floor. It's a very clean vertical line, with just Earth Orbit ledge to offer a solid place to put your feet for a momentary break.

Soloing a big wall is extremely demanding—and equally satisfying. The planning, the packing, the equipment management, the entire workload are all yours. It's a 100-percent commitment to being self-sufficient. For every single pitch, you must climb the route and self-belay with your own rope, rappel back down the pitch, and climb it again to clean your gear off then pull the haul bag of supplies up after you. Unlike partner climbing, where the workload is shared, rope soloing means nearly triple the work. There is also no rest period, and if you make a mistake, it's up to you alone to find a solution or rescue yourself. Escape off a route like Spaceshot is not really an option. After you get a few pitches up, the route is so steep and exposed that rappelling down is impossible because you cannot swing yourself back into the wall; instead you'd dangle out in space, unable to get back to the anchors. Though the difficulty of this route was within my abilities, the commitment was sobering.

After a full day of climbing alone, I settled onto Earth Orbit ledge for the night with the mice and the moon to keep me company. Eating my can of tuna and staring across the valley, I realized that the climb had become a rite of passage. The only sounds were the wind, my breathing, the climbing gear clanking on my harness, and the Virgin river below. There was no one to share my thoughts with; there were no social media posts or cell phones to shout my achievement to the world. I was alone with my internal soundtrack, the beautiful red sandstone, and the newfound confidence that I was a real rock climber. I was going to make it to the top of this sheer cliff alone, as I had set out to do. It was my first act of true self-reliance.

By the time I got back down to the truck, I was not the same person who had left the ground two days earlier. I had a new clarity and strength. Setting a stout goal and then succeeding elicited a powerful feeling, and I had to have more of it. I began to see my body as a useful tool I could rely on and something I should be proud of. The muscles in my arms, back, and legs served the purpose of taking me places. The eating disorder and body image I'd struggled with when I was younger were in the rearview mirror. I now viewed myself as an athlete.

MOMENTS OF TRANSFORMATION are so often followed by an event that puts the authenticity of that transformation to the test. In 2000, a friend from the climbing gym asked me to take part in a project he was doing called Stone Nudes. Yes, naked climbing. The proposition was intriguing, flattering, and embarrassing all at once. Dean Fidelman is an illustrious climber himself—part of the infamous

Stone Masters history of climbing—and a photographer who had been documenting the climbing culture in black-and-white images since the '70s. His photographs impressed me for how they melded person and place and captured a subject fully present in a moment in time. So when he approached me to be his first subject in this new project, I said yes, hesitantly.

Naturally, I was intimidated about the idea of climbing naked. I don't know anyone who is 100 percent confident about the way they look without clothing. Maybe some people are comfortable parading in front of an audience, but I have never been much of a showboat, clothed or unclothed. I did, however, believe in helping Dean launch his ambitious project. I wanted to see what he could create and if these photos would evoke a desire to climb, uninhibited and free.

Joshua Tree National Park is steeped in rock climbing history and was the site of my first leads and early guiding work, so it was appropriate that we would start there. The following year, Dean asked me to do another photo shoot, this time in Yosemite, where I'd climbed my first big walls. Both photo shoots began with trepidation, embarrassed laughter, and insecurity. With zero modeling experience, I felt overly conscious of my body and sort of clumsy. My hands were sweaty and I missed the security of my chalk bag hanging from my waist. But as soon as I turned away from the camera and touched the rock, my inhibition faded away and the feeling of the texture under my fingers took over. I took a deep breath, inhaling the smell of the stone. I forgot all about Dean and his camera and became absorbed in the pure, simple act of movement.

When I look at the photos now, I don't see my body. I see the climbing universe and my own intimate experiences of the sport. I see the waterfalls in Yosemite, the textured stone and patina in Joshua Tree, the dirt under my fingernails, the blood and chalk on my hands, the cactus blooms and mountain wildflowers, the countless campfires and starry skies, the restless nights on a portaledge, the mountains of well-worn gear. I feel the fear in my throat and the elation of the summits. Mostly, I see the smiling faces of my climbing friends. All of it makes me feel grateful to be able to call myself a climber and a Stone Nude.

BETWEEN ROCK CLIMBING, outrigger canoeing, white-water rafting, and river boarding, I thought my sporting dance card was full, but it wasn't long before I was whisked into my next activity, which would combine all the athletics I'd ever done, take me to places all around the world I'd never dreamed of visiting, and push me to new limits.

While I was working at the gym, all these Lycra-clad adventure racers would come in and ask for rappelling lessons. I had no idea what sort of racing they were talking about; all I knew was that they didn't fit in with the typical climbing crowd. They were not interested in the physical challenge and intellectual puzzle of climbing. They simply wanted to use the wall as a ladder so they could learn the mechanics of how to get back down. Trying to keep a straight face and an open mind, I would explain that nobody just rappels. That's how you get down. The real joy is in the ascent, not the descent. But they had their minds set on rappelling because it is a required skill in adventure racing. I felt perfectly fine accepting their money for the instruction.

Over time, I was able to look past the silly Lycra tights. I even converted a few adventure racers to climbers. I forged some really great friendships with many of these athletes, and as I exposed them to the climbing world, they solicited my expertise as a climbing instructor and rope safety rigger for some adventure racing training camps. I was happy for the extra work outside and got a glimpse into their sport. One of those friends was Cathy Sassin, a trainer and nutritional consultant at Gold's Gym who had been pulled into adventure racing after winning a contest put on by Mark Burnett, the TV producer who was bringing Eco-Challenge to the United States. Shortly after winning, she came in to Rockreation to learn how to climb in preparation for a race in Borneo, and we hit it off.

In 1997, when Burnett contacted Cathy about needing experienced people to help lead the way at his 24-hour adventure race in Malibu, she decided that she was going to persuade me to race, even if she had to drag me kicking and screaming. My friend Andy Petranek still needed a female team member for his team, so he joined Cathy in convincing me. When they first asked, I laughed at them. I didn't even own a bike, and 24 hours sounded like a long time to do anything, even sit on a couch. But from where they were standing, I'd been a runner and was now a climber and paddler, which loosely covered most of the adventure-racing disciplines. And they figured that anyone can pedal a bike. But the most persuasive argument was that they genuinely needed another woman in order to race. Adventure racing requires a four- or five-person team with at least one member of the opposite sex. So in this male-dominated sport, strong women are a hot commodity, even a woman who hadn't ridden a bike in years and had never touched a mountain bike.

Of course I succumbed to the peer pressure. Adventure racing sounded a little outrageous and very challenging, but what I really needed was something to motivate me over the winter months. In the summers, I climbed outdoors every week and was now racing outrigger canoes with an internationally renowned team. However, winters in the climbing gym were leaving me feeling out of shape and uninspired. I needed something new to feed my competitive nature until the climbing and paddling season rolled back around. So I agreed to give it a shot and went about confronting my weakest (okay, nonexistent) skill: the bike.

This was my first personal encounter with mountain biking—and it was a reluctant meeting, to say the least. I had zero interest in the sport, but there was no getting around it: I had to learn to ride if I was going to do the race. I purchased a used bike from a woman who used to race downhill and was much shorter than me. It was a heavy bike, and no one educated me on how to adjust the suspension for my body weight. It was a chore wrangling it where I wanted it to go, but I just assumed it was my lack of experience that made it so hard to ride. I never considered the possibility that it was actually the wrong tool for the job, and no one told me otherwise.

For the four weeks leading up to the race, I simply put in time being active. I didn't know about structured training, so I just spent time paddling, running, and climbing. I knew nothing of the sport and had no intention of doing another race after that one. But I did want to pull my own weight, and I was getting increasingly concerned that my male teammates were going to have to tow me around, especially on the bike. I had been searching for motivation to get active and fit again over the winter months, and it was working.

Team ROAM (an acronymn for Rebecca, Owen, Andy, and Mike) did a few organized workouts in the Los Angeles area. Owen Shea, Andy, and Mike Hobbs did all of the planning, and I tagged along, trying to learn as much as possible in a short amount of time. They coordinated sea kayaking workouts in the ocean, rock climbing sessions in the gym, big monster hikes in the Santa Monica Mountains, and, of course, mountain bike rides. We practiced carrying stuff in backpacks, and I used a Camelbak for the first time. I was totally fine with most of our weekend adventures—except when mountain biking was involved. It was a crash course in cycling, with virtually no instruction except "Follow me" and "Get your weight back behind the saddle for the downhills."

Our weekend adventures in the Santa Monica Mountains were multi-hour excursions, but we did nothing that lasted 24 hours. I was becoming increasingly concerned about how I would race around the clock. I've always cherished my sleep and never, ever been a morning person. Growing up, my mom continually struggled to get me out of bed and off to school on time. Although my sister would be awake with the sun, I could easily sleep until noon on the weekends. The physical demands of enduring nonstop activity for 24 hours (especially with three big, strong guys) had me worried, but so did my lack of cycling skill.

My anxiety grew as the race neared. In fact, the week before the start I was in tears as I tried to visualize what the experience would be like. I was certain that I'd be the weak link, unable to stay upright on the bike, struggling to survive the duration of the event with three disappointed guys yelling at me. I cursed myself for agreeing to something that seemed utterly impossible and ridiculous. But I felt a sense of responsibility toward the team; I knew they wouldn't be able to find another woman on such short notice. I couldn't back out now.

The race was incredibly difficult and eye opening. I didn't know what was what coming next or even what I was expected to do. My focus was 100 percent on not screwing up or slowing down my team. I followed dutifully, maintained concentration, and pretty much kept my mouth shut. I had disturbing visions of having to be dragged and pushed through the bike section to the finish. Some of the teams were gunning hard for the winning prize: a trip to Eco-Challenge Australia. They had organized team names, matching uniforms, and were dialed in on winning. I just hoped to survive.

The race started on the beach at Sycamore Cove. Huge waves crashed on the sand as the racers charged into the water to launch their kayaks. Many of the teams took multiple tries and many mouthfuls of seawater to punch through the Pacific Ocean swell. One team's race ended right there when their kayak broke in half after being smashed back onto the beach. Another woman's race ended with a trip to the hospital after having her face drug across the ocean floor. Luck was on our side, and we pierced through on our first try, rocketed the paddling section, and were quickly among the top teams. Our biggest advantage was that Andy had trained in the military and was an exceptional navigator. With designated checkpoints to hit but no marked route for miles in between, an adventure-racing course is open for each team to interpret. Andy nailed the navigation, and we literally bumped right into every single checkpoint without error. Naively, I assumed every team was doing the same thing. Instead, there were tons of teams wallowing around lost in the Santa Monica Mountains. I would find out much later how vital and rare a good navigator is in adventure racing. We moved through the course steadily. I kept waiting for my body to say, "Stop. Let me go to sleep." But it didn't.

Just before midnight, and hours ahead of the predicted schedule, we reached the mountain bike section. As Andy plotted the bike course on our map, all I could see was that it went up and up, forever, and he told us we'd be riding uphill for many hours. I braced myself for the inevitable. We rode in silence, and I entered my own world of steely concentration. Soon Mike, a strong firefighter, was wavering, and both Andy and Owen had to put all their attention into helping him up the hill. This meant they would not be available to help push me up. Although the possibility of needing their help had been haunting me, having that security blanket snatched away was a rude awakening. I was the girl on the team. If anyone was supposed to get help, it was me. If two of us needed help, there would be no way to get to the top. I rode a bit ahead of the team to regain my focus and make sure I didn't fall behind. I also hoped to get out of earshot of Mike's groaning because I feared it would suck me back into my own panic. Behind me, the three guys moved in unison as they took turns pulling and pushing Mike. I had never ridden or seen a hill this big. I started playing little counting games to keep me motivated. First,

I just focused on counting 10 pedal strokes at a time. I told myself I wouldn't stop until 10, then 10 became 20, then I began to count to 100. I have no idea how much time passed climbing that hill, but finally in the middle of the dark night, I could see the road flattening out and there was nothing above me except moonlit sky. We were at the top of the hill—I'd made it on my own power.

It turned out I didn't need any additional help from the guys during the event. We ended up winning the race, and despite my massive insecurities, I was one of the stronger members of the team—certainly not the weak link I expected to be. I had no idea how it had happened, but I was able to race alongside three very strong, athletic men who had a lot more endurance sport experience than I did.

The prize for this 24-hour race was a trip to compete in the Australian Eco-Challenge. I stood on the very top step of the podium to accept our award, which now seemed like a death sentence, not a prize. Twenty-four hours on a racecourse was the biggest, longest competition I'd ever done, and now we were being offered the "opportunity" to do this again for a week straight, covering more than 600 miles of scorched earth and deadly snakes in the Australian outback. But we took the coveted entry to the biggest adventure race in the world, and I agreed to go along. Truth be told, I was just in it for the free trip to Australia. I had been an exchange student there in college and loved the people and the place. I'd take the trip, do my best, and get back to rock climbing when I returned home.

Our rookie team never made it to the finish line in Australia. We had two sick teammates—Patrick Czismasia (Owen's replacement) was hallucinating, sure he'd been bitten by a snake even though there was no evidence of a bite, and Mike, our firefighter, suffered serious blisters that no amount of duct tape could cover, and he couldn't muster the desire to go on through the pain. We made it through two days. I was surprised at how heartbroken I was to be pulled from the race when I was feeling physically strong and able to continue. Andy and I actually petitioned the race director to allow us to go on unranked, but we were denied for safety reasons. We stayed in Australia to watch the other teams finish. I was envious of those exhausted, elated racers—many of them my rappelling students from Rockreation—as they stumbled onto the beach and across the finish line after a week of non-stop human-powered travel. I wanted to stand in their soggy, bloodied shoes. I vowed to come back and finish at least one expedition-length race. I wanted to see if I could go the distance.

ONCE I GOT BACK to Southern California, even though our team hadn't finished the Eco-Challenge, word had spread that I had potential to be a decent adventure racer. The teams were required to be coed, which meant at least one woman and one man per team. Women with multisport skills and the desire to go days without showering were rather scarce, so the core community was eager to find new talent. Meanwhile, I had discovered that those adventure racers flocking to Rockreation to hone their rappelling skills were the best in the world in this growing but niche sport. John Howard, Ian Adamson, Cathy Sassin, and Robyn Benincasa were revered racers. I hadn't realized that until I witnessed their prowess in Australia. I had been clueless all the while, but having the ear and the advice of the cream of the crop worked to my advantage.

After the DNF in Australia and with the desire to finish one of these expedition races, I decided to take matters into my own hands and go about trying to form a legitimate adventure racing team, one where I could participate in selecting the team roster. Eco-Challenge founder Mark Burnett and my new adventure racing friends encouraged me to go for it and see what happened. I would just take it one event at a time.

In Australia we raced as an unsponsored team, so we had picked our own team name and sold T-shirts to friends, family, and climbing gym members to help fund the trip. I knew that formula wouldn't work again, so I put my marketing degree to work and started soliciting sponsors, creating budgets, and talking to potential teammates. I went about building a racing resume and establishing relationships with partners like Pearl Izumi and Montrail. As the team built momentum over the following years and more opportunities for international adventure races were presenting themselves, it became blatantly obvious that something had to give. I was still managing Rockreation at the time. The job was fantastic—a dream job—but it didn't allow me enough flexibility to be away racing for weeks at a time throughout the year. If I really wanted to make a go at this and pursue adventure racing full time, I would have to quit my job at the gym. It was the only logical course of action.

Of course, the problem with quitting one's job is paying one's rent. Although our new sponsors were generous in their support of the team, they weren't going to be cutting checks to my landlord anytime soon. The biggest races in the world might have a cash purse of $50,000, but I couldn't count on winning as a rookie racer trying to break into the scene. Even with a substantial team budget, once you take into consideration the $15,000 entry fee for an expedition race, international airfare for four people, and food and miscellaneous equipment costs for multiple races a year, that budget quickly vanishes. I've always been frugal and didn't need a fat paycheck, but the accounting on this was going to put me well below the poverty line, especially living in Southern California.

That got me to thinking further: Los Angeles wasn't the ideal training environment for me. I was really hooked on this adventure racing thing. I loved the survival aspect of it. It was like no sport I'd ever seen or experienced. You never know what's coming next, and the route before you offers multiple options, so you have to be present mentally and make strategic decisions on the fly. The athletes who succeed are not necessarily the most fit, but they are the smartest and the most well-rounded. Sheer physical strength is not the winning formula. Of course, you have to be insanely fit and capable in multiple sports, but it's really the tenacity, backcountry smarts, and cooperation that make for the best teams.

In addition to my growing love for adventure racing, it was also a great time to be in the sport. In the late '90s, adventure racing was one of the newest and fastest growing sports in the world. Mainstream brands like Wendy's, Ford, and ChapStick were fully onboard, promoting their products through the sport. Races were being televised by MTV, the Discovery Channel, Outdoor Life Network (now NBC Sports Network), and even NBC. The 1999 Eco-Challenge was broadcast in 145 countries to 144 million households worldwide. Now was the perfect time for me to dive headfirst into this lifestyle.

I weighed the options and figured out that if I wanted to quit my job and pursue adventure racing, I would have to be homeless for a while. So I made the decision to move into Betty and travel wherever the spirit moved me while racing full time. I gave notice at Rockreation, hammered together sponsor proposals, and decided I'd give myself five years to see if I could make a go as a professional nomad and adventure racer.

The wanderer inside me was buzzing with excitement, and I got to work calling up friends I knew would put me up for small stretches of time. I had some vague plans and locations I wanted to visit, but no set agenda to speak of. I knew I had to fit myself and my belongings into my truck and keep expenses low. I wanted to stay out West in the places that inspired me most—Yosemite, Moab, the Sierras, and the Rockies—where I could climb, kayak, trail run, and explore endless mountains and deserts.

Then came the hard part: condensing my life, boxing up and storing my possessions, and packing my gear. It was torturous to decide what I would need for such an open-ended trip. I had to be ready for anything, from mountaineering and glacier travel in New Zealand to rock climbing in the Utah desert. Every article of clothing and piece of gear was subject to scrutiny. I also needed cooking and sleeping supplies for times when I wouldn't have a roof over my head. I sifted through my belongings, hell-bent on simplifying my life and freeing myself from so many possessions. After weeks of packing, repacking, consolidating, and filling a storage unit, Betty was jammed to the ceiling with gear for climbing, paddling, cycling, and camping, along with repair tools, a computer, a cell phone, personal files, books, cooking gear, cameras, a can of Mace, journals, CDs, and even a little cactus glued to the dashboard to keep me company. The truck looked like a traveling sports store. It was so full that I couldn't see out of the windows or fit a passenger in beside me.

Betty was fairly reliable, but she was old, cramped, got lousy gas mileage, and was a bit finicky at times. Just driving hundreds of miles in that truck was going to be an adventure in itself.

I had informed friends, many of them new adventure racing friends, that I'd be on the road a while in search of good places to stay. Invitations came flooding in. I expect some of those people never really thought they'd hear me knocking at their front door. My best friend in Arizona offered a room, a friend in Utah offered an empty trailer in Moab, and another acquaintance offered up a guest room in Truckee, California. Of course, there were invitations from my family members in Michigan, Texas, Illinois, and Washington, D.C., but they didn't meet the travel criteria of staying out West. Because my climbing and adventure racing friends lived in more intriguing places, I hit them up first.

A friend's empty double-wide trailer in Moab, Utah, was my first stop, and it seemed like heaven. Maybe I'd never leave this place. I had access to a washer and dryer, a place to park and work on my truck, space to unload a bit of gear, a real address, and lots of other dirtbag climbers and cyclists roaming around town. So far this homeless thing was a breeze. I quickly registered my truck in Utah, got a Utah driver's license, changed all my bills to automatic debit, and got a post office box in Moab as a sort of home base to collect mail every once in a while. Once the anticipation of leaving California and setting out on my adventure was behind me, the reality of my situation was setting in.

I was alone in an unknown town with no plans, no friends around me, and the responsibility of creating a new life for myself was a little daunting. I had no regrets, but I was scared and unsure of where to start or what I wanted. I hoped that opportunities would present themselves, but I also knew that I couldn't sit around inside the trailer waiting for a knock on the door. I had to step outside and create my own future.

The five years came and went. I was every bit as much a professional nomad as I was a professional adventure racer. I traveled to 15 different countries, raced a raft down the holy Ganges River in India, walked across the Himalayas from Tibet into Nepal, rope soloed multiday climbing walls in Yosemite and Utah, spent countless hours under the hood of my truck, and became a connoisseur of canned tuna and gas station food. I could never have predicted that either title—adventure racer or nomad—would have suited me for so long. At one point, I had keys and an open-door policy to four different homes in four different western states.

I was lousy about writing holiday letters, remembering birthdays, sending cards, and all the kinds of things that one always intends to do but usually doesn't. It seemed I was always off in some other country doing another race. My mom became the official team correspondent and was responsible for informing friends, family, and sponsors of my whereabouts. All I had to do was drop an e-mail or phone message to her and the international communication tree was in effect. Even though I was well into my 30s, my mom was still looking after me and making sure that everything was under control.

During that time, I was racing as much as possible, building a team, working with sponsors, and essentially constructing a life. There were bouts of loneliness and uncertainty when I thought maybe I really was crazy to be living like this. There were times that I longed to unpack my truck and have a sense of place and belonging. The month just after a long race was always the hardest. Coming back from such an intensely emotional and physical overload always left me feeling depressed, lost, and lacking motivation. I had no savings, no home, and no illustrious 5- or 10-year plan. I lived from race to race, recovering, training, and planning for the next one in between.

Along the way I did a smattering of work as a climbing and adventure-racing instructor, stunt double or rigger for commercials, and cross-country ski center ticket checker, and I helped frame a couple houses and did some motivational speaking for extra income. But the jobs were few and far between, and none of them were in the same state. Filing taxes was interesting because I had no official residence and no official income. My accountant had a hell of a time justifying my "business" as an adventure racer. It was a spartan existence, and I loved it. Despite being homeless and broke, I was free and seeing the world. And for nearly a decade, I never looked back.

5

Learning Management Skills in Morocco

I n business school the curriculum is bound to cover the specifics of communication, teamwork, and human behavior, but my real education came in the form of 10 years of adventure racing in all corners of the earth. Racing through far-off expanses of pristine wilderness alongside three or four other people you need for sheer survival, let alone success, will give you an advanced degree in the dynamics of teamwork, how to motivate people, how to lead and how to follow, how to cope with failures and disappointments, how to overcome adversity, and dozens of other life skills.

In 1998 the next Eco-Challenge was going to take place in Morocco, and I desperately wanted to be there. After having to drop out in Australia, I had vowed to complete an expedition-length race. I was friends with some of the top adventure racers in the world, but I was afraid no team would invite me. The trouble was that I had so little adventure racing experience and no expedition-length finishes to my name.

At the time, I was still living in Los Angeles and frequenting the same Venice Beach Gold's Gym as Eco-Challenge race founder Mark Burnett. We had a heart-to-heart one day on the beach, and he prodded me to create my own destiny instead of waiting for an invitation that might never come. We came up with an audacious idea: I would captain my own team, one predominantly composed of women.

Most adventure racing teams fill the coed requirement by having just one female. The lone woman is often viewed as the de facto weak link, mandatory equipment to be acquired and checked off along with the rest of the gear that must be hauled around. Early in my career I came to believe that it was the athlete, not the gender that makes a good adventure racer. The performance gap narrows and eventually disappears in ultra-endurance events. If I could build a reverse coed team, one that flipped the ratio of men to women, I could drive that point home. Energized by my new mission, I went about securing sponsorships and building my squad.

I exploited every contact I had to find the ideal women for this fledgling team. Even though my own experience wasn't deep, I wanted to surround myself with the most awe-inspiring women I could find. I was able to secure Kim Csizmazia, ice climber and Survival of the Fittest winner, and Nora Tobin, Alaskan mountain runner, backcountry skier, and uber-athlete. Both women carried superextreme resumes that included things I didn't even understand, and they'd been kicking guys' asses for a while. They loved the idea of doing that on a big stage like Eco-Challenge. Rounding out the team was ultra-athlete and navigator Kirk Boylston, a soft-spoken, sensitive guy whom I thought would work well with three type A, strong-willed ladies. Kim, Nora, and Kirk all had more experience than I did, and together we were a perfect combination of aptitude and attitude for this groundbreaking team.

We would be racing as Team Rubicon, reminiscent of Julius Caesar's famous decision to cross the Rubicon and take a step from which there was no turning back. Racing with a reverse coed team had never been done before, and success or failure, it was a bold statement. Equally thrilling was the fact that I had successfully pulled together funding and organized a team for my second-ever expedition race. We were going to Morocco!

But in the weeks leading up to the race, my grand vision started to crumble before my eyes. My hotshot women called within days of each other, delivering the difficult news that they were out. Kim had injured her hip, and Nora had discovered she was pregnant. I was heartbroken, deflated, and left scrambling for not one, but two replacements. At this late date it would be nearly impossible to find good women who were both willing and able to compete in adventure racing. This close to the race, the best were already committed.

After considerable struggle and casting a wide net, I was able to land experienced adventure racer and army sergeant Cathy Callahan to fill one slot, and I then signed on journalist and accomplished triathlete Lisa Jhung to round out the team. Both were complete strangers—I had to rely on references and be open to working with whoever was available at the very last minute. It was the ultimate blind date and Lisa's first adventure race. Hardly ideal, but we had to run with what we had. I couldn't give up before reaching the start line.

ALL ADVENTURE RACES are brutally hard. A typical course covers hundreds of miles of mixed terrain with every sort of nonmotorized travel you can imagine. The course is unmarked, and the clock never stops: Those two components set adventure racing apart from other sports by introducing route finding, strategy, and sleep deprivation into the mix. The race is a team format where all members must travel together, which means you're only as fast as your weakest link—but you can potentially be faster and smarter as a unit than you would be alone. Morocco presented its own unique set of challenges that could make or break the toughest teams. At elevations upward of 13,000 feet, the Atlas Mountains could wreck your race if you pushed too hard and didn't recover. In the desert, temperatures can swing from well below freezing at night to over 90 degrees in the heat of the day. There would be paddling in the frigid and rough water of the Atlantic Ocean. We'd be rappelling cliff faces more than 30 stories high and trekking rugged terrain for days on end, including a trip over North Africa's second highest peak, Mount M'Goun. Hypothermia, altitude sickness, injuries, and illness awaited us at every turn, yet we all still paid good money to be there and lined up anxiously to sample a bit of all those things. According to the official course description, we would have 11 days to navigate the 315 miles to the finish in Marrakesh. In addition to the typical adventure racing disciplines required to cross vast expanses of land and water, there would also be camels.

Yeah. Camels. Burnett took delight in keeping racers on their toes with special surprises that showcased the culture of the host country. Teams gathered from around the world in the ancient fortressed town of Essaouira, on the coast. For centuries this place had been an important military outpost, Morocco's principal seaport, and, in the '60s, a cultural hangout for famous artists and musicians. The pedestrian-only fortified medina, or historic town center, is a UNESCO World Heritage site. As we strolled through the ancient ramparts and onto the glorious beach, I couldn't get the Jimi Hendrix song "Castles Made of Sand" out of my head. The walled city, the ocean, the camels all provided a surreal backdrop for our race start.

Imagine 55 teams, 220 racers in all, loaded down with packs and nervously perched atop the humps of bellowing, spitting, braying camels. It was the most insane race start I've ever seen, rumored to be the biggest amassing of camels since the filming of *Lawrence of Arabia*. A piece of rough rope secured around the nose of the camel gave us the impression that we would somehow have the ability to steer. Race organizers equipped us with a twig from the animal's owner and the Arabic words for "go," "stop," and "kneel down." I couldn't even form the words in my mouth, so using them to control this gangly beast was not going to happen. The saddles were crude, hard wooden frames running the length of the camel's back, covered with a sturdy piece of burlap. It was hell on your legs, so many racers opted to wear their life jackets like a diaper, with their legs through the armholes.

When the gun went off, total mayhem ensued, with frightened camels, wide-eyed athletes, and Moroccan handlers scattering in every direction. These camels are locals' lifeblood and their most significant piece of property, so many Moroccans ran the miles alongside us, robes flowing, screaming Arabic commands to ensure their animals were not lost or hurt. TV cameras, production crews, 4x4 vehicles, and a few helicopters made the melee complete.

This was the only section of the race where teams were not required to stay together, so it was every man or woman for themself. We would wait for one another at the camel drop-off. Even though it was spitting and braying, my camel seemed willing to bounce along in a straight line and generally follow the pack, but it was a jarring ride. My hands were nearly bloody from gripping the rope so tightly. Around me, saddles were spinning underneath the bellies of the camels, dumping riders left and right. Some camels strolled casually away from the scene as if they were drunk, and some took off like rockets. Others frantically ran in circles whenever a helicopter hovered overhead. No doubt the animals were as scared as we were. On reaching the next transition zone, I was relieved to see that all of my teammates had arrived in one piece so we could really start the race in earnest. We made it to the beach without incident, sitting in about the front third of the pack. I was totally fine with that.

Once at the water's edge, we began traversing the rocky shoreline on foot—or "coasteering," as Eco-Challenge described it. Thankfully, the tide had not yet come in, so we were able to scramble along the seaside cliffs and rocks for a few miles without much interference from the crashing waves and surging water. Teams behind us were forced to swim much of this section as the ocean grew more violent, pushing them and their heavy, waterlogged packs toward the jagged rocks. A 50-mile open ocean paddle was waiting for us just ahead.

The sea kayaking leg of the race crossed some of the roughest water in adventure racing history. With swells well above six feet, multiple trips to shore and in and out of the surf to navigate the checkpoints, stout currents, and cold 62-degree water, this leg would test even the world-class paddlers: Eight of the 55 teams would not make it through this section of the course. Early in the kayak leg, Lisa, who was riding tandem with Kirk, became seasick and began nodding off, her head bobbing and swaying like a rag doll. She effectively stopped paddling, so Cathy and I had to slow our pace to keep the boats together. We were on the water like that for two days. When we finally reached the shore, all of us were shivering, chilled to the bone by the constant wind and cold ocean spray. We got pummeled by the surf on the beach exit, our bodies, gear, and boats all flung unceremoniously onto the sand. But I was relieved to be off the water and safely on terra firma.

Camp 1 looked like a MASH unit, filled with hypothermic, dehydrated, disoriented racers wrapped up in Mylar like hot dogs, receiving IV drips and supplemental oxygen. Lisa was still cold and nauseous, but on her own two feet. It was worrisome to be contending with illness so early in the race, but I was optimistic that her situation would improve now that she was off the rocking ocean and back on land.

Over the course of an adventure race, you repeatedly trade one type of toil for another. Using a different muscle group or embarking on a more familiar element can help you bounce back. Because Lisa was a runner, I thought she would liven up for the next leg. As she stood there immobile and quivering on the beach, I got to work gathering our explosion of paddling equipment and changing into trekking gear while Kirk prepared the maps. We were headed into the infamous high Atlas Mountains, a place Winston Churchill called "simply the most lovely spot in the whole world." I'm pretty sure he hadn't viewed it as up close and personal as we were about to do.

We would travel nearly 107 miles through this labyrinth of rugged terrain, and no matter how arduous it was, I intended to have my eyes wide open so I could soak in the beauty. The mountains here were nothing like the green alpine environments I had seen before. It was a harsh, unforgiving expanse of rock and sand. The giant peaks were scoured clean by the hot, dry Saharan wind that ripped unencumbered across the high plains. American Team Vail captain Billy Madison nicknamed the place "more rock oh," and it was an apt description. The colors of Moroccan geology range from amber to crimson, and at sunset the rocky sandstone landscape lights up like glowing embers. It was gorgeous and eerie, especially at dusk when we'd occasionally hear the call to prayer echo through the canyons.

The only break in the monotonous color scheme was in the gorges and river beds. The casbahs, or walled villages, would appear in an explosion of green fruit trees, brilliant hibiscus, bougainvillea, and bursts of colorful clothing the Berber people wore. It was a feast for our eyes, but then as we departed and marched on, the terrain would again become devoid of life.

There's a Moroccan proverb that advises you to "choose your companion before your road." It's something adventure racing hammers home. Being bone tired, hungry, scared, and potentially lost magnifies every aspect of your personality. Your true self is stripped bare, like the landscape here. This is why even in light of the physical nature of the event and the danger it presents, it's team dynamics that truly make or break the experience. You may like someone personally, but are they the right companion for the arduous journey? On the flip side, you might find someone with all of the skills for the excursion, but can they operate and collaborate in a group setting? The whole must be stronger than the parts. You need to function as a single unit out there, so it's paramount that each member be on the same page.

In this case, Lisa was the odd woman out. It wasn't just inexperience; it was attitude. You must have a fierce desire to put yourself through that extreme level of sleep deprivation, fatigue, and suffering. In retrospect, I think she simply had no idea what she was getting herself into. This was no triathlon, where lithe athletes carry just ounces of food and water and efficiently pace themselves toward the finish line. In adventure racing, you haul the gear you need on your back, and distance and pace are unpredictable. For this section through the Atlas Mountains, our packs had food for five days, a first aid kit, rock climbing gear, water, a water filter, and clothing for temperature fluctuations of more than 50 degrees. It all added up to nearly 40 pounds, and Lisa groaned as she shouldered her load. At this point, just two days into the race, I'm guessing that the realization hit . . . she was in way over her head. The days and nights that followed would be a crash course in team leadership.

Sixty-three miles of mountainous desert stretched before us, a sea of sand and rock working its way up and up and up over 10,000 feet where we would need to navigate canyons and eventually ride feisty military stallions to Camp 2, our next resupply point. My mind couldn't even fathom how far we had to go or what we would encounter along the way. As we prepared to embark on this next segment, locals from an indigenous Berber tribe came out from their sandstone villages to send us off in traditional style. The steady beat of the drums and singing filled me with gratitude. There was nowhere else I wanted to be than right there in that beautiful spot, heading off into the unknown in the dead of night.

Under the beam of a headlamp, the topographical map looked like an optical illusion. On most maps there's at least one distinguishing feature, but this one was a succession of tight squiggly lines, aptly reflecting the sameness of the mountainous terrain we moved through. As our navigator, Kirk had the added pressure of finding the path of least resistance. I did not envy his job in the least—not only did he need to keep his body going day after day, his mind had to be razor sharp. He couldn't for a moment zone out and trudge along, lost in his own thoughts. It's a heavy responsibility, made increasingly difficult when bone-deep fatigue begins to set in.

It was now Day 3, which I've always said is the moment of truth in an adventure race. Any chinks in the team's armor make themselves known then. It could be a small blister that suddenly turns into full-on foot rot or an overzealous rookie team realizing they are now paying for the mistake of going too fast. No matter how well trained you are, the body and mind begin breaking down. The mental fatigue means more navigational errors. Because you cannot keep up with your calorie expenditure or recover from exhaustion, your body is in a state of deterioration, literally cannibalizing itself to survive. From here until the finish line, you must tap your mental reserves to take over where the physical cannot. Every cell in your body is screaming at you to stop moving, and your mind must override those signals as you stumble on.

The hardscrabble, trackless terrain was a mix of rock and sand winding between the canyon walls. The passage narrowed, forcing us to walk single file through a stream of water carving its way across the canyon floor. It was one of the very few rivers with life-giving water we would find. The mixture of sand and water was beautiful—and just about lethal for our primary mode of transportation, our feet.

One of the only guarantees in adventure racing is that your feet will take a beating. Regardless of how carefully you select your socks and shoes and how diligently you lubricate your feet, you will find that hot spots, excessive swelling, bloody blisters, and blackened toenails are par for the course. You must be prepared to manage them appropriately or be hobbled. By nightfall we hit Passport Control (PC) 9, where we needed to get a time stamp in our official Eco-Challenge passport. Lisa was on the ground, shoes off, trying to peel the skin back on some broken, weeping blisters on the bottom of her right foot under her big toe. I stopped her.

"I want to peel the skin off," she told me.

"Don't," I said. "The skin is actually good to have on there. Just leave it. It's okay." I knew from experience that the old, dead skin acts as a cushion to protect the raw, tender skin underneath.

"It's not okay. I just don't want it to hurt. I can't move my toes."

This was new territory for Lisa, so the only way to get her to accept her fate was to show her we were all in the same boat. I looked at her for a second and then reached down to take off my shoes and socks and show her my own hamburger feet.

"Eww!" She reeled back, laughing.

"I don't want to hear you complain!" I teased, trying to lighten the mood.

"But *this* hurts!" she said, pointing at her foot. "Yours doesn't hurt that bad."

"It *does* hurt! I'm just not whining about it," I poked back.

"Oh come on, I wouldn't whine if it didn't hurt," she said.

I just shook my head and let it be. Arguing back and forth wasn't getting us anywhere. Everyone was suffering, but we had to productively manage and work through the pain.

I'd be lying if I said I wasn't a bit frustrated. But I knew this was all so unfamiliar to Lisa. When you haven't been in these extreme environments, it's easy to get scared and overwhelmed by the immensity of it all. Lisa needed some nurturing, and it was clear that I needed to step up and play that unfamiliar role as best as I could. Instead of charging on, I helped clean her wounds and pulled out the duct tape to wrap her feet and numb the pain. The only way to keep our team moving forward was to stop and address this issue.

After a few more hours of walking on painful, tender feet and leaning on our hiking poles as crutches, we found ourselves in a cold, dark canyon with the sinking sensation that we were not where we needed to be. Worse, it turned out that we didn't know where that was. We were off course *and* lost. Nobody wanted to bunk down on the freezing canyon floor, but we had no choice. In the dark of night we had zero hope of finding our way. We pulled out our tiny space blankets, made a Mylar nest among the jagged rocks, and settled in for some group shivering until the sun came up and we could see where we were going.

At first light, Kirk felt rested and more confident with the navigation, so we started our ascent to the peak of a steep, rubbly mountain, toward PC 10. We picked up a few other teams along the way, and the social interaction made the painfully slow going a little less awful—that is, until we got to the top and the true error of our ways became horribly clear. We were on the wrong mountain. In the darkness the night before, we had walked through a rough riverbed and followed it to the right. I vaguely recalled a channel forking to the left. It was oh so faint, but I had seen it, pondered it for a split second, and walked on silently as Kirk led us to the right. Now our prospects looked bleak, and what should have been a celebratory summit was a morale-crushing blow.

Nature called, and there were no port-a-potties out there in the desolate terrain. I crouched behind a rock, resting my elbows on my knees and cradling my weary head in my hands as I took a rare moment of stillness and solitude. Gazing far across the valley I could see the sunrise just cresting the majestic peak we were supposed to be standing on. I had only myself to blame for not speaking up at the intersection the night before. Since Kirk was an experienced navigator, I assumed he had it all under control. Who was I to tell him how to do his job? I could have saved us hours and hours of walking in the wrong direction on sore feet if I had just said something in that critical moment. Now we would pay the price for my silence.

Still, we had to keep moving. So I chalked the mistake up to inexperience, pulled up my pants, and we got back to work. With the ground literally crumbling beneath our boots, we began a painfully slow descent to get back on track.

We had slipped from 21st to 24th place, which was the least of our problems. When we finally reached PC10, Cathy shocked us all by doubling over, gasping and crying. Altitude sickness would mark the second phase of my leadership training.

In sharp contrast to Lisa's regular status updates on her pain and suffering, Cathy's military training had taught her to keep her mouth shut and gut it out. Since we were relative strangers, I didn't recognize that her stoicism and independence could go too far. If we had only known she was starting to feel the effects of altitude, we could have taken her pack or slowed down. But with reassurance from a race medic, rest, and support from us, she pulled it together and we pressed on.

There was nowhere to go but forward. We had yet to reach some of the biggest challenges of the race—more than a dozen rappelling sections, a horse section, another huge trekking section to the highest point in the race, then a 120-mile mountain bike segment to the finish line in Marrakesh. I tried not to think of the magnitude of what still lay ahead. Instead, I remained focused on holding together our crumbling team and moving forward to just the next passport control point.

During the night Cathy spiraled downward. The intent was to keep progressing to get her to a lower elevation. She was sobbing, gasping, and shivering uncontrollably. We had to stop. We unpacked all of our equipment, food, and clothing to create a nest. She was absolutely freezing, so we took off most of her clothes and mine and I got into her sleeping bag to provide her with body heat so she could relax and calm her breathing. By now we were in survival mode and were forced to consider calling for help.

Every team is equipped with an emergency two-way radio in a sealed envelope. Crack it open for assistance and you are disqualified. There was only one exception, which had been communicated to us at the pre-race safety briefing. If we elected to use the emergency altitude sickness medication each team was issued, we were required to call to alert the medical staff and receive instructions.

As the team captain, I decided this was a true emergency. I broke the seal, turned on the radio, and called out to race headquarters: "Team Rubicon to HQ, come in, please." Nothing. No reply. "Team Rubicon to HQ. Come in, please." Radio silence. We were left to our own devices for the long, cold night, and my focus turned back to Cathy and how to best help her. Lisa and Kirk got some much-needed sleep while I dozed in and out and tended to Cathy as she shivered and moaned in the near-freezing temperatures.

In the dawn hours, we finally picked our way slowly down the mountainside. With each foot of descent in elevation, Cathy steadily improved and was soon back to herself. It seemed like a miracle recovery, and I was nearly dancing with joy. We'd dodged another bullet, and our teamwork had gotten us through a very dark patch. The old Cathy was coming back, Lisa was no longer complaining about her blisters, and the sun was shining. Maybe we were getting the hang of this and it would be okay. *Just take care of each other and patiently keep moving forward*, I thought. *We can do this.*

My outlook was improving, but it wouldn't last long. Hours into our trek to PC 11, we reached the grim realization that we were once again lost in the Moroccan maze. The sameness of the terrain was so infuriating. There were no distinguishing features to separate one peak or valley from the next. I couldn't blame Kirk, because I really had minimal navigation skills. He was doing the best he could, but our team honestly couldn't afford all of the extra mileage.

We were so far off track that the race organization eventually sent out a helicopter search party outfitted with a gyrostabilizer camera that could zoom in and read race numbers from the air. It took them hours, but they finally located us barely making forward progress over a boulder field near the mouth of a gorge near the town of Tinghir. We'd been wandering for 26 hours and finally managed to get back on track and hit PC 11. But now we were in a precariously dangerous place. And Mr. Big, Mark Burnett himself, was waiting for us at the checkpoint with arms crossed.

The race's safety team didn't want to let us proceed into the next section because we would need to perform 14 difficult rappels through the Todgha Gorge. This is dangerous enough during daylight, but far more so now that night was falling. From the pathetic look of our team and the snail's pace we were traveling, the safety officials didn't think we could manage it. I was sure that we could. Though they look daunting to the uninitiated, these ropes sections are often a welcome mental and physical break from endless trekking and stumbling on uneven terrain.

Quietly, I took control and whispered to the team to quickly gear up with helmet and climbing harness and to act supremely confident. I felt we were on the rebound, and the thought of being stopped at this point was unacceptable to me. After all, I was a rock climbing guide. I had climbed El Cap. I probably had more rope experience than most of the race officials themselves. If there was any portion of the course I was capable of shepherding the team through, it was this.

After much debating and a stern warning from Burnett, we were allowed to continue on the condition that one of the safety officials follow us at least halfway down the gorge to make sure we were managing. He came with us for a while, then, convinced that we were okay, cleared us to continue on our own in the dwindling light.

Five hours later, at the end of Day 5, we finally reached the last monster rappel. It was time to step off the 340-foot cliff on the north face of a rock formation called Jebel Oujdant. I was tired but energized by our success and completely in my element on these ropes. Part of me actually envied the team of climbing riggers who had set up the ropes and were watching us now. I flashed back to my climbing days, and a piece of me longed to stay there with them with the bundles of ropes and carabiners. But they wouldn't get to see all that we had ahead of us. We fastened our harnesses and dropped into the blackness below. One more section was now behind us instead of looming in front of us.

We were nearing the next major milestone, the horse segment, where we could give our weary feet some much-needed rest and soak in the atmosphere. The rocky canyons and uneven footing had done more damage to Lisa's feet, and she was hobbling. We took turns carrying her pack to alleviate some pressure, but she needed to get off of her feet completely. I was thankful for a relatively easy section of the course. I'd had my doubts along with everyone else about whether we were going to make it to this place. But we'd pushed through so much already, and we were finally starting to feel like a team. Perhaps the worst was behind us. Maybe the horses were just the right assistance we needed. Then Lisa started vomiting.

When we reached PC 16, we were 36 hours behind the leaders, who were now nearing the finish of the entire race. After taking a break to change gear and get ready for the next leg, we were finally prepared to mount our horses when Lisa collapsed and began retching and weeping. Once again, we were at a crossroads as the sun began to sink in the sky. My shoulders slumped and I struggled to make eye contact with her. Between sobs, she told us to go on without her, but we refused to let her off the hook that easily. Instead we each took a turn talking to her, sharing our experiences, negotiating to take one section at a time.

It was the only way to tackle a beast so enormous: one step, one segment, one challenge, one day at a time. Nearly an hour later, our coaxing and pleading wore her down and she reluctantly agreed to proceed just to the next checkpoint. As she mounted her horse, her expression was one of defeat and misery. She muttered barely audibly, "I can't do this. It's too hard." With some encouragement we hoped to pull her through this dark spell and revive her once again. I still believed the yo-yo recovery effect could help her. We'd sit on the backs of the horses for hours, eating, hydrating, and resting our weary bodies.

I had been trying to motivate Lisa for days. My pushing and prodding had made her angry. She blamed us for making her go on, for pushing her past her limits. So I changed my tactics in the hopes of taking her mind off the fatigue and the suffering. I'm not a particularly chatty person, but that night, I rambled on and on from sundown to sunup. I rode next to Lisa and peppered her with questions that would take her mind far away from this place: questions about her life, her triathlon running, her family, her boyfriend. I engaged her mind, told jokes, kept her awake and moving but distracted. We all got to know each other much better that night, and I started to understand what made Lisa tick. Once she got her mind off quitting, she started enjoying the ride, and Day 5 gave way to our most enjoyable night on the course.

Like a true oasis, Camp 2 finally appeared before us at the start of Day 6. It wasn't a mirage: colorful tents glistened in the sun amid the hustle of hundreds of race staff, teams, and media. It was the most welcomed site I'd ever laid eyes on. My fatigue vanished, my pack lightened, and I felt high as a kite. We could get fresh, warm food, crystal-clear bottled water, chairs to sit on, and the miraculous rejuvenation our team so desperately needed. Simple requirements like food, water, shelter, and human interaction felt utterly luxurious in our downtrodden state. I almost wept as I piled couscous, chicken, and fresh fruit onto my plate from the buffet. We'd persevered through so much, but one of the biggest hurdles remained: a 12-mile hike up into the clouds to reach the 13,000-foot summit of Mount M'Goun, North Africa's second highest peak. Altitude sickness and blisters would likely rear their ugly heads again for our team, but we were now well versed on dealing with them.

Several hours later, the inevitable happened. Lisa started vomiting again—repeatedly—and we were on a steep trail with a dangerous drop-off. There was no way she could stagger on, even if she came through this. She was dizzy and her stomach hurt, likely from a stomach bug that she could not shake in her weakened state. I was facing my own exhaustion after trying to bolster her physically and emotionally. I pulled out the race radio with no fanfare and no discussion. We finally raised the white flag.

Seven days after we started, Lisa was medevaced out by a helicopter longline. Since the terrain was so steep and narrow, a landing was impossible. Her rescuers were lowered down to us on a cable. They attached a harness under Lisa's arms, and the helicopter hovering above hoisted her up. Her eyes were closed and her head hung to the side. As I watched her limp, drained body get lifted into the air, I was awash in emotions: sadness, frustration, pride, fatigue, and determination. The intensity of everything we'd gone through for the last seven days finally hit me all at once.

The sound of the chopper faded away, and we were once again alone. Each of us had to come to terms with what had happened to our team and where to go from here. I did not want to quit; we'd come too far. Kirk and Cathy wholeheartedly agreed. Each of us entered this race determined to finish. Regardless of placing or unofficial ranking, the three of us vowed to ride across those colorful Berber carpets at that finish line in Marrakesh.

We still had miles to go, and it definitely wasn't easy. But we were a team with a unified mission. That alone made our burden feel lighter.

We made it to the rocky summit of Mount M'Goun and biked the 120 miles of intricate paths and roads to finish the race. As we got closer to Marrakesh and our reentry, the desolate terrain was slowly replaced by the signs of civilization. We were unranked and nearly dead last. The race winners had finished about four days in front of us.

Despite or maybe because of all the hardships we'd endured over those 10 days, Morocco ended up being one of the most rewarding and important races of my life. It was a true education and the ultimate test of my leadership skills. I realized that I was actually good at this sport and had a passion for it. I learned to voice my opinion regardless of my experience level. Furthermore, I realized the value of soliciting opinions from everyone around me, from the expert to the novice. You never know where your next nugget of knowledge will come from.

FACEBOOK CHIEF OPERATING officer Sheryl Sandberg made headlines with her book *Lean In*, in which she talked about how women unintentionally hold themselves back. She challenged women to take risks and pursue goals and, most important, lean in and work together to create more equality, especially in predominately male domains. Sandberg's ideas resonated with me. From the girls' cross-country team in high school to women's paddling teams to rock climbing with female partners, I had experienced the rewards and community that come from leaning in before I even knew what that was.

Although I have always enjoyed the camaraderie of hanging out with women, I was actually introduced to climbing, paddling, and adventure racing by a string of amazing guys who went on to mentor me. At the time I was discovering outdoor sports, men were often the only mentors and teachers available. I soaked up all the know-how and knowledge I could get from them. If I'm being honest, I would've never gotten where I am today without those guys. I'm eternally grateful, because without them, I never would have found these passions or smashed through so many of my own limits.

However, I have always thrived on sharing knowledge and bringing more women along with me. And the real rewards came from embracing that role reversal. Going from student to teacher and back again elevated my experience and forced me to stand on my own rather than use a more seasoned athlete as a crutch. Had I just kept following the guys, I wouldn't have grown into the person I am now.

In Morocco I was both teacher and student. It was a colossal adventure and just the beginning. I knew I wanted more. I recognized that I could do better next time and bring some other great women with me. Although my vision of this first Team Rubicon didn't smash the glass ceiling or prove all that women are capable of, it did offer a glimpse of what I could accomplish and what might be possible with the right combination of teammates.

Betty Bronco was my hands-on study in mechanics and my home base through my adventure racing years. She was a gas-guzzler and hardly a smooth ride, but we suited each other well and hit all the cool spots.

Morocco Eco-Challenge was my first expedition-length adventure race, and there was no way to prepare for what we would face—starting with the camels.

The Eco-Challenge had a knack for making something hard even harder. The intensity of this coastal swim was magnified by the incoming tide and jagged rocks, not to mention our soggy backpacks and shoes.

The beauty of the Moroccan landscape was mind-blowing. The villages we encountered in the Atlas Mountains were full of life and color—a real contrast to the barren landscape.

In a multiday expedition race, the smallest things become luxuries. As we neared Marrakesh and the finish line, we took a short break to celebrate 10 days of intense effort. You can find Fanta pretty much anywhere, and it tasted wonderful in this moment.

Adventure racing is a cerebral sport and a team effort. As our team solidified, Patrick Harper became our primary navigator in charge of preparing the maps, but the rest of us kept our heads in the game, absorbing complicated race instructions and supporting route choices.

Because I was comfortable in the vertical world, the rope sections of a race always set me at ease. It was a time to rest and take in the scenery.

Living out of my truck was good practice for the intense gear organization in adventure racing. The gear box was our lifeline, with food, clothing, and extra equipment meticulously packed and compartmentalized in color-coded bags. Transition areas offered a chance to resupply and quickly repack until the next time we'd see the box days later.

Expedition racing required an army of support staff—checkpoint personnel, medical teams, rope safety teams, and photographers. They were often working just as hard as the athletes, nestled in the midst of some gorgeous terrain.

This glacial lake marked the start of the 1999 Eco-Challenge in Argentina. Each team had two swimmers and two kayakers. Lucky me, I was swimming.

Stumbling upon a place like Cerro Catedral always fueled my desire to keep racing. To see something like this and then head straight into the puzzle was exhilarating.

We made history in Argentina as the first three-woman, one-man team to finish at the front of an elite expedition race. It was a hard-fought, fourth place finish. Race director Mark Burnett stayed up for days to welcome every single team across the finish line.

Mount Tronador sits on the border of Chile and Argentina in the Andes Mountains, the perfect stage for the final battle to the finish line.

Borneo Eco-Challenge might be the most physically disgusting race I have done. The jungle was nasty, and the heat was sweltering. Picking leeches off each other took team bonding to a new level.

The Borneo rivers were teeming with parasites, but the water was often the fastest way through the jungle. Swimming was far from refreshing. Worse yet, there weren't chlorine drops strong enough to kill what was festering in this water, but we had to drink it anyway.

We were never so happy to see daylight as when we climbed out of the dark, dank, bat-infested caves in Borneo. It felt like ascending from hell.

Vietnam welcomed the 2002 Raid Gauloises with open arms, and tons of locals came out to see us off at the start. For me, this race would represent not only a competition but also a personal journey.

There were many races in which we had to assemble a raft or boat using traditional materials. In Vietnam our raft-building skills had us cruising down the river and having a great time doing it. We didn't always fare so well.

The finish of the Raid Gauloises Trans-Himalaya was a place I thought I'd never see. This race taught me the true meaning of suffering and friendship. In a week, I lost 10 pounds and damaged a fair amount of lung tissue, but our team stuck it out and clawed our way back to the highest-ever finish for an American team.

We were immersed in local culture and welcomed with open arms everywhere we raced. Nowhere was the hospitality as amazing as in Fiji. Villagers offered us clean water, shelter, and food from their tables. They had very little, but they gave us anything we needed.

Big expedition races like the 2003 Raid Gauloises in Kyrgyzstan tend to start with a bang, and teams fall into a fast-moving conga line. Navigational prowess doesn't truly factor into the first few days, and then the racing really starts.

Unknown teammates are inherently risky and unpredictable. While animals gave us a chance to get off our aching feet, we never knew what sort of beast we were going to get—proof that you can lead a horse to adventure, but you can't always make him race.

Kyrgyzstan was a spectacular obstacle course, and Team Montrail emerged victorious.

Primal Quest Washington was a high-stakes adventure race with the biggest prize purse in the history of the sport. The world's best teams lined up for this event in 2004.

We encountered more than our fair share of hike-a-bike during Primal Quest.

We joined forces with Team AROC, and our two teams were leading the competition when we reached the checkpoint atop Illabot Peaks. Our Aussie friends stopped to scope out the terrain, and Nigel Aylott (second from left) was the first to descend into the gulley below.

The fateful moment descending the gulley off the high point of Illabot Peaks—the events that unfolded changed us all dramatically.

Teamwork is essential to adventure racing. The group must move and operate as one unit, and the strength of the whole is greater than that of the individual.

I was having the time of my life as we enjoyed a gravity-assisted run down Lanín Volcano. I've visited Argentina many times since the 2005 Raid Gauloises, and it remains one of my favorite places in the world.

6

If at First You Don't Succeed...

As a kid, I was always the girl running around in scrappy cut-off jeans rather than putting on a dress and acting like a lady. On the rare occasion when I sported a dress, I considered matching sneakers to be the perfect complement. When the boys took off their shirts on a hot summer day, I followed suit, having no idea that "little girls don't do that." Because I wasn't privy to traditional male and female roles in my daily life, I've never felt limited by my gender.

From my grandmother, mother, and sister to my paddling teammates and firefighter friends, I've always had strong women to look up to. I didn't think twice about rebuilding a truck, guiding rock climbs, or becoming an adventure racer. I was simply chasing down my dreams and doing what came naturally. But somewhere along the line the naiveté fell away and I realized that everyone else didn't see it quite the same way I did. And that renewed my sense of purpose.

I was well aware that some people thought we didn't make much of an impact in Morocco because we were a predominantly female team. Determined to prove them wrong, I piloted a second "reverse coed" team (three women, one man) for the 1999 Eco-Challenge Argentina. This time, I was able to lock in the absolute best and most experienced athletes in the sport: adventure racing world champion Ian Adamson, internationally renowned fitness trainer and my friend and personal adventure racing mentor Cathy Sassin, and firefighter and adventure racing champion Robyn Benincasa. I still considered myself somewhat of a rookie, but because of a rule change I was now joining the most elite adventure racers in the world as their team captain. The tables were turned: Instead of being one of the strongest on the team, I was certain to be the weakest. For me, it's more natural to be in the position of offering support than it is to be the weak link, swallowing my ego and accepting assistance the entire way. I think for many people it's easier to give help than to receive.

Robyn, Ian, and Cathy had all been racing for years in the elite echelon on multinational teams. Most of the top racers and events were in Europe and New Zealand. The sport was just catching on in the United States, so there were only a handful of Americans on the forefront of the wave. In 1999, Eco-Challenge introduced a new rule requiring team members to be entirely from the same nation. This left many conventional teams dismantled and some of the best racers stranded without a squad. I took advantage of the opportunity and asked the best of the best to race with me and make history. Given my experience level, it was an audacious move, but I had the coveted sponsor commitment (we would be racing as Team Atlas Snowshoes/ Rubicon), and Ian, Robyn, and Cathy needed a home. Normally they all lined up as my opponents. It would be compelling to have them pin on the same number, and they loved the idea of seeing what a mostly female squad could do. Despite enthusiasm from them and the spon-

sors, I sensed that everybody shared my doubts about whether someone so green could rise to the occasion.

The race was being held in Patagonia, at the southernmost tip of
South America, a region that is twice the size of California with the
bustling population of Siberia—I'm exaggerating, but only just. The
place where we'd be racing has been called the least hospitable place
on earth, and for good reason. The towering, jagged granite-spired
Andes drive a giant wedge between the Atlantic and Pacific halves of
the region, inviting chaotic weather that can turn from mild to mael-
strom in a moment's notice.

We would face 200 miles of some of the most radically contrasting
terrain in the world. But I also knew the race played to our strengths,
with plenty of kayaking (Ian was a world champion), trekking, orienteering, mountaineering (among us we'd bagged multiple summits),
rappelling (rock faces were like a second home to me at that point),
white-water rafting (we were all great paddlers), and no biking, which
made me extremely happy. If there was ever a perfect course for me,
this was it.

The race was set to begin at 8:30 a.m. under brilliant blue skies.
At the moment, the glacial lake was as smooth as glass, but at any
moment the infamous Patagonian winds could produce whitecaps
and dramatically change the scene. At the signal, the teams would
swim across the frigid 41-degree glacier-fed water and belly flop into
their boats before heading off into the horizon for a 56-mile paddle.
Surely the race organizers could have just started us all onshore in our
kayaks, but the artic swim just added a layer of drama and chaos that
made for good TV. After all, we really were unpaid actors—the first
generation of reality TV stars.

I felt dwarfed as I lined up next to the giants of the sport. I still
had virtually no legitimate expedition race finishes to my name. Robyn,
Ian, and I stood on the northern shore of Lake Correntoso along with

200 other twitchy, anxious racers, while the other quarter of the field was afloat with the kayaks 500 feet offshore. We had to gear up for the icy water temps, but we also had nearly a full day of paddling in the hot sun ahead of us, so we were all dressed in dry suits with multiple layers underneath.

Ian and Robyn were both former triathletes, so it was a given that they'd do the swim. Cathy and I had drawn straws for the third swimmer, and my heart had sunk when I drew the short straw. I sink like a stone in the water, and it scares me. Not only was I worried about my inexperience showing through, but now one of my weaknesses was also going to be on display right from the start.

Mark Burnett shouted, "GO!" and there was no turning back. The ice-cold water knocked the breath right out of me. I struggled to negotiate the water as my dry suit ballooned and the shoes on my feet grew heavier by the minute. I was getting kicked in the face and was flailing my arms for both propulsion and protection. I was gasping for breath like a carp, but when I looked up, I was relieved to see that I wasn't too far behind my heroes. It was an aquascrum as racers tried to locate their boats, but we managed to reunite with relative ease. Okay, 10 minutes down, and several days to go. We found ourselves out in the front of the pack, along with Foster's Team Australia, New Zealand's Team Greenpeace (captained by adventure racing legend John Howard), Finland's Team Halti, and a few other strong local and international teams.

Even in the heat of competition, the beauty of this place was mesmerizing. Lake Nahuel Huapi and the surrounding area became Argentina's first national park in 1934. Carved by glaciers and dammed by natural mountain moraines, the lake is up to 1,500 feet deep and stretches over 200 square miles from the base of snowcapped Patagonian volcanoes. The water was still as we glided past the lushly forested shoreline of Tiger Island jutting out into the middle of the lake. We would paddle the immense blue expanse all the way to its outlet at the Limay River.

If you've never paddled for a full day and into the night, it's an exercise in moving meditation. After the novelty wears off and the chit-chat dies down, it's you and the water and a far-off point on the horizon. You and your partner fix your eyes on that point and paddle in unison for hours on end, breaking rhythm only to drink and eat. The dip of the paddle stroke and your own labored breathing are the only sounds. The faraway shore moves closer in painstakingly slow increments. At times, I was paddling with my eyes closed, peeking every so often to see if the shore was any closer. With Robyn sitting right behind me watching my every move, I was intent on paddling my absolute best. We found a fluid rhythm and functioned like a well-oiled machine. We hit the first checkpoint in third place after just 2.5 hours, only 5 minutes off the lead.

Nearly 12 hours later, aching to stand up and give our arms a break, we reached the river's edge along with the top half-dozen teams. It was time to haul our 18-foot, 130-pound boats onshore and swim across the surging, ice-cold Limay without being swept downstream. Ian, who is known for his calculating mind, strategized, and we made a team decision to swim into the middle and then turn into the upstream current and ferry ourselves across. We huddled together and swam like a pod of dolphins for safety. It was short and intense, but it worked, and we were safely on the other side, hearts pumping and ready to leave the boats behind.

Here, we met with our new teammates for the next 41 miles: beautiful, athletic horses. We would travel by horseback through dusk and into the night toward the Andes foothills, where the real challenge, the big mountains, awaited us. On paper it seemed like an easy leg, but these were working gaucho horses used to a fast pace and a confident handler, unlike the docile trail horses we had practiced on. Gaucho horses are feisty and ready to run, and they will take control if you don't; a few teams were already out of the race at this point after being bucked and thrown. We were solidly in the mix in fourth place, less than 40 minutes off of first. Although it was second nature to the rest of my team, I'd never seen the front of an expedition race before. Not even close.

We had the fortune of negotiating the hardest part of the horse segment, through the wild Argentinean pampas, in the waning daylight, and we were absolutely flying across the stunning grasslands. I felt like I was in a tourism commercial, charging through this beautiful scenery on horseback. They were incredible athletes, and I was anxious but exhilirated by the ride. By the time we hit the transition area at Checkpoint 6, we were essentially in a tie for first with New Zealand's Team Greenpeace and Team Aussie. I kept my mouth shut, my ears open, and my feet moving. I was soaking in as much experience and knowledge as I possibly could while trying to care for myself and not look too much like an imposter.

Twenty-three miles of trekking and difficult navigation were on the agenda for the third leg of the race. I had never seen a bamboo forest before, but now we were going to get up close and personal with one. The bamboo was so dense you could barely see the racer in front of you. No light shone through the trees because there simply wasn't any space for it. Every single move forward was like pushing through a thick green curtain and taking a high step to get through. At times we were crawling over the dense vegetation on our hands and knees, traveling just half a mile an hour. There were places where our feet didn't touch the ground as we found ourselves balancing above the forest floor on bouncy, bendy bamboo stalks. With every move we had to push and separate the green curtain. We wore cycling gloves to protect our hands, which were every bit as valuable as our feet, and sunglasses to keep the bamboo from slapping our eyes.

Ian was supremely focused, with his face in the map and an eagle eye on the compass. His world-class navigation skills were being put to the test for sure. I still have no idea how he was able to plot any sort of course through that mess. It's times like those when you're grateful to reach any discernible landmark that confirms you're on track, but this time, there were no landmarks, just a sea of green. After wandering and floundering and ultimately being disqualified in Morocco, I was grateful to be racing with a human GPS. Ian seemed to be able to make route-finding decisions quickly and effortlessly. At least I could be assured that we probably wouldn't have to do any bonus mileage on this course.

Sometimes you end up banding with other teams and traveling with them for a portion of the race, simply because you're going the same pace and have made similar navigation decisions. That had been the case with us, Team Halti, and Team Greenpeace in this race, but several miles into the bamboo, Halti decided to split from us to search for what looked like an enticing shortcut on the map. We weren't convinced it was worth the gamble, so we stayed the current, more predictable course with Greenpeace. It would end up being a costly mistake for the Finnish team. They crossed the wrong river and got disoriented in the bamboo, losing three hours in the process. Other teams would struggle for hours in the maze as well. Mark Burnett was impressed with our two teams, saying, "Ian and John chose the one perfect route out of a hundred possibilities." I was hugely relieved that Ian had made the right decision. Had we made a navigational error, I'm not sure I would have been able to sustain our pace.

The intensity of racing at the front was entirely new to me, and I was nearly redlining and wondering to myself how long we could possibly keep this up. We were now in a footrace with Greenpeace, and nobody was giving an inch. The friendly banter gave way to labored breathing. No one was talking about us as "the girls' team" anymore. John Howard later said that he knew us all well as friends and competitors and that we were as good as any of the best men in the field. We were contenders for the win, and the mood was tense.

Eleven hours after starting the hiking leg, we hit Camp 1, locked in a duel with Greenpeace under still-blue evening skies. At each of the three transition areas over the course of the race we could access equipment and food. Every team member had his or her own giant gear box, which was stacked in an enormous tent and arranged by team number. It was our chance to refuel and recalibrate. We pored over the maps to estimate travel time, weather conditions, and terrain for the course ahead in order to make an educated guess on how much food, what clothing, and what equipment would be needed. It's a fine line between keeping your pack light and having enough to survive. Striking that balance meant we would surely be cold and uncomfortable but hopefully safe and with just enough food. The discomfort would motivate us to reach the next transition area.

Teams sometimes sleep at these transition areas, where you have warm sleeping bags and additional clothing. We were exhausted, but Greenpeace had bolted out of camp ahead of us and daylight is at such a premium in adventure racing that we decided to push on while we could still see where we were going, then grab some sleep out on the trail somewhere. After we decided on our strategy, Ian cracked the whip to get us out of camp: The media had dubbed us *Las Diosas*—the goddesses—and were hounding us at every access point. It was flattering to be in the spotlight for being near the front instead of the shit show my team put on in Morocco, but it was distracting. We hustled away and back into our isolated world.

We chatted in the waning sunshine and enjoyed the camaraderie as we departed the low ground and started ascending into the Andes. After almost two days of racing, it was the first moment I felt really relaxed and could soak in what was actually happening. I was racing with adventure racing's dream team. Not only were they fast, smart, and efficient, they were all caring and nurturing. There was no posturing, competing against each other, or a shred of negativity. They were professional enough to know that the fastest way to the finish line is to take care of each other physically and emotionally.

Ian, as the sole male, fit in perfectly. As the navigator, he was clearly the leader in our route choice, but when it came to the rest of the team strategy decisions, he was completely a team player, involving us all in a democratic process. Robyn was as hard core and competitive as they come but also had a healthy sense of humor and was constantly lightening the mood by singing *South Park* songs and making wisecracks about anything and everything. Cathy, my friend and mentor, had an attentive, mothering instinct about her. She knew when to quietly ask how I was doing or offer a bit of advice. I felt respected and cared for, which allowed me to be my best and truly enjoy the ride.

Shortly after Camp 1 the forest grew thick and dense and the path narrowed to near nonexistence. But fortunately we were now at higher elevations, above the bamboo nightmare. Before long our trek became a trudge, which gave way to a slow vertical crawl up the face of the mountain over thick roots, rocks, and crumbling dirt. We reached a clearing and stopped to look up. Before us was the most spectacular rope section I'd ever seen, heading straight into the teeth of two of the region's most daunting peaks. It was straight the hell up loose rock and a fully exposed, slippery cliff face, and I felt completely at home. We clipped into the ropes and started our ascent up Angostini Wall, gaining 5,000 feet in less than a mile. We had basically taken an elevator route to enter the Cerro Catedral, a dramatic sawtooth ridge of towering spires that formed the stony maze in the sky between us and PC 10.

Winning teams need endurance. That's a given. But they also need a bit of wile. And let's just say Team Greenpeace's grizzled adventure racing vet John Howard is a wily man. We were still charging after them. And I was figuring that as long as they kept going, we'd keep going too. I was just giddy that we were duking it out for the top spot with the best in the business. Well, unbeknownst to us, somewhere between PC 9 and PC 10, Howard had ordered his squad into a hidden, protected nook between the rocks for some sleep. He had known we would take the lead, but since we didn't have line of sight to the front team, we wouldn't know we'd taken the lead. He predicted we'd continue to chase hard, wearing ourselves down, which is precisely what we did as we scrambled through the entire night.

As dawn broke on Day 3, we were walking on the tiger's teeth of the spires, suffering from sleep-deprivation-induced cranial rectal inversion (the technical term for judgment-impairment disorder, commonly referred to as "head up one's ass"). We needed to get off the ridge, but we couldn't find the best way down. Fortified by a little shut-eye, Greenpeace proceeded to run straight down the 5,000-foot descent through the ankle-deep scree. We, on the other hand, took the longer, more gradual way down the ridge—a decision that would cost us our lead.

We finally made it to PC 11 at the shore of Lake Mascardi, where inflatable rafts were waiting. The idyllic lake funnels into the Rio Manso, a lively river with Class IV rapids. This was potentially disastrous in our current sleep-deprived condition. After 48 hours of racing without rest, we decided to take advantage of some dry, sheltered bunks and sleep for just one hour. I desperately longed for more rest, but I let Ian, Cathy, and Robyn make the strategy decisions. A blink of an eye later, we were on the water. It was cold and raining, and as we would learn later on, the fabled Patagonia weather had finally unleashed its fury and hit the high mountains behind us. The storm dumped snow and sleet and pummeled the middle and back of the field with 70 to 100 mph winds. For safety reasons, the ascent up Angostini Wall was shut down and many teams were rerouted. We were one of only seven teams to escape Cerro Catedral before the storm hit and buried the craggy peaks in snow. That system was now coming our way.

Greenpeace was still in the lead when the raging storm reached the lowlands. The wind was howling, spraying freezing rain in our faces and nearly pushing us back upstream. Having spent hours leaning into the storm, expending a ton of energy and making little progress, we elected to get off the water and wait it out while we tried to get some much-needed sleep. We huddled under a rock, wrapped in our tiny space blankets and every stitch of clothing we had with us. We took turns being on the exposed side in an attempt to get an equal shred of warmth from each other. After a very fitful sleep with a great deal of shivering, we were relieved to see the storm finally slowing. We started paddling back down the river, not because we were rested, but because we needed to get warm and get the hell out of there.

The relentless Rio Manso, however, never let up. The current was fast and furious, and the frigid water splashing in our faces kept us awake. We came to an area thick with spectators: That should have been my first clue that there were dangerous conditions ahead. A huge, plunging rapid filled the river before us. Cathy and Ian went first and made it through the drop with no problem. Robyn and I were less elegant.

Ideally, a boater faced with an unknown challenge should find an eddy, get out of the boat, climb up onto the bank, and scout the best line. Well, we missed the eddy and plunged right into the rapid. Backward. Robyn was ejected and was floating downstream in the ice-cold river. Of course we were swaddled in dry suits, helmets, and life jackets, but the current was twirling our boat like a beach ball and Robyn was about to be swept downstream. Our wide eyes locked as she latched onto the side of the boat and I heaved her back in. We had bounced through the rapid thanks to a combination of luck and skill and gave the spectators the show they came for.

With a million more challenges ahead in the coming days, there was no time for discussion or celebration. We just continued to push toward PC 13, exhausted but safe. From there we would embark on the course's biggest undertaking.

It was time to change into mountaineering gear and head up and over the 11,000-foot Mount Tronador. At this point in the race, it was a death march. We were trudging through the snow, breaking trail, nearly going in and out of consciousness from the exertion in our addled state. Halti, just behind us, had been intelligently following our path, conserving energy. We were approaching Camp 2 at the base of Tronador with the top three teams, but before we could reach the camp, we needed to complete a series of rappels down a 500-foot waterfall. It was akin to dropping off a 15-story building, in the dark, through blowing snow. We were barely aware of our surroundings, save the task directly before us. Halti was so close they actually had to wait their turn before rappelling down.

The storm faded as we reached Camp 2. Greenpeace had chosen a route they hoped would be quicker, but it wasn't, so we bumped into them again at camp, and Halti joined us shortly thereafter. We were within 23 minutes of each other after three days of racing—evidence that sheer speed and stamina are only part of the equation. Strategy, team dynamics, and navigation are perhaps even bigger factors than outright fitness, especially in this case, when there was a lot of race left to play out, including the massive summit ahead.

After food and a short rest, we set off. Mount Tronador, an extinct volcano with a summit of 11,453 feet, hosts eight glaciers on its flanks. The volatile Patagonian weather and dangerous, crevasse-riddled access to the peak kept mountaineers off the summit until 1934. On this particular day we enjoyed clear skies, but the windchill was 65 below. We tethered ourselves together to prevent anyone from falling away, and we followed a fixed line that ascended and descended along the same route. We were still in second place, with the Finns biding their time, letting us break trail for them as we tried to chase down

Greenpeace. At that point, after days of near-perfect racing at the front of the pack, we started unraveling. The cumulative fatigue was gnawing on us like rats, leaving us exposed and fragile.

Traversing toward Tronador, the sun beat down and the reflective warmth off the snow was actually lulling us to sleep even though we were on our feet. We were walking zombies, weaving side to side with our heads rolling. Robyn literally fell over in the snow. "I'm sleeping while I'm walking," she moaned into the thin air. My tunnel vision was so bad that I could barely process my surroundings. Robyn's words sounded like an echo, but I couldn't locate where the sound was coming from. Then the bickering started, all of it nonsense. We knew we needed rest, but none of us wanted to let our near lead slip away. It was right there within our grasp. We agreed to take a 15-minute power nap on the side of the mountain, propped up on our backpacks. A short reprieve could give us the tiniest bit of clarity and fortify us just enough to get up and down the mountain. The early morning mountain air was still and clear, without a cloud in the sky, making for a window of opportunity that could change at any moment. We didn't want to fall too far behind and risk a bottleneck of teams on the ropes leading to the summit.

But while we were passed out, Halti tiptoed by, and Spanish Team Sierra Nevada, which had been steadily making up time on us, closed in as well. We awoke groggy and continued trudging like a line of ants up 11 miles of ice and snow. In the immense white landscape we could see all four teams, tiny black dots sprinkled at various spots on the mountain.

Our legs and lungs burned with ferocity, but we were silent in our mutual suffering. The ghostly wind, the crunching of our crampons, the clinking of climbing gear, and our labored breathing were the only sounds to be heard. Methodically, I focused on my steps. I clipped and reclipped my safety slings to the rope as we ascended, more out of instinct than conscious thought. My brain was numb from fatigue and exertion, and a mistake would prove costly, but all of my previous climbing experience was paying dividends here.

The path to the peak got so steep that we placed our hands on the snow in front of us and crawled vertically. The barren, windswept summit finally materialized, and it was like no place I have ever seen—like being on the top of the world. Tronador stands more than 1,000 feet higher than the surrounding ring of volcanoes that dot the landscape. I turned in every direction and saw nothing but more snowy peaks.

We took a brief moment to hug and lean into each other before the technical descent. I was grateful that it was a high-risk part of the course, because the ropes and the concentration they required actually helped keep me awake and took my mind off the pain in my legs.

I was starting to feel tendonitis in my shins and could hear crepitus as I flexed my ankles. I knew this was bad. My legs were now a ticking time bomb that I hoped could survive until the final paddling section. I flexed my jaw and bit the inside of my cheeks until they bled to take my mind off the searing pain in my shins. Running down the mountain would have normally been a welcomed break, but this time it was sheer torture. I was near tears, and Robyn could see what I was going through. She put a hand on my shoulder, looked into my eyes, and said, "I know how you feel. I'm sorry." It didn't take away the pain, but her acknowledgment was an emotional salve that kept my tears in check.

Otto Meiling Refuge, named after the mountaineer who made dozens of ascents of the peak, is perched at the base of Tronador and was our shining beacon. There we could purchase hot food and drink to reenergize ourselves for the final leg of the race. We were reeling and on the verge of collapse. Our relentless pace and lack of sleep early on had taken a toll. At the refuge, my head was falling into my plate of pasta, and Cathy was in the same pathetic state. We had slept precious few hours over five days, and my inexperience was starting to show. I just couldn't stay awake, even with the end of the race now less than a day away. There was just no adrenaline left to tap into. The warmth and security of that mountain hut was lulling me to sleep, and try as I might, I couldn't fight it off any longer. Ian and Robyn wanted to keep moving but reluctantly realized they had to do what was best for the team. Knowing we'd slip down in the rankings, they agreed to allow us two hours to sleep, and then we'd go all the way to the finish.

The teams behind us, Sierra Nevada and Argentinian Team Condor, passed us while we slept. By the time we left the checkpoint, ready to finish the race, we were sitting in fifth place—until Team Halti, who had brashly predicted a race win, became hopelessly lost, losing hours in their error. As we paddled the final miles of Lake Bahia Lopez to the finish, we heard a rising chorus of "*las diosas!*" being chanted by the spectators. The emotion of it all swelled up in my throat. We hadn't held onto the lead or even second or third, but it was a historic finish that would change the way this male-dominated sport viewed its "fairer" competitors.

Even Andrea Murray, the woman on winning team Greenpeace, called us out in her podium speech as the most impressive performance of the race. Her words and the respect we earned from the other teams were more significant than any trophy. When we started the race, no one expected us to be battling at the front, myself included. It was not only a team triumph, but also a personal victory. I got a taste of competition at the front end of the field and found out that I could hold my own with the best adventure racers in the world.

7

Exploring My Limits

A t the awards ceremony in Argentina, before the blisters on my feet had time to heal, I was tapped to be part of a top American team for the Trans-Himalaya 2000 Raid Gauloises in Tibet and Nepal, a race even more historic and prestigious than the Eco-Challenge. The invitation came from a conventional team that included Patrick Harper, an expert ski racer, kayaker, new adventure racer, and a whiz with a map and compass who had joined the Trans-Himalaya team as a last-minute replacement; mountain bike and adventure racing champion Mike Kloser; strong-man-in-just-about-any-sport Isaac Wilson; and Marshall Ulrich, mountaineer, ultrarunner, and seasoned adventure racer. They needed a strong American female to complete the roster. My single performance at the Eco-Challenge with *las diosas* had catapulted me into the spotlight of adventure racing. In just one year I went from being unranked and pulling up the rear to racing at the pointy end of the field.

I was astonished by the abrupt invitation to race on an experienced team, but also hesitant about racing with a hodgepodge of strangers after my Morocco experience. Having witnessed firsthand how the best in the world can operate as a seamless unit, I never wanted to race any other way again. I was also nervous once again about being the weak link and the only woman. I felt passionate about upending the prevalent attitude that women were "mandatory equipment" that the team is forced to carry, but I also felt more comfortable racing on a predominantly female team.

In no other sport are men and women scored on the same playing field the way they are in adventure racing. The fact that some of my first big expedition races were with mostly women's teams is no coincidence. Yes, it had been my choice to captain these teams, but I did it on my terms, which gave me security, eased the learning curve, and allowed me to be myself without censorship. Regardless of performance abilities, men and women are different creatures, and the care and compassion that I had felt in Argentina would be hard to replicate with a group of men I didn't know. Would they respect me? Could I be honest about my emotions and my shortcomings? Would I have to hide my fears?

Like so many times before, I had to put aside my trepidation and say yes to an opportunity that had the potential to be equally terrifying and gratifying. I gladly accepted the amazing invitation to travel to the roof of the world and see the Forbidden Kingdom of the Dalai Lama. I went in with a new confidence, knowing I had been able to keep pace with the most elite expedition racers. Why would this be any different? These men had experience, but they were not yet at the caliber of my teammates in Argentina. I also knew that in the adventure races I'd done so far, I'd never been the one to quit. Come hell, high water, or hamburger feet, I keep going.

It's often said in adventure racing circles that just getting to the start line is the hardest part of the race. Not only does training exact a toll that includes injuries and illness, but the races themselves are held in far-flung locales that make *Planes, Trains and Automobiles* look like a documentary. In this case, the flights to Nepal were the easy part. We checked in at the host hotel in the chaotic, polluted city of Kathmandu and boarded a plane to Lhasa, Tibet, located 12,000 feet above sea level. There, we got a brief respite and spent a couple of days acclimatizing and exploring the Potala Palace, the historical residence of the Dalai Lama. The place was spellbinding. The highest peaks in the world provide a breathtaking backdrop for the intricate, ancient architecture. The air was filled with chants, the whir of spinning prayer wheels, and the smell of the constantly burning yak butter lamps. The two-day break in our journey was just long enough for me to become entranced by the history and the beauty of this culture.

The next step was a brutal, bumpy two-day bus ride on the Tibetan Highway, which, contrary to its Western-sounding name, was actually a dirt road. It's the world's most dangerous, highest, and punishing road. We journeyed through the barren high-desert plateau, a cold and windy place with little in the way of life to call it home. The sweeping mountain views were only occasionally broken by stupas, gold-roofed monasteries, and prayer flags streaming in the wind. The bus ride itself was so arduous that we had to camp midway between Lhasa and the start village of Sherda Dzong. We hunkered down with hundreds of competitors and crew on a windy patch of hard ground, huddled between the gear trucks to escape the incessant wind. The journey continued to wear us down: Coughing reverberated through the bus, and you could see the fatigue starting to build in people's eyes. Well before the start gun went off, it was clear that this was going to be a truly unique adventure and that the hostile elements would play a decisive role in each team's success or failure.

The start area, at 14,000 feet, consisted of another barren camp nestled next to a tiny village where we could look forward to a second night of meager, dehydrated food, high winds, and parched air. We assembled our bikes, readied our packs, and were tested for blood oxygen saturation levels to ensure that the five-day acclimatization program had prepared us well enough to start the race. Normal blood oxygen levels are 95 to 100 percent. Anything below 90 percent and you're considered hypoxic—there's too little blood oxygen for you to function normally, so the race organizers would forbid your team from starting. Even though it felt like we were breathing through straws, everyone on our team scored in the 90s, so we were cleared to race. We had survived the first obstacle: getting to the start line healthy enough to begin.

By race morning, our team was worn out from the pilgrimage but otherwise healthy, acclimatized, and anxious to finally begin the race. The wind and dust were intense, so we wore surgical masks and Buffs (a versatile, light head cover) over our mouths in an attempt to keep the dust from infiltrating our lungs.

The Himalayas loomed bold and beautiful in the distance, but the torture of mountain biking at 14,000 feet through the "foothills" into a headwind was utmost in my mind. We would start the race with a quick 2-mile trek. Then it was onto the bikes for 52 miles. Then we'd trek again for 35 miles, all the way up to 17,500 feet—the highest point on the course—before saddling up once more for a 73-mile mountain bike ride back down. This ambitious first leg of the course would end up halting nearly one-third of the field.

We made quick work of the 2-mile trek and mounted up for the bike leg. This first bike section was even more brutal than I had imagined. The winds clocked in at 30 mph, the dust and altitude choked our lungs, and the hard dirt quickly turned to sand. I stuck close to Mike, using his body to block the wind and taking cues from his mountain bike skills. We finished this part of the race exhausted and already coughing but overjoyed to be in third place.

It was nearly dark when we packed up our bikes and selected a Tibetan pony as our packhorse for the next leg. Bessie, as we named her, was loaded down with our packs and towropes. We began the long walk up to 17,500 feet. As we headed into the night, three of the five of us were suffering from a dry, raspy cough that we attributed to the dust and dry air. I wasn't about to admit it, but I was suffering terribly, and it was only the first night. I felt like I might be in the worst shape of anyone on the team.

From dusk that first night until well into the third day, much of the race was a blur accompanied by a symphony of coughing. We would find out a full day later that three of us were coming down with bronchitis, which, when combined with high altitude, is an ugly, dangerous combination. It was so ugly, in fact, that there came a point when Isaac's vision went blurry and his arms began feeling numb. Marshall started vomiting and could keep down nothing but water. My own breathing was shallow and scratchy, and the pain of my incessant coughing was intense.

Bessie and our two healthy teammates, Patrick and Mike, miraculously dragged us through the freezing night, higher and higher into the snow. We were barely moving, and our sickness grew worse as we climbed higher. Around 2 a.m., about 18 hours into the race, we spent 90 minutes at Bessie's required vet check. Multiple teams were huddled into a small yurt where locals were burning yak dung for warmth. We crowded in and snuggled against any warm body we could find while we breathed the foul, smoky air. I was sure that the smoke was aggravating my lungs even more, but it was so cold outside that we had to trade one misery to avoid another. Beneath our tightly cinched hoods, everyone in the yurt was hacking. The vet check was designed to ensure the safety and health of the ponies, but Bessie was far better off than the humans on her team. Once our pony was cleared, we dejectedly pressed on into the cold night, post-holing in the deep snow and hanging onto Bessie.

As the sun rose over Shishpangma and the surrounding glorious peaks I had read about in mountaineering books, my black mood lifted for a moment, but I soon became numb again to the stunning beauty around me. My two sick teammates appeared to be feeling a bit better and began talking. The rising sun can often lift your mood and warm your spirit, but that wasn't happening for me. I had spent much of the night walking in half steps, laboring for every inhale and unable to move without the support of my teammate Patrick. I remember telling him I couldn't breathe, that I was afraid I'd choke. Now I was spiraling into a dark place. Just one day into the race and I was more tired, frightened, and hurt than I'd ever been in my life. All I wanted to do was reach our high point and then get out of this altitude prison as soon as possible.

The race medics had a different plan. At over 17,000 feet, they stopped us for an hour while they monitored Isaac's breathing and watched us, their demeanors stern. They showed no compassion for our struggling team. The next checkpoint was just a couple of hours away, and there would be a full medical facility there. It would also be the high point of the trek. After some fast-talking from Mike and Patrick, the French medic said he would watch us walk away and see if we were fit to go on. I remember Mike hissing at me that I'd better walk like I'd never walked before or we'd be disqualified. He was a fierce competitor. I wanted to dutifully follow his instruction, so I willed my body to cooperate.

I mustered all my energy to take about 10 slow steps before leaning over my poles to suck more air into my lungs. It felt like there was a vice grip on my chest. My deep cough had turned from dry and raspy to gurgled and mucous filled. But the medic let us go on.

Isaac, Marshall, and I made the slow walk to the high point by alternating shifts on our pony, who was thankfully doing just fine. Sitting on Bessie's back was wonderful, and I dreaded getting off. Isaac and Marshall would hold onto the pony and let her drag them along like deadweight. Dropping Bessie off at the next checkpoint would be hard to do—she had become a crucial part of our team's survival. We would not have made it without her.

The medics from the last checkpoint had radioed ahead about our condition, so our hopes of continuing the race were met by a firing line of medical officials. We were immediately ushered into the medical tent for a full evaluation. It felt like an interrogation at a police station. While Marshall, Isaac, and I rested for an hour, they hooked us up to oxygen saturation meters, checked our pulses, and monitored our breathing. They were observing us to see if rest would bring us into a healthier state. Mike paced around the cots, willing us to improve. I turned away from him, succumbed to the exhaustion, and went to sleep. After an hour, my pulse was still extremely high and my blood oxygen saturation was only in the 50s.

They put me through what amounts to a field sobriety test. I had to touch my nose and walk a straight line, and they checked my pupils. They were intent on us spending the night there to rest so they could reevaluate the situation in the morning. The problem was, we were at 17,500 feet, our health was deteriorating, and we had no tent or shelter to spend the night in. I knew I had to get down to a lower elevation to allow my body to heal. It was clear that staying put would make matters worse. The next checkpoint was a measly 8 kilometers away and 2,000 feet lower. I listened to the medics jabbering away in French about my health as they took long pulls on their cigarettes, and I wished they would just make a decision to either yank me from the race or let us get the hell out of there. After three more hours of waiting, we'd slipped to about 25th place and 20 teams had dropped out, all within the first 24 hours of the race.

More fast-talking by Mike and Patrick convinced the medics to let us shuffle out of there and begin our descent. It's always been my opinion that the medics were so annoyed by the pushy Americans that they agreed to let us go so they could enjoy some peace and quiet and get back to smoking their cigarettes. The guys were elated to escape, and even Isaac and Marshall seemed to be energized after our rest. I still felt like I was circling the drain. For me, walking the next 2.5 miles of flat ground felt like climbing Mount Everest. But I knew if I could make it across this first stretch, the terrain would drastically drop away and deliver us to the warm, moist air in Nepal. I was delirious, seriously ill, and petrified about what was happening to me. I knew my symptoms were much more than just simple altitude sickness; I had no pack on my back, was being towed by a bungee cord behind Mike, and could still barely put one foot in front of the other. I was in pain, dizzy, experiencing blurred vision and extreme shortness of breath. I was struggling physically and mentally, and I was afraid I was seriously damaging my health. At this point, I was no longer concerned with whether or not we would finish the race—I feared for my life. I made it about a half mile before I fell to my knees, sobbing between sharp, labored breaths. I knew that after the next checkpoint, the terrain would drop us quickly out of the mountains. I just didn't think I could make it there.

After being the one to talk my fellow racers off the cliff (literally and figuratively) in previous races and the one who watched our race hopes vanish with the illness or injury of a teammate, it was now my turn. I struggled with the realization that my failings would be the team's failings, but I simply couldn't go on. My body was betraying me. Mike turned around and barked, "Come on. You don't want to be like Lisa!" Mike had been a member of the winning Team Vail in Morocco and had finished five days quicker than I had. He knew of the struggles my team had with Lisa complaining and dragging anchor for days before finally abandoning. The insinuation that I was just quitting because I was uncomfortable or unmotivated only increased my agony.

Mike and Isaac seemed to think that if they adopted the approach of walking far ahead and yelling back at me, I would somehow be motivated to keep up. Their words hung useless in the thin air. Marshall, who had still not fully recovered, kept his distance from them and from me. He looked sheepish in the face of the conflict, avoided eye contact, and remained quiet. Neither strategy—ignoring me or shouting at me—was helping. I was at a level of fatigue and illness I'd never felt before or since; I was beyond caring about whether or not I was keeping pace with the boys. I was truly putting one foot in front of the other in a life-saving effort to get myself to safety.

Amid the hazy memory of that day a singular moment is crystal clear. After pushing and pulling me for 24 hours without judgment or blame, Patrick put his arm around me while I dropped to my knees and cried. He privately told me not to worry about letting the team down, that he would stand by whatever decision I made: to go on or to stop. Either way, he would stay with me. That was all I needed, a gentle human touch and an honest word that it was okay to make the decision that was best for me. No pep talk or "you can do it" sermon could reach me. What I needed was to know someone else out there cared more about me and my health than about finishing the race. Patrick forever altered my view of what it means to be a true teammate. His reassurance calmed my panic and brought me to my feet.

"Let's go," I said.

The following days rewarded me with antibiotics for my bronchitis, a 10,000-foot mountain bike descent, and arrival into the warm, moist air of Nepal on the shores of the Bhote Kosi river. The discouraging behavior from my teammates gave way to respect as I returned to my normal self and could once again pull my weight. Mike even said at one point, "This is the Rebecca I was waiting to see again." Our lung infections slowly healed throughout the race (though I'll always wonder if a later diagnosis of exercise-induced asthma was a by-product of that beating I put my lungs through in Tibet), and we worked our way back up to a seventh place finish—the highest-ever finish for an American team.

When you receive the support you need from people who care about you as a human being, it's amazing how unbelievably far your body can go. Sometimes all you need is permission to fail in order to succeed. Patrick's loyalty to me high in the Himalayas that week laid the groundwork for a long-term adventure racing partnership and cemented a lifelong friendship.

With Patrick and me as the backbone of the team, I would continue racing as part of predominantly male teams for the remainder of my adventure racing career. Even though I cherished the experiences with predominantly female teams, women were still a vast minority in the sport. Due to a bigger talent pool, it was easier to build a cohesive, dependable, elite team with men. Racing on these teams became a multiyear education in gender dynamics and firsthand confirmation that women are from Venus and men are from Mars.

A typical training day would go like this: One of the guys would call me up and ask if I wanted to join a training run. I'd take a deep breath, a hit of my inhaler, and mentally evaluate whether or not I was feeling up for an "easy" run with my testosterone-laden teammates. Thirty minutes into my run with the guys, I'd be watching them disappear around the next bend, wondering why they'd bothered to invite me in the first place. It was always a blow to my confidence. If I couldn't keep up with my teammates on an easy run, how was I ever going to keep up with them in a 600-mile expedition race in the middle of nowhere? I figured they couldn't help themselves. They were born with an overabundance of that magic hormone that made them treat every workout as a chance to exert their dominance. After all, any athlete in their vicinity was a potential predator who might snatch away the day's victory—even if it was just a ride to the coffee shop.

When it came time to race, the competitive fire burned even hotter in my male teammates. I would roll my eyes or cuss under my breath (or for all to hear) at some jackass thing that one of my teammates would do: bolt ahead and then get separated from the team; avoid asking directions; not admit to suffering like a dog, only to come completely undone a few hours later. Despite training, racing, and sometimes even living together for months on end, I often struggled to understand what made them tick.

I know the feeling was often mutual. In the years that followed it wasn't uncommon for me to overhear the guys bickering over who was going to go back to "deal with Reba" in a particularly grueling section of the race.

"You go. I did it last time!" they'd argue back and forth.

If I hadn't been gasping like a fish on dry land, I'd have told them to suck it up and just come tell me a story to get my mind off the suffering. Their avoidance felt like criticism, and I certainly didn't need to be criticized . . . I'm my own worst critic. There are exceptions to any rule, but I always found that I often wanted camaraderie while the guys wanted competition. As different as we were in our tactics, the team was successful because we were all bonded by a unified goal—the desire to redefine our limits and test our endurance.

ADVENTURE RACING LEGEND John Howard once said he was sure that one expedition race takes years off your life. The sleep deprivation, calorie deprivation, physical and emotional stress, the extreme highs, and the extreme lows all take a heavy toll on an otherwise healthy athlete. Add to that list overuse or traumatic injuries, stomach ailments, sunburn, skin rashes, foot blisters, mouth sores, and parasites.

Nowhere do your vulnerabilities feel more exposed than in the jungle. The 2000 Eco-Challenge took place in Borneo, a large tropical island off the coast of Southeast Asia. I have always preferred mountains to jungles. I'll just say it: I hate jungle races and the jungle climate. There's just a creepy-crawly, sticky, extra-uncomfortable factor that, when added on top of the already intense nature of a race, messes with your mind in a much more vivid, weird way than the mountain races. Borneo, the jungle of all jungles, drove that point home in spades.

We had been biking, kayaking, and trekking for four days on just two hours of sleep per night. The clock never stops, so gambling with sleep is a huge factor in race strategy. Stop more to sleep and move faster, or sleep less and keep moving: those are your choices. It's always a roll of the dice to calculate which will yield the fastest overall pace. For this late riser who normally cherishes 8–10 hours of sleep a night, 2 hours of sleep per night for a week straight is torture, but it's par for the course among the top teams in expedition races. Sleep deprivation is hell for the body, one of the toughest and most extreme parts of racing. In Borneo, my body was breaking down as well as shutting down, and I was trying to fortify it any way I could. While Patrick reviewed the maps during a quick stop, I fished some vitamins out of my pack.

I dumped the capsules into my palm. Staring through half-closed eyes, I looked down to see bugs engulfing my hand and scurrying up my forearm.

I shrieked, tossing the vitamins high above my head and running in circles to escape the horror. Patrick started laughing so hard he nearly fell to the ground.

"Glad those vitamins didn't get ya, Reba," he said as gales of laughter erupted from my other teammates. Hallucination is a very common occurrence after four or five days of sleep deprivation.

Borneo, in particular, was a mind screw because sometimes what you thought and wished was a hallucination was actually real. The jungle was absolutely alive. For one, it was deafening because of all the insects, birds, monkeys, and other creatures we couldn't identify and often couldn't see. Judging from the *huge* droppings they left behind, there were elephants around too. At one point I dropped a wrapped food bar, and when I bent to pick it up, the jungle floor literally started moving with creatures scurrying out of the way—that was *not* a hallucination. Between the noise and the overpopulation of creepy crawlies, any sleep was fitful and nightmarish. We constantly imagined what was crawling on or even into us as we dozed off.

We laughed when we saw that machetes were listed as mandatory gear for this event, but the joking was over when we actually started traveling through the jungle. The foliage and brush were so dense and thick that we could barely see 5 or 6 feet in any direction, and we all became adept at swinging the blade to clear an opening that would simply close right behind us.

In the massive limestone Madai Caves we waded through knee-deep mounds of bat guano. There were centipedes of cartoonishly large proportions and beetles that rolled up into a ball about the size of a small orange if you touched them. We wore surgical masks inside the caves to keep from breathing in all of the floating particles of who knows what.

It was bad enough having the bugs and snakes all around me, but the worst, hands down, were the leeches. After days of slogging through the rain-soaked Sabah jungles, we were covered in leeches. They were all over the jungle, and as we brushed against the foliage, they'd sense our body heat and hitch a ride. We had hundreds of these blood-sucking, slimy, horrible creatures stuck to us everywhere, and I mean everywhere! One athlete was temporarily blinded because a leech got into her eye and secreted some sort of poison. Another guy opened up his race radio and called for help because a leech had gone into his penis. I was terrified to pull my pants down to answer nature's call, and when I did, it was standing tall and in the biggest clearing I could find. Any cuts or open wounds would soon be covered with a clump of writhing leeches, fighting each other for our warm blood. These tiny, nightmarish beasts could get through anything and everything, including your shoes, socks, and any article of clothing. We would take our shoes off to care for blisters, and soon clumps of leeches would be stuck between our toes and wriggling into our open blisters. There was no way to shield ourselves from those devils. The most natural reaction was to scream and get them the hell off your body. Practically speaking, leeches are truly a threat because they can cause infection, especially given our depleted state. Staying healthy felt like a nearly futile mission but an important part of our daily existence in the jungle.

You can't really grab on to leeches because they stretch as you pull and they burrow in deeper. If you do get them off one body part, they stick to your fingers and get to work there, or they move on to whatever body part you brush against as you try to flick them off. It's a never-ending cycle that you cannot win. The Borneo locals told us to put a leaf between our fingers so the leech would not stick to the skin and we could then toss it away. We also tried to put salt on them or use a lighter to burn them away. These strategies worked, but they resulted in us spending a great deal of time picking over each other like a pack of monkeys. It was a fruitless and maddening task that occupied much of our precious energy. More than seeing the finish line, I wanted to stand in a hot, leechless shower naked and sleep in a clean, bug-free bed.

The jungle experience stayed with me. About six months later, in the comfort of my leech-free temporary Lake Tahoe home, I used the toilet and as I turned to flush, I caught a glimpse of something in the bowl. "Holy shit!" I yelled. I called Patrick, who was now my boyfriend, into the bathroom. (Not exactly the most romantic gesture, I know, but when you adventure race together, you are pretty used to seeing all sides of someone.)

He came in, glanced into the toilet bowl, and said, "Holy shit!" There was a worm about the diameter of my pinkie finger and three times as long. Patrick got a fork and fished it out (the things we do for love), and the three of us went to the hospital. The doctor looked at the worm with horrified curiosity. "Have you been traveling?" he asked. I laughed and ripped off the long list of exotic locales I'd been to in that past year alone. He left the room and came back with a team of doctors, and they all hovered around, scratching their heads and flipping through pages of a fat medical journal. Wide-eyed, they stared at me, then at the worm, then back to the pages, trying to identify this foreign thing. Knowing something had been living in my body, sharing my food, hitching a ride for months, and that there might still be members of its family remaining was unsettling, to say the least. I wanted some exceptionally potent medicine to wipe out the colony and rid myself of the parasitic horror.

"When there's one, there's usually more," the doctor told me as he signed the prescription. I named that worm, a roundworm parasite bigger than any the Tahoe Medical Center had ever seen, Nermil and bade it a less-than-fond farewell. Aside from the numerous gummy worms my family sent me as gags, I'm happy to say I never saw another worm come from inside of me.

IN 2002 THE RAID GAULOISES in Vietnam took us back into the jungles. From start to finish, the race was 1,000 kilometers, the longest adventure race in history. We were going crazy from the incessant, stifling heat. After three soaking wet days of hiking through rice paddies and jungles in brutal sun or pouring rain, our clothes were literally rotting on our flesh, which also felt like it was rotting. We stunk in a putrid, unhealthy way and were all developing prickly heat rash—even the light touch of clothing on our skin was becoming excruciatingly painful. So, I did the sensible thing: I took off my clothes. Everything except my shoes. And so did John Jacoby, Novak Thompson, Gary Southerland, and Tony Molina. Me and four guys, my teammates and my friends, strolling silently through the jungle. We used just one headlamp between the five of us to save batteries and enjoy the privacy of the darkness. The air on our naked skin felt delicious, and it was one of the most peaceful and enjoyable moments of that entire race.

The usual social norms of privacy did not apply. We were in survival mode, and our skin was getting blistered and chafed, so walking down the road in the nude was a perfectly logical thing to do. As we came out of the deep jungle and approached the outskirts of a village, the spell was broken. Even painful skin rash and sleep deprivation had not washed away *all* of our social etiquette, so we stopped to gingerly pull back on a few items of sweat-soaked clothing. The breezy, refreshing reprieve was over, and we went back to trading one type of discomfort for another.

It's the toughest environments that leave the biggest impression. Even though the memories of all of these races, countries, and landscapes often run together in my head, I have moments of clarity about each race, moments that changed me in ways subtle and significant. The 2002 Eco-Challenge Fiji is the race I think about when I need some perspective on my life at home. We didn't do particularly well, but it was still a great race (albeit in the jungle). Traveling through the remote world, there is a strange sense of isolation from reality and dependence on your tiny pod of people. There will be no convenience stores, no trail fairy to tell you where to go, no mother to give you a hug and make it all better. You are totally reliant on yourself and each other. When you fall down, you pick yourself up, wipe your own tears away, and keep going to the finish line. What you have for the journey is on your back, and that's it—but sometimes it's not enough and something magical intervenes.

In Fiji we finished a paddling section down a brown ribbon of water that slashed a navigable path through the jungle. Tony had been sick and was alternating between retching and sleeping in the kayak for hours. Due to his illness, we were behind schedule, which meant we were stressed out and running low on food.

A swarm of Fijian villagers with the whitest smiles and darkest skin I had ever seen helped us ashore. It felt like a homecoming, even though we were complete strangers and had never before set foot in this place. These people lived in simple thatch huts; they had no shoes and had never seen a car. We showed up wearing native sarongs that we had procured in a previous village, but aside from that, I'm sure we looked completely foreign to them with our multicolored backpacks and high-tech running shoes.

The villagers had no understanding of what we were doing, but they knew that we were traveling through their country, and they could see in our exhausted expressions and body language that we needed help—and that was enough for them. They lifted our heavy loads, took us into their homes as family, spread out blankets for us to rest on, and gave us much-needed food. We chowed down plate after plate of cassava root (which tastes a bit like potato)—it was heaven to our empty bellies. Following a glorious nap, the woman of the house had tea ready for us, and one of the strongest men in their community used gestures to communicate that he would escort us to the next village so we didn't lose our way. He dipped his wooden torch into the fire and ran ahead of us with his fire stick raised high. He darted and scrambled shoeless over river rocks and logs while enthusiastically motioning for us to hurry and move along. He was getting sucked into the excitement of the journey and was a contributing member of the team for a while. His supreme athleticism was incredible to witness and made me feel like an imposter in his backyard.

When it was time to part ways, he politely motioned to us to ask if he could have one of our headlamps. It broke my heart to deny him. We couldn't explain in his language that we needed this tool to keep moving or that his fascination would be short-lived when the batteries ran out. We were touched by the charity and true goodness of these people we will never see again. We were truly visitors in this place. Despite our differences, the universal needs for food, shelter, and directions span the globe and overcome any language or cultural barriers.

Over the years of adventure racing we had many experiences with locals that both humbled and amazed me. They forced me think about the day-to-day luxuries that we take for granted: hot showers, clean sheets, an ice-cold beverage. We have so much, but it seems like we often lose sight of what it means to be happy. Meeting people from all over the world and experiencing a small piece of their way of life was one of my favorite parts of racing, even if those encounters occurred in a creepy-crawly, sticky jungle.

MY MOM HAS ALWAYS been very supportive of my gypsy lifestyle and my adventures around the world, even when her friends thought I was crazy. "She graduated 10th in her class with a business degree and could have written her own ticket anywhere, but she's living out of her car and crashing on people's couches . . . Aren't you disappointed?" her friends would ask. But I wasn't on drugs, in jail, asking for money, or any combination of the above, so Mom figured she didn't have any reason to complain. For the most part, I was happy and choosing what I wanted to be doing, so that's what really mattered to her. I think some of those judgmental comments only served to make her even more determined to show the world how proud of me she was and to give me as much support as possible. Over the years, she traveled to a lot of the races and helped us by crewing, following our progress, collecting photos and articles, and writing detailed race reports for the folks back home.

It was great to be able to share some of these big travel experiences with my mom, but deep down, I always carried a bit of sadness that my dad wasn't there too. In high school I'd often dreamed about having coffee with him and telling him about how I played the flute and ran cross-country and loved camping and the outdoors. I wondered if he would be proud of me. What would he think of the adult that I'd become? When he was shot down in Vietnam, I was only three, so I have no personal memories of him. My impression is woven together from a hodgepodge of tales my family members have shared with me.

My grandmother would sit me down with photo albums and talk about how my dad loved animals and would bring in strays and nurse them back to health. My mom would tell me about his love for fast cars and folk music by Woody Guthrie, Pete Seeger, and Tom Paxton. My uncle would tell me what a great musician my dad was and how they loved jamming together. There are enough themes that hit a familiar chord for me to feel connected to my dad, to know I am truly his flesh and blood. However, none of the memories are my own. So, when I got word that the organizers of Raid Gauloises were holding their 2002 competition in Vietnam, where my dad spent the last nine months of his life, I knew I had to go and see if I could piece together some of my own memories of him.

It was another roller coaster of a race, with our team taking an early, dominating lead for five days before one of my teammates was struck with an intestinal bug that knocked us back about 10 hours and out of contention. It was an important race for me, not just because of my father's history there, but because I ended up being the strongest member of the team for much of the race. Instead of just hanging on for dear life, I was truly a contributing member of the team, even carrying John Jacoby's backpack for a spell. We managed to fight our way back to a fourth place finish, which was disappointing considering we'd been tasting the win for most of the race, but totally respectable. Once the race was over, a more personal adventure began.

My mom and I flew to Da Nang Airfield, where my dad was stationed from July 1971 to March 1972, when his F-4 Phantom jet was shot down near Saravan, over the Ho Chi Minh Trail, in southern Laos. From there, my mom arranged a car and driver to help us retrace his steps through the country so both of us could see and feel where my dad had been. I could imagine him, a nomad like myself, traveling among the temples and pagodas and elaborate tombs of the Nguyen dynasty's emperors. I could imagine him feeling hungry, lost, and scared. In a very small way, my team's experience of this terrain was similar, but also radically different. I had chosen to come here and had no hate, anger, or firearms pointed in my direction.

My dad was a lot of things: an activist, a pacifist, a wanderer, and a musician, traveling around the country in a mail truck–turned-camper, playing protest music and speaking out for civil rights and unions and against the Vietnam War. With a very low draft number, he decided to take the bull by the horns and enlist in the Air Force so he could be an officer rather than a drafted grunt on the front lines. Ironically, he liked it enough to reenlist and was serving as a captain, stationed in Puerto Rico, when I was born. Six months later, he reenlisted and was accepted into Officer Candidate School.

While we were in Vietnam, Mom and I went to China Beach, where the U.S. servicemen would go on weekend passes for R and R. As we stood on the beach, she remembered some of his happiest letters coming from here, and she could finally connect the words he'd written all those years ago with this place. We strolled through the hallways of the Vietnam War Museum in Hue, reading about what the Vietnamese call "The American War." From Hue, we drove north through the countryside to the border of North and South Vietnam to venture into the tunnels at Vinh Muoc. This labyrinth burrowed nearly 100 feet underground and housed a village of 60 families from the intense bombing in this volatile region. Nearby, the only remains of the Khe Sanh Combat Base are a small museum, a few abandoned aircraft, and the remnants of a bunker. The rest of this bloody battleground is now covered in lush green banana trees and coffee plants. The earth has recovered, but the still air and eerie silence tell a different story.

The adjacent demilitarized zone (DMZ) didn't hide the scars of war as well. Here, much of the land was still barren from the continual bombing and Agent Orange defoliant that was dropped daily for so many years. It was a sad sight, and there are no words to explain how I felt staring across the bald terrain.

Mom and I finished our tour with a trip to what is left of the infamous Hoa Lo Prison (nicknamed the Hanoi Hilton). From 1964 to 1973, the concrete fortress was used by the North Vietnamese to house, torture, and interrogate more than 600 American prisoners of war, most of them pilots who had been shot down like my father. We silently passed through the cement cells, unable and unwilling to imagine the horror and atrocities that filled those rooms, and I hoped with all my might that he had not spent time here. I had no way to know, because in 2002, 30 years after his plane went down, my father's remains were not yet identified. Had he died in the crash? Or did his MIA designation mean he had survived the crash only to be kept as a prisoner and tortured before his death? Or had he survived the crash and was living another life, perhaps a happy one, right here in Vietnam? I wouldn't know the answers to these questions for five more years, when the government officially located his remains and confirmed that he was killed in action.

I cried more than I expected to on this trip and felt closer to my dad than I ever had. Being in Vietnam on the same ground he had stood on or flown over, I could know a portion of his life. I left with a more complete picture of him, a better understanding of a beautiful and damaged country, and a genuine reassurance that my dad and I would have gotten along very well. My mom and I grew closer on the trip too. I saw a more tender side of her. She let her guard down and allowed herself to share painful memories that she had been harboring for 30 years. This spectacular journey also planted a seed—one day I would return to spend more time close to my father and eventually visit his crash site. My search for answers had left me with a desire to someday go even deeper into that jungle.

8

Proving Grounds

By this point in my adventure racing career, I'd been close enough to smell victory. I had traversed different types of terrain in so many different countries and had adapted to handle countless situations along the way that I could now visualize a big win happening. With a steady roster of regulars, I believed our team (now called Team Montrail) finally had the maturity and skill to do it. But an overall win in a big expedition race remained stubbornly elusive. Unlike mountain bike races, marathons, or even triathlons—where speed dictates the win—adventure races are about being able to make forward progress in many different modalities, through all sorts of adversity, alongside three or four other people. Being fast is an essential trait, to be sure. But you also need to be skilled and smart and resourceful and frankly just plain lucky to get to the finish line at all, let alone before everyone else.

I knew it was more common to have more failures than wins and that failures are the prerequisite and preparation for success. The teams I captained saw our fair share of falling short, but we had some significant achievements too. We got lost and were covered in leeches in Borneo but still fought our way up to eighth place overall. We had to pull out of the Southern Traverse in New Zealand after a teammate succumbed to hypothermia in the mountains. We fended off heat and snakes in Vietnam to hold a seven-hour lead until a teammate caught a bug and we lost it all and then some. We made a disastrous bamboo raft in Fiji that plummeted us to 30th place right off the bat, but then we clawed our way back to first after an endless trek through the jungle, a treacherous mountain-bike leg, and some ocean and white-water kayaking. At one point we'd built up a two-hour lead. And then another teammate with a stomach bug caused us to abandon the race. Another strong finish slipped through our fingers.

The list goes on and on. Despite our failures, however, my team was building a reputation as a force to be reckoned with, if only because we refused to give up. So when, in 2003, my team was one of only three U.S.-based teams to qualify for the prestigious Raid Gauloises World Championships in Kyrgyzstan, we were pegged as a team to watch, according to the race web site, which ran the following:

> MONTRAIL (US)—For almost two thirds of the race, Rebecca Rusch and her teammates dominated the 2002 Raid Gauloises in Vietnam, before falling foul of fatigue and slowing their speed to recuperate. This year, Rebecca is back as captain with a slightly modified team, including the twin pillars of Thompson and Harper, both enormously respected on the North American circuit. They won't be far off the race-front.

I was elated reading those words. It's exciting to be a favorite. It's also daunting because there's no flying under the radar. Everyone is watching your every move, looking for a chink in the armor. We really *did* have an amazing squad, however. I would be trekking, kayaking, rafting, rope climbing, and horseback riding through this raw, wild part of the world with three amazing guys who were now the core members of my most successful and longest-lived adventure racing team. We had honed our skill and relationships over the years, and we really had a shot at capturing a win this time—and we all wanted it . . . badly. Judging by the course description, it would take every bit of our collective race experience to get it.

My team was a crew of men, primarily Aussies, who are notoriously macho men. Thankfully, most of them also had a softer side, like Patrick Harper (the non-Aussie), whom I had first raced with in Tibet in 2000. His experience growing up in the Idaho wilderness, competing as a cross-country skier and ultrarunner, and paddling first descents in many Idaho rivers gave him the perfect combination of athletic prowess and savvy wilderness knowledge. Patrick was thin, wiry, and much stronger than he looked, and he'd become one of my favorite teammates and best friends over the course of the many races we'd done together. We even dated for a while, but eventually we decided we were better off as friends. The fact that we were able to continue racing together after that just proved how strong our friendship really is.

The Raid rules allow mixed nationalities, so our team was U.S.-based with two Americans and two Australians. The lack of proximity made training days together few and far between, but we'd spent so many hours together in races that we now knew each other like family. Novak Thompson was the other pillar on our team. I'd raced with him in Vietnam and was blown away by his navigation skills and hard-core attitude. I had not witnessed navigational prowess like his since racing with Ian Adamson in Argentina. Nothing seemed to rattle Novak physically or mentally. He is a man of few words, and he does not put up with any crap at all. His background in the Australian military taught him how to navigate and suffer efficiently. His triathlon racing built his lightning-fast speed, and living on the beach sculpted him into an incredible paddler. Like Patrick, Novak's lanky, thin physique belies his true strength.

The final addition to our core group was Australian kayaking legend John Jacoby. John had been adventure racing for longer than any of us and had raced with the best in the world. He is big, strong, levelheaded, and extremely easygoing. He actually seems too big to move quickly and appears to lumber along ungracefully, but he still posts extremely fast marathon times. He is never fazed by other teams, difficult situations, or personality conflicts.

With this core team of regulars, we were feeling confident—as confident as you can feel about a sport with so many uncontrollable variables. We were all experienced racers, and each of us had our own training regimens locked down, so our biggest task was prepping our gear for the daunting logistics.

Equipment management for a race like the Raid is very complicated. Before the race even begins, you have mandatory gear and equipment checks. We packed up six different gear bags, five gear boxes, and four bike cases, all of which were numbered and distributed to various points along the route. The course was 514 miles long, with 14 different transitions and discipline changes, so it was critical that the right gear be in the right place. John cautioned us that the race could be won or lost on transition times alone, so we went about our preparation especially carefully, since we all knew we'd never be able to live with ourselves if some little mistake or oversight ended up jeopardizing what felt like a really big opportunity for a win.

THE RACE STARTED EARLY, at 6 a.m., in lush, green foothills that would take us into the high mountains right out of the gate. It was tough going. After a brisk jog up a hillside, jockeying for position with the lead teams, we started a 32-mile trek up to 3,500 feet, where a late winter has deposited a blanket of deep, heavy snow. We were sitting in with the top 10 teams, making steady progress and trying to keep the race reasonably close without making mistakes. In a race this long the opening hours are not typically decisive. It's important to stay in contact with the lead, but also to be patient and not take the lead until the timing is right. There is little opportunity for navigational brilliance when teams are in close proximity, just following the leader.

Twelve hours later, we were off the mountain, had sailed through a rowdy stretch of white water down the narrow, twisting, brush-riddled Kyzyl-Suu River on our inflatable canoes. We were now paddling on the massive Lake Issyk Kul, the largest high-altitude lake in the world. This stretch was 62 miles, and our paddling would take us into the night before we would trade our boats for bikes and embark on a 47-mile mountain-bike leg over the jagged Celestial Mountains.

We left the water in fifth place and kept moving. When we arrived at the location for Checkpoint 5, we found no one. It was like a ghost town. We double-checked the maps to be sure we were in the right place. We were. We looked at each other as a terrible sinking sensation came over us: Something bad—really bad—must have happened. We had to get credit for making it to this checkpoint before we could move on, so we sat down and waited.

As the teams piled up at Checkpoint 5, I finally got the news of the accident from Michael Lemmel of Team Sweden. Dominique Roberts of the French Team Endurance-AGF had been dragged into the branches of a partially submerged tree, known as a strainer in river speak, and had been flipped and trapped beneath her boat. The paramedics were on the spot, but they could not revive her. I wept as a stunned silence fell over the group of athletes—it was a grim reminder of the risks that lie around every corner. After what felt like a very long time of confused, hushed milling about, talking with friends, hugging, and reflecting on what we were all doing out there, the race proceeded in honor of Dominique. The next section was cycling, and we rolled out with all of the other teams intermingled and still in shock.

We were riding, mostly in silence and reflection, but it didn't take long for us to realize something was not right with Patrick. He was lagging back and struggling to keep up, even though we were barely a day into the race. Typically for the first 24 hours, I'm the one struggling to keep pace with the guys. This time it was different, and I kept looking back, wondering what was happening. He finally fessed up that he was sick with a stomach bug and had been pulling over frequently with diarrhea. Novak and John were visibly annoyed that Patrick was off the back and slowing the team's pace. I hung back with him and offered what support I could, but I was sadly watching the race roll by. How could we have this bad luck so early in the event? He had been fine when we started that morning.

The team kept our heads, relieved Patrick of his pack, and did everything we could to simply make forward progress. I bridged up to John and Novak and told them we had to help Patrick and that we needed to ride together for moral and physical support. I even made the team take a forced rest stop in the middle of the day so we could nurse Patrick with electrolytes and fluids. Novak and John were furious as we watched multiple teams pass by, look over at us, and count us out of contention. I insisted that because it was so early in the race, there was still time for Patrick to recover. If we kept pushing him beyond his breaking point, we certainly would have no chance of a good finish. If he recovered, we'd have a chance and could start chasing again. Patrick had supported me in the same way in the Tibetan mountains, and now it was my turn.

For the rest of the bike leg and into the following trekking section, which included ascending over rocks and glaciers at 14,000 feet, he was sluggish but improving. As a timely blessing, there was a mandatory six-hour stay at the camp midway through the trek, which gave us a chance to rest in a yurt, nourish ourselves, and recharge. I mothered Patrick, fed him, helped organize his gear, and got him to sleep as soon as possible. By the time we needed to roll out and finish the trek, Patrick was back to himself and ready to pull his own weight again. Novak and John were charged up by seeing that we'd not fallen too far back.

We now faced a monster mountain-bike leg of 119 miles. In light of Dominique's tragic accident, the race directors removed a section of white water and now had us covering that distance by bike. I was bracing myself for a massive struggle. At this point, I'd never ridden more than 100 miles in my life. Add to that our very heavy packs filled with winter mountaineering gear, the sleeting rain, and a howling, icy wind, and you can imagine my dread. The tables would turn from me giving support to receiving it.

The bike course was extraordinarily long with lots of gravel roads. I fixated on efficiency, watching my teammates' pedal strokes, trying to mimic their body position and stay in their slipstream. I focused on making sure I was eating and drinking, even though my cold hands could barely unclench from the bars and dig into my pack for food. It took skill and unflinching concentration for me to keep up with the rest of the group. On top of the physical stress, the mental stress of being out of my element was exhausting. It was cold, dark, and raining for much of the miserable ride. I was grateful that Patrick and Novak are navigational wizards, so we didn't get off course in the endless web of hills and valleys.

Most teams have just one lead navigator. Our massive advantage was that we had two. Of course we could all read a map and knew how to use a compass, but having the skill to plan, strategize, and interpret the tiny squiggly lines on a topo map, all while flying along on a bike and taking care of ourselves, was a huge challenge. With two navigators, we had backup, and Novak and Patrick switched the roles so each of them got a mental break. It kept us from making mistakes and wearing out one person too much.

We continued on, not charging forward but riding steady, picking off teams one by one and moving back up near the front of the field. Midway through the ride we were within striking distance, just 10 or 15 minutes back of the leaders, Team Sweden. All of those teams that had discounted us earlier looked a little shocked to see that we'd brought Patrick back from a deep, dark hole. Personally, I couldn't believe we were actually making up time on a *bike* section. We caught Team Sweden in the last 20 miles of the ride and formed an eight-person pace line that steamrolled through the rain. No one spoke, but we shared the work, even though we were competitors. We all knew that as a bigger group, we could distance ourselves from the rest of the field and narrow down the competition. We would postpone doing battle with each other until later.

We rolled into the next transition area together, giddy at having this hard bike leg behind us and a gap on the field, but my team was also carefully eyeing Team Sweden, looking for signs of fatigue or weakness. We rummaged through our gear boxes and readied ourselves for a huge, high mountain trek, then Team Sweden and Team Montrail walked out of there together, knowing one of our teams could likely hold on to a decisive lead in this next section. Patrick, Novak, John, and I felt we were a stronger team navigationally, so we worked hard to create a gap. We even hiked without our headlamps on for a portion of the night to slink away from Team Sweden. Novak and Patrick made some critical navigation decisions, and our strategy worked. We entered the next section ahead of the Swedes.

There we found ourselves joined by some new teammates— horses. These horses, however, were not waiting for us saddled and brushed. They were loose, and, like rodeo clowns, we had to catch them, saddle and bridle them, and then ride 36 mountainous miles through the night. As to the quality of our mounts, let's just say these "sturdy Kyrgyz horses" were a bit more like broken-down nags. They were sinewy and small as a result of the harsh environment and certainly not accustomed to carrying heavy athletes with large packs for hours. Big John looked especially ridiculous in the saddle because his legs nearly brushed the ground. Sprinting out of the gate, the horses were charging in every direction and protesting the weights on their backs. Mine would repeatedly race ahead at Mach speed then, without warning, take a hard left turn in an effort to be rid of me. Soon enough they realized their protestations weren't working, and they began to settle down. And then they really settled down and ran out of steam entirely. At one point, Patrick's horse lay down on the cold ground with Patrick still on its back. (Thankfully, we were not the only ones with bum steeds. We were told later that the Swedes attempted to pour Red Bull down the throats of their horses to make them go.) It ended up being a long slog of walking, pulling, pushing, and coaxing Patrick's horse to the next transition, where we arrived still in first place but with no idea by how much. What should have been a recovery segment with some time off our legs was anything but that. We were happy to say farewell to the horses.

Now we were staring down another bike leg to a river section, then to a hike, then to the final paddle. Slowly the segments of the race were stacking up behind us instead of in front of us. For the bike and river sections, we were chasing a dark zone cutoff: For safety, teams had to be off the water by 6 p.m. or pull over on shore for the night. We knew we would be chasing the clock to get to the end of the river section and that it was likely we might not make the cutoff. If we did make it, we would have a huge buffer between us and the rest of the teams. If not, the race would essentially start over as all the teams piled up together at river's edge. Of course this realization hit during another cycling leg, and the guys turned on the gas, pushing me to ride better and faster than I ever had before. But I was running on fumes.

The course to the river was a descent through a sandy, eroded wash that seemed like a luge with banked edges, big ruts, and rocks. I turned off all the doubting demons in my head and just stuck on Novak's wheel, following his line. I was white-knuckled as I flew down some of the most technical terrain I'd ever seen, but I told myself that getting to that river was our finish line. Get there on time and we could relax and take the pressure off; maybe we'd even get to eat while sitting down and sleep a little more.

We finished the descent with my body and bike intact, but there was no time for me to pat myself on my back. We threw all of our gear into the boats, launched, and paddled like crazy. At every bridge we passed under, we could see the race director, Sylvain Thuault, overhead, marking our progress. As the afternoon wore on his face looked increasingly stern. Looking down at us he pointed at his wristwatch. Ticktock.

We made it to the transition and pulled off the water with just 10 minutes to spare. Sylvain, who was now smiling, and his staff applauded us as we flopped out of the boat onto the sand and lay there, panting. The next 10 minutes were nerve-wracking as we waited to see if Team Sweden would make the cutoff or if we'd be the only team to get through the checkpoint. We kept sneaking looks upstream as we organized our waterlogged gear, but they never appeared. We still had days ahead of us, but with a buffer like this, the race was now ours to lose, and we could look over our shoulders a little less often. But I am never one to celebrate until after a finish line, so after only a small celebration and sigh of relief, we trudged off to begin the last big hiking leg.

When we completed the hike, it was 1 a.m., and despite our lead and a slightly more relaxed pace, we were blind and stumbling with fatigue as we reached the transition to the final leg, a lake paddle. It was unanimous that there was no way we could launch at this point—we would end up asleep and adrift within minutes. Sometimes you can fight sleep for a while in a hiking or biking section, but battling against your natural circadian rhythm while paddling is exponentially harder. Sitting down is just that much closer to lying down, so without any lower body movement, you begin the slippery slide into a dream state more easily. Adding darkness to the struggle is a double whammy. So we took one of the many calculated risks you take in adventure racing and bunked down right in our boats to wait for sunrise.

When you're in the front of an adventure race, there are no race radios to tell you how far back the next team is. Your mind plays tricks as you try to calculate the threat. With the river dark zone, we'd known at the start of the hike that we would have at least six hours on the teams behind us. However, we hadn't set any speed records on that hike, and the other teams would be coming off of rest from the mandatory river cutoff. Throw in some better navigation decisions than ours, and, in our worst nightmare, Team Sweden could possibly be knocking at the door. There were also still too many factors that could change the outcome, like a damaged boat, sleeping through our alarm, or a rejuvenated Team Sweden. If we slept for four hours until sunrise, there was a very real chance that they'd come strolling in and we'd have ourselves a paddling sprint finish at the end of seven days of racing. But seeing as how we were falling over, we had to take the risk and sleep. We pulled on our paddling clothes, fastened our life jackets, wrapped ourselves in our crinkly Mylar blankets, and nestled in. If another team did happen to catch us during our sleep, we would be ready to immediately sit up and paddle frantically while they were changing into their gear. This could give us a small jump, and we were a strong paddling team, so that gave us a little peace of mind about our decision. However, the possibility of a close finish made me sick to my stomach after how hard we had worked to get here. I'd been close to big wins in the past only to watch them slip away.

Thankfully, our readiness wasn't tested. No one came. We woke up to our watch alarms just before first light, looked around nervously, and smiled at each other. We launched at sunrise, paddling side by side all the way down Song Kol Lake against a backdrop of snowcapped mountains. It was the perfect victory lap. As I looked across the water at my teammates, I felt such a strong bond of friendship and respect that only our shared effort could have built. We were elated, and the scene was both beautiful and surreal.

Our success in Kyrgyzstan was a long time in the making. It took me six years and thousands of miles of adventure racing to finally piece together all of the elements necessary to win a big event. It was only the second time an American team had won the prestigious Raid Gauloises. By strategizing, working as a team, and adapting to the challenges that presented themselves, we reached the absolute pinnacle of the sport. It felt so good to finally feel rewarded for all of the hard effort. With my team's dominant execution, I had earned my rightful place among the world's best adventure racers, male or female.

Everyone camped in yurts on the beach as we waited for teams to finish one by one. There was time to reflect, welcome our friends and competitors to the finish, and bond as a group. When every team was accounted for, we paddled out into the middle of the lake and linked all of the boats together in a huge circle to honor Dominique. We floated there in silence, filled with gratitude for our adventure racing family and for the opportunity to spend time together in this magical place.

IT'S SAFE TO SAY I have failed more times that I've succeeded. Of course victories are the marker of success when you are a professional athlete. Failure devalues your currency, threatens to make you irrelevant. But if you can sustain determination and passion, failure is a practice run for future success.

If there's one thing that's universal, it's the fear of failure. *Everyone* has it. It's what you do with that fear that determines whether or not you will actually succeed. Some people choose not to try at all rather than fail. Others seem to be immune to the sting of failure. I fall somewhere in the middle. Despite some great successes, I've never been overly confident in my abilities, and it was apparent even as a kid. My fourth-grade teacher, Mrs. Green, wrote in a note to my mom: "Encourage Becky not to hide her light under a bushel basket." I didn't know what a bushel basket was, but I knew she was encouraging me to believe in myself. That comment from so long ago stuck with me, and now I realized that our demons and personality traits are part of our DNA. We cannot erase them, but we can surround ourselves with people who prop us up and let us shine our light.

The pressure of being the only woman on the team hovered over me in my years of adventure racing, and no matter how fast I went, I couldn't outrun it. Because men and women literally compete on the same playing field, the success or failure of many teams rests firmly on the woman's shoulders. We actually have to be better than the men on our team to make up for the physiological differences. At the start line of every single adventure race I faced the fear of being the weakest link and letting my teammates down.

Although there were plenty of failures over my career, I can proudly say that my individual performance never forced the team to drop out. Some of this was pure luck, some of it I attribute to my durability and stubbornness. That's not to say there weren't plenty of times that I was the slowest person on the team. For the first 24–48 hours of almost every expedition-length race, I would be dragging behind the guys, redlining while they seemed to be casually chatting just up ahead. I waged a silent battle with the demons in my head who were telling me how slow and pathetic I was. And sometimes I believed them. In those moments I would vow to never do a long race with men again—no one would ever want to race with me again anyway. Like clockwork, by the dawn of Day 3 my pack would feel gradually lighter, my stride would lengthen by a few inches, the gap between me and my teammates would close, and the black cloud of self-doubt would lift. Once the early race speed mellowed, my endurance kicked in and I could be a full-functioning member of the team and push those fears of failure back into the dark recesses in my mind, at least until the next time.

By building experience and diligently preparing and by surrounding myself with the right teammates I was able to manage my fear of failure. Even today I don't enjoy supreme confidence in my abilities, but after all these years, the bushel basket is at least tipped over so a bit more light can come out. As much as it's been me lifting up the edge of that basket, there has been a small crowd of friends, coaches, and teammates who have lifted the basket and propped me up too. And I had no idea how important that would become.

9

Heavy Sits the Crown

Adventure racing continued to evolve into faster, more competitive, and more cutthroat events. The sport was catching on, and it was growing by leaps and bounds. Gone were the days when just a handful of teams were gunning for the lead. By 2004 there were tons of top-notch international teams that could win any event. Granted, the basics were still the same and competitors remained a tight-knit community, but the stakes were higher. We were all attempting to make a humble living in this sport. When your passion becomes your profession, regardless of how much passion you have, things change. You become reliant on the paycheck, which is in turn reliant on consistent performance.

As the team captain, it was my job to pick and choose the races we had the best chance of winning. My responsibilities began well before the start of each competition and extended long after the finish. I needed to rally sponsors, maintain the budget, juggle endless logistics, all while finding the time to train for a half dozen different sports. Most important, I needed to believe in myself and my abilities and have the courage to stand by my choices—or at least fake it well. After years of hammering out this unconventional existence on the road and around the globe, it was becoming increasingly difficult to manage it all.

Further complicating things, ever since winning the Raid in Kyrgyzstan, my team had encountered a string of terrible luck. We seemed to be trapped in a revolving door of injury and illness, and Patrick looked to be on his way out. His IT band was severely injured from years of abuse. He faced a long road to recovery and the possibility of not returning to adventure racing—it was a devastating blow to the team. Patrick and I had built this team together, starting in Tibet in 2000. As one of world's best navigators, he was pivotal to our success. On a more personal level, he was one of my best friends and we had stood by each other in some desperate moments, so it was nearly impossible to imagine racing without him.

Setbacks suck, especially when you string them together. Although it's hard to see past the difficulties, there are really just two choices: give up or move forward. Despite how disastrous the year had been so far, I wasn't ready to walk away. I had become a jack-of-all-trades, master of none, but I loved the diversity of skills adventure racing required.

Going into my seventh year of being a professional adventure racer, I resolutely believed that my team still had what it took to be champions. We had been there before, after all. We just needed to shake this monkey off our backs and keep marching onward, away from our string of injuries and defeats, to make the magic happen again. The hit to our team roster was another obstacle I was just going to have to overcome.

In hopes of closing out 2004 with a podium finish and some sort of redemption, I set my sights on Primal Quest, a 400-mile expedition race in Washington's San Juan Islands to be held that September. It seemed like the perfect place for Team Montrail to stage our comeback. For one, it awarded a massive prize: $100,000, the largest prize purse in the history of the sport. After our string of unsuccessful races, we all desperately needed a paycheck. The race director boasted about the demands of the course: extraordinarily difficult navigation, intense mountain trekking, and sustained paddling sections. All three played to our team strengths, so we were motivated to prove once again that we belonged with the best in the world.

Our first priority was to fill Patrick's spot and integrate the new team member as quickly as possible. In keeping with the year's chain of events, our usual alternates were all sidelined with various injuries. John and Novak suggested a fellow Aussie, Guy Andrews. Given our goals and expectations, I was leery of going into a challenge of this size with a blind date, but John and Novak had both raced with him and gave Guy their stamp of approval. I had been to the ends of the earth with those two men, and I trusted them with my life. So it seemed logical that I should trust them with this decision too. I agreed to allow Guy to come on board sight unseen.

Guy immediately set my mind at ease. He was affable, outgoing, and motivated. He was confident but not cocky. It was a huge opportunity for him to jump onto one of the best teams in the world with a chance to win one of the biggest races out there, very similar to the opportunity I had been given to race with Ian, Cathy, and Robyn in Argentina. Guy took his new role seriously, and he brought a great attitude and tons of energy.

So the roster was set. We had three out of four of our dream team members and a very strong alternate. The extent of the technical terrain was rumored to be unprecedented. Physical prowess alone wouldn't get you to the finish line first—or at all, for that matter. There were many a sculpted Adonis preening and strutting around the start line. Their egos would be deflated by the scrappy men and women who would inevitably pass them in the woods somewhere on the way to the finish. Preparation, navigation, decision-making, patience, creativity, and teamwork were the true indicators of success. John, Novak, and I were a well-oiled machine—the harder and more technical the course, the better our chances. Finishing well would mean financial security for us for the remainder of the year and a good shot at renewing sponsorships for the following year.

On Day 1, all 56 teams pushed off from Rosario Resort on Orcas Island, one of the many misty, quiet coves that embody the beauty of the Pacific Northwest waterways. Some teams surged ahead on the 51-mile kayak in the frigid Salish Sea, which creates the roiling dividing line between Washington and British Columbia. Others seemingly dropped anchor and drifted back until there were boats strung out for miles along the inlet, like scattered leaves. Already the leaders had a considerable time advantage on those trailing behind.

More than 10 hours later, we pulled our boats onto the mainland with four other teams. We faced an 8-mile trek followed by a long, arduous cycling section, and the temperatures were falling as the sun dipped into the Pacific. We decided to roll the dice and push through this first night with no sleep—as did many of the top teams—to force an early selection in the front of the field and separate ourselves from the pack. We breezed through our transition area, changed gear, and pushed on. Around midnight, we got on our bikes and rode into the night. So far, so good.

What lay ahead was a brutal 75-mile mountain-biking leg through Mount Baker–Snoqualmie National Forest. This section would be the undoing of more than a few teams. The forest was unforgiving, forcing teams to bushwhack at times. Many of the riders who tried to pedal through the dense vegetation ended up with dangling derailleurs and broken chains. Some teams were moving less than a mile an hour through the night—it was that bad. Our team got to be adept at shouldering and hiking with our bikes. There were long sections where I wondered why this was a mountain-biking leg at all, and I considered removing my pedals so they wouldn't keep bashing me in the shins while I was walking.

We spent much of that section yo-yoing with Team AROC, a good-natured Aussie squad that had been leading the event from the gun. There were tricky navigation points where we'd split off, but we somehow always came back together again. Neither team was able to shake the other.

As we pedaled into the second night of the race, our team decided we had to take care of ourselves rather than focus on what Team AROC and the others were up to. The hiking section ahead was rumored to have seriously difficult navigation, so we elected to take a two-hour sleep at our transition area, where we met our crew. We snuggled into warm sleeping bags with full bellies while Team AROC blasted through, still running on no sleep.

Sunrise on Day 3 found us bumping into Team AROC yet again for the start of the first foot section. Although we were racing for a massive prize purse, we had to laugh when we all saw each other. It was getting a little ridiculous how evenly matched our teams seemed to be, but I didn't mind the company.

In racing there are teams you enjoy as competitive friends while others are strictly adversaries. Team AROC was definitely the former—a group of happy, hilarious, well-adjusted athletes who clearly loved the sport and the outdoors, and they let their abilities do the talking. It was a pleasure to be around them. And frankly, we were in need of a pleasant distraction. The nonstop pace had aggravated an old knee injury for Guy. He was in considerable pain and visibly limping as he struggled to keep pace with the pack. The more company and support we had going into what promised to be one of the most difficult parts of the race, the better.

Knee pain in the first half of a multiday adventure race seems an obvious indicator of a team's demise. Sometimes it is, and this is why you must address even the smallest blister or tweak before it grows into a catastrophic problem. These races are so long and arduous and take every ounce of strength you can muster. Your body must cooperate. However, we had plenty of experience nursing teammates back to health and coming back to finish strong or even win. We did this in the Raid when Patrick was sick, and we did it in Tibet when we clawed our way more than 20 places to finish higher than any American team in history, despite my illness. So, while Guy's knee pain was disconcerting, I was attentive but not yet panicking. If our team could support him through this tough hiking leg, we would move on to paddling and cycling, where he could give his knee a break and have a chance to recover.

By midafternoon, our two teams were racing comfortably at the front with the third-place team hours behind. With two of the best navigators in the race on our two teams, we could join forces to safely and quickly get through the most onerous and technical terrain before nightfall and put a big gap between ourselves and the other teams, which would be slowed by darkness. All eight of us were in 100 percent agreement. We knew this strategy could make it a two-horse race.

Race strategy aside, my team was also having a blast traveling with Team AROC, belting out Australian drinking songs, sharing stories, and breaking up the mental monotony while our bodies suffered through the course. As the lone American in the group, I was basking in the laid-back attitude, colorful commentary, and camaraderie of my now seven-person Aussie posse. I also really loved hanging out with my friend Alina. It was great having a female companion along to temper some of the male energy. As our navigators, Novak and Matt (an AROC racer with similarly razor-sharp map and compass skills) walked out front with their heads together and noses in the maps; the rest of us trotted behind and socialized like schoolkids.

We homed in on fun topics like finding a girlfriend for Nigel, which AROC always joked was one of their team's global missions. Nigel was 38, goofy, and elfish. He loved nothing more than an adventure of any kind. We agreed that the lucky lady would have to love the outdoors, though maybe not be a racer herself, and would definitely have to be okay with a guy who doesn't own a car, travels the world for months at a time, and doesn't shower all that often. Somebody suggested she should be a big German woman who makes pancakes and gives massages. Fräulein Nigel! That brought a huge laugh from Nigel, which led me to believe we might be close to the truth.

The conversations continued to drift among us like the bright green grasses waving in the surrounding alpine meadows. We traded food as we exchanged jovial chitchat. Tom, a boyish, sandy-haired guy who seemed to never take anything very seriously, was telling me how he might quit racing soon and start a family with Alina, his wife and teammate, who was hiking along in front of us. I tried to picture this big kid having a kid of his own. I glanced around. There were wildflowers as far as the eye could see, and a clear blue stream carved through the meadow under the warmth of a late summer sun. At that moment it felt so much more like an afternoon hike in the mountains with friends than an elite, high-stakes race where $100,000 was on the line. It was one of the happiest, most enjoyable days I have had in all my years of adventure racing. Of course we couldn't just ramble on, swapping stories and popping chocolate-covered peanuts and bison jerky into our mouths all day. As we reached the end of the meadow, I glanced up at the mossy, jagged, rocky peaks ahead and realized it would soon be time to get back to serious business.

We grew quiet as we ascended out of the peaceful green valley and into the thick woods. The fertile ground gave way to fields of loose, often deep scree. Guy was in a lot of pain at this point and could barely bend his left knee. He was using hiking poles as support, and I could see he was clenching his jaw with every step. The collection of high points known as Illabot Peaks loomed in front of us, with an unmanned checkpoint atop the nearly 6,000-foot summit of the highest peak. We would have to climb the peak, mark our navigation passport, and then find a route down the other side leading to the next checkpoint.

We had a full view of the peak, which appeared to be very loose shale with slick lichen and grass growing between the cracks in the rock. As an experienced climber, I didn't like the look of any of the routes. It was all just one giant pile of unstable, crumbling rock. We stopped to discuss our options.

None of us could see an obvious way to the summit. There was no marked trail or even a path of least resistance. The only reasonable approach we saw was to traverse a slippery, wet slope below the steepest part of the face, head left to the lower angled shoulder, and then scramble up the remaining few hundred feet on the southwest shoulder. This was by no means the most direct route, but it appeared to be the one with the mellowest angle, and we could see the entire route from where we stood, so we knew we wouldn't encounter any unexpected cliffs. Both teams nodded in agreement and began making our way to the top.

As expected, the traverse was slick, but the slope was at a fairly low angle and the rocks were embedded, not loose. So while this section of the climb required focus, it didn't make the hair on my neck stand up or my hands sweat. The next section was another story.

The final push to the summit was steep and technical and would demand a high level of rock climbing ability. I worried about Guy. Climbing might appear to be an upper-body sport in which you pull yourself up the rock face, but you use your legs to push your weight as much, if not more, than you would ascending a ladder. Making these moves with a badly throbbing knee that was swollen stiff would be demanding at best. There were plenty of small ledges to stand on and rocks to grab, but the slope was near vertical in some sections, and many of the rocks were unstable. Falling was absolutely not an option given the exposure, so every move mattered.

If Guy doubted his ability to make it, he wasn't letting on. He and all the rest of us were keenly focused. I was personally very thankful for my years of climbing experience and doubly thankful that we hit this section of the race in broad daylight. I questioned what the middle- and back-of-the-pack teams were going to do, especially with rain looming in the forecast.

Slowly and surely we pushed upward. Every single person in that eight-racer "Aussie Army" had climbed, paddled, cycled, and hiked around the world, covering thousands of miles as adventurers. Each of us had encountered tough situations along the way. This ranked near epic for each of us. Novak, whom I regard as perhaps the toughest and by far the most stoic and silent, groused aloud, "Where the fuck are the fixed ropes? And why weren't we told to bring helmets?" That drove home the gravity of the situation. Nobody spoke another word. All eight of us were now fixated on each handhold and foot placement.

One by one, we scrambled toward the tiny, pointed summit, each of us breathing a small sigh of relief at reaching the ominous wooden cross that marked the checkpoint at the pinnacle. We marked our passports and quickly saw that although we were at the top of the mountain, we were far from being out of the woods. Anxiously perching on the knife-edge of the summit, we evaluated our options for the descent. The next checkpoint was in a valley below to the north. Based on the tight squiggly lines on the topo maps and what we could see from our vantage point, most of the routes looked dangerously steep or were obscured from view. We had no way of knowing if we'd end up cliffed out.

We narrowed our choices to two feasible options. We could reverse our steps, heading away from the next checkpoint, and climb down the loose, exposed ridge that we had just climbed up. Or we could carefully pick our way down a narrow rock gully that was a direct route and visible from where we stood on the summit. Neither of the two options was optimal, and none of us were comfortable with the situation. The mood was tense. How do you make a good decision when all of the choices seem bad? Still, we had to get out of there. We agreed that the steep, narrow gully would be faster and more efficient than backtracking, and being able to see the entire route down was a plus.

Nigel offered to take the lead and play scout. He nimbly darted into the narrow, steep gully to check it out. We waited anxiously as he surveyed the terrain. After a few minutes he gave us the thumbs-up, calling for us to follow. I felt somewhat relieved upon hearing his rich Aussie accent cutting through the cool alpine air. "It's good!"

Despite his assurances, we knew we had to be extremely conscientious. There were loose, jagged boulders everywhere. We tentatively began to drop into the gulley one by one, first Nigel's team and then my own. Guy, who was negotiating the terrain gingerly, was the last to reach the peak and to approach the edge of the gully. I was the sixth in line to climb into the slot. The whole peak was a pile of rubble, and I warned everyone within earshot to be careful of loose rock and extremely deliberate about where they placed their hands and feet.

My teammate John followed directly in my footsteps. As he began his descent, he grabbed hold of a large boulder at the lip of the gully. Then, the unthinkable happened: John dislodged the razor-sharp microwave-sized boulder that six of us had already climbed over and pulled on. He attempted to stop the missile with his leg, and it sliced through his calf muscle like a knife through butter as it tumbled down the gully.

"Rock!" The word fell out of my mouth as instinctively as my breath. My brain had not yet registered what was happening. In an instant, my concentrated climbing focus gave way to utter confusion. Instinctively, I dove close to the rock wall, covered my head with my arms, and waited for the deafening, thunderous noise to stop. The rock hurled by me so closely that I could hear and feel the wind it created. It bounced against the opposite side of the canyon right next to Alina and continued on its trajectory with increasing speed. More than 100 feet below, Nigel was approaching the area where the narrow gulley started to open up into a giant rocky fan. The rock struck the back of his skull, propelling him forward as it crashed down the mountainside.

I remember a deadly silence, and then the screaming. The next minutes were spent in shock as the seven of us, still in the danger zone, took stock of each other and our surroundings and gingerly reversed our steps back toward the summit.

As we regrouped, I gravitated toward Novak, who remained strong and calm in the face of this nightmare. He was also the person I felt closest to. He looked me straight in the eye and told me how close I had come to being hit. I could see the anguish and the severity of the situation written plainly on his face, even as Alina and Tom embraced each other and yelled down to Nigel, "Hold on, we'll get you out of here." Alina started moaning, "He's not moving. Why is he not moving?" Guy broke out the race radio and took charge of communicating the accident and our location to race headquarters.

The only other souls for miles around were Rob Raker, a professional rock climbing guide, and race photographer Dan Campbell, who had climbed to the summit to take pictures of the teams as they reached the peak. Rob offered to make the technical climb down to Nigel to check on his condition, an offer we immediately and gratefully accepted. Meanwhile, Novak and I raided our first aid kit to begin treating John, whose sliced Achilles and bone-deep calf laceration were filling his shoe with blood. We could see straight to his tendon and bones. There was no way he was going to get out of there on his own power. We needed emergency evacuation.

Minutes later, Rob radioed up and confirmed our darkest fear. Nigel was dead. Killed instantly from massive head trauma. As I sat there, stunned by the reality that was at once shaking me to my core and yet still stubbornly refusing to seep in, I was silently thanking Rob for taking the responsibility to check on Nigel. I was grateful that none of us, his friends, would have the horrific image of his mangled body burned into our minds, forever clouding our recollection of him. Instead, we would always have the goofy, elfish, laughing Nigel to fill our memories.

We quickly realized that we had to keep moving or we would surely suffer more casualties. Nightfall was approaching, and John's injuries were too severe for him to move. Our safety on the peak was tentative at best. If the rescue helicopter could not land, we were in for a horrible night, during which we stood a good chance of losing John too.

We worked well together and kept our focus on evacuating the rest of the team. Novak, Rob, and I opted to stay with John on the peak and do our best to stabilize him while Alina, Tom, and Matt from Team AROC joined Guy and made the slow, cautious 500-foot descent to an organized helicopter-landing zone in the meadow, where the race officials would meet them. We were still perched on the treacherously loose rock at the head of the gully. The only place the helicopter would be able to evacuate us was from the very top of the peak, 15 feet above us. Those 15 feet were slippery, loose climbing with devastating exposure. Novak and I managed to assist John as he crawled to the summit. We laid him down on packs and insulated him with our space blankets and sparse extra clothing. We elevated his leg and kept pressure on the wound while listening to the helicopter pilot attempt, time and time again, to put a skid down long enough to pick us up.

It had been hours since the accident. Our window of opportunity continued to close as the helicopter repeatedly tried to execute this difficult maneuver. The adrenaline had long since worn off, and the cold reality was setting in. John was turning white, shivering, and losing way too much blood. He had soaked through all of our medical supplies. We waited and shivered in silence, not knowing what to say. Finally, just minutes before dark, the pilot hovered long enough above the peak for us to lift John into the chopper. I dove in with him and, with no space left in the helicopter, left Novak and Rob on the peak to walk out in the dark. The helicopter took us directly to a medical facility, where John received 30 stitches in his leg. Soon afterward, we were driven back to the race camp and reunited with the rest of both teams and our crew members.

The gravity of the day's events set in while we huddled together in sadness, shock, and despair. We were required to meet with a race psychologist for an official debriefing on what we were to do in the hours that followed in order to stave off depression. I sat dumbfounded as he instructed us to hydrate, avoid alcohol, and do some light exercise. Who the fuck was this guy, and did he really not have any idea what we had been doing prior to the accident? In the true Aussie tradition, we piled into the car and drove one block to the nearest pub.

It may not have been what the doctor ordered, but the Aussie "piss up" seemed to be just the type of therapy we all needed. Throughout the evening, members of the film crew, our support crew, and others who were affected by the accident trickled in. We closed down the bar and all camped together under a big tarp in the transition area. I felt such sadness about Nigel's death but an incredible sense of closeness to this clan. I have never felt two antagonizing emotions so strongly in my life. Oscillating between love and anger and joy and despair, sleep finally overtook me, and I collapsed into a numb, exhausted slumber.

The next few days were as surreal as the accident. Time seemed to have no meaning, and my memory of those days is disjointed and jumbled. In the wake of Nigel's death, the race had come to a screeching halt. It had taken another full day until rescue teams could safely recover his body. The organizers held a memorial service by the river we were meant to be paddling on. Teams had been pulled from their various positions on the course and gathered at this transition area to remember Nigel. After the service, when emotions were still sparking like exposed wires, the organization started the serious and contentious discussions about how to handle the remainder of the race.

They took input from each team captain and deliberated for hours. Racers were sharply divided on whether or not to continue. A few fellow racers whom I had known for years and considered friends shocked me with their lack of sympathy and overly competitive nature. I was disgusted that some individuals were still chomping at the bit to race for a piece of the prize purse—a prize purse that most likely would have been awarded to Nigel and Team AROC had it not been for the accident. American Danelle Ballengee, one of the best athletes in the world, suggested that we all continue the course together in a noncompetitive tribute to Nigel and donate the prize money to his family. That sounded like the most fitting way to honor Nigel and bond together as a race community. The majority voted otherwise. After hours of group deliberations, the race officials elected to continue the event, minus the mountain section where the accident occurred and minus the two teams who'd been leading. The race surged ahead full steam, with a black cloud hanging over many of the staff and participants.

Instead of coming together as a community in the face of tragedy, we were pulled apart. In the wake of the accident, people sadly but predictably started pointing fingers and looking for someone to blame. Some racers blamed the race organizer, saying the course was too dangerous and that we never should have been forced onto that peak. Others blamed us, criticizing our teams' decision to descend via that route. In the blink of an eye, I felt like an outcast in my own community and abandoned by my peers. Of the seven survivors from the accident, a few got vocal about safety in adventure racing, one got really silent, and the rest of us were somewhere in between, defending ourselves, cringing at the chatter in the media, and wanting it all to just go away.

In all of my experience racing in very extreme, remote situations, this was only the second death to take place during an event. The statistics are remarkable when you consider the terrain we travel, the conditions, and the circumstances. I thought back to the Raid in Kyrgyzstan when Dominique drowned in a white-water river section. In contrast to Nigel's death, Dominique's was a true accident, despite there being safety measures in place. The river section in Kyrgyzstan was challenging. However all of the teams were geared up with helmets, life jackets, throw bags, and other required safety equipment appropriate for that section. There were also river safety crews along the shore to assist in any necessary rescue. They were on scene when Dominique's kayak overturned. Despite their efforts, they were not able to save her. The athletes obviously mourned for their friend and fellow racer, but there was no finger pointing or blame being thrown around. We understood these risks when we lined up to race. We were all truly sad and shaken by the accident, and it drew us together.

Conversely, Nigel's death had a polarizing affect. Many athletes, including me, felt that the peak was a bad place for a checkpoint and that the accident was preventable. Yes, adventure racing is dangerous, and we didn't expect a race director to keep us entirely safe, but none of us were out there with a death wish. And being able to make navigational decisions is one of the appeals of adventure racing. However, placing a checkpoint on Illabot Peaks, with exposed loose rock and no clear option for descent, amounted to poor course design and unnecessary risk. The navigational challenge would have been the same if the checkpoint had been located in the saddle below the dangerous peak.

To this day, I still don't understand why they chose to push teams up there. I also had a hard time accepting the critique of our route choice from other racers who never saw that part of the course. No one else had the firsthand information necessary to evaluate the severity of the terrain. Nigel's death forced me to ask some bigger questions too. Had adventure racing finally been pushed too far? Was the extreme amount of prize money changing the way we raced and treated each other? All I know is that I was seeing an unexpected ugly side of the sport and I wanted no part of it.

When I got back from the race, I plunged into a self-imposed hermit lifestyle at my condo in Ketchum, Idaho. After years of living the nomadic lifestyle, I had slowly and unintentionally started to put down some roots after visiting Patrick and falling in love with Ketchum. I thought I was just going to rent a place for the summer before moving on, as usual, to my next location, but I never left. It was the place where I felt most comfortable and welcome.

When I received an unexpected inheritance from my grandfather, I thought, *I'd better not piss this away*, so I bought my first real home, a condo in Sun Valley. I'd gone from living out of a Bronco and surfing couches and rentals to being a homeowner in what felt like a really short amount of time, and for me it was a really big deal, especially since I was doing it with an unpredictable paycheck. In my classic "calculated risk" style, I did do some math first and figured that if shit went south and I ended up without a job the next year, I could always sell my condo for more than I bought it for. So there was a safety net—or at least that's what I told myself. Regardless, the commitment was daunting, but it also felt really nice to finally have my own place as a safe haven, especially at a time like this.

I stayed holed up, communicated very little with anyone, didn't train, and searched my soul for why I raced. I was depressed and needed to process the experience and all the feelings that followed it. I had to decide if I wanted to keep racing and taking part in a sport that I loved in spite of all of the grief it had caused me. My career and passion had swiftly evaporated out there in Washington. I felt lost and alone. My sense of purpose was gone.

Time does funny things to your memory. On that day, I saw absolutely no better choice for a safe descent off that peak. Yet the more days and weeks that passed, the more vicious my thought processes became. I second-guessed everything about that day. Was it my fault? Should I have been more vocal about the climbing dangers? Of the group, I had the most rock climbing experience, and my hackles were definitely up during that section. It wasn't safe. But how do you define "safe" in the backcountry anyway? Would I do something differently the next time? After all these years, I still don't know the answers to these questions.

What I do know is that no one ever expects an accident to happen. Time and time again, we skate through exhilarating moments in the outdoors that cause us to look back and feel lucky to have squeaked through. These moments add color and character to our stories and our lives. Yet the same situations that make us feel alive can turn deadly in an instant. You never fully appreciate that . . . until they do.

Despite the inherent risks of spending time in the backcountry, I have never fancied myself an excessive risk-taker. I am passionate about being outdoors, and I thrive on challenging myself physically and emotionally, on breaking down my own barriers of what's possible, but it's never been about the thrill of cheating death or any type of cavalier attitude like that. I always recognize the dangers and take them seriously; the fear is always there, but it's manageable. I can usually put my head down and push through even the most difficult, arduous, and, yes, potentially dangerous circumstances. But now I was scared to climb again.

I also questioned what my passion for this sport was really all about. For seven years of professional adventure racing, it had seemed like the most amazing way to make a living: sharing the outdoors and physical challenges with like-minded souls from around the world. Now I was struggling to keep that perspective, because all those wonderful things were overshadowed by what felt like a soulless quest for prize money, race results, and personal glory. I was lost.

Even today, most of my best friends in the world are the people I met adventure racing. They are people I saw only a few times a year at gear checks, along the trail in the middle of nowhere, and at race parties. I barely know what they do with the rest of their lives, but still we share a deep friendship and respect because of our common interests and struggles in racing. I cherished those connections and didn't want to lose them. I also knew that I never wanted myself or anyone I know to have to suffer through such a horrendous disaster again.

The only way out of the darkness was through it. I spent months trying to answer the big question: Why? Why had I been there on that peak to begin with? What had led me to that place?

When I first started racing, the attraction was the travel, accomplishing seemingly impossible goals, and team kinship. The danger didn't excite me, but the unknown did. I was drawn to the big mysterious adventure—the uncharted courses, the long rigorous physical journey, and of course, the intense emotional journey. As I thought back to my favorite races, they weren't necessarily the ones we'd won. Instead, the races in which we overcame adversity, worked together, and grew closer were the ones I was most proud of and recalled most fondly.

I thought back to the Moroccan Eco-Challenge. My team was unranked and finished nearly dead last, but it was the first race that I captained and the first time I actually crossed the finish line. Then there was the Patagonian Eco-Challenge, where my predominantly female team finished fourth and smashed some glass ceilings in our sport. I looked at the pictures I'd hung on my fridge. There was one from Raid in Tibet, another favorite, where I'd been plagued with bronchitis at 17,000 feet and was nearly pulled out of the race by the medics. We had dropped from 3rd place to 27th, but my teammate stood by me, we kept moving forward, and we ended up 7th overall. I knew that if I intended to keep adventure racing, I must find a way to return to those core attractions that had fueled my desire for so many years.

In retrospect, it's no surprise that Novak, always my pillar of strength on the team, was the one who eventually pulled me out of the darkness and ushered me back into the wilderness. Before the accident, our team had been planning to defend our victory in the Raid in Argentina. John had developed a blood clot following his injury at Primal Quest and would be out for the season, but Novak was still game to go, and he pushed me to consider it. It was rumored to be a long course with difficult navigation in high mountain terrain and with a huge amount of paddling. It was just the type of course that we normally excelled at. My mind started spinning with the possibilities, just like the old days. The appeal was not money, exposure, or the podium. Instead it was the lure of the location and the desire to once again feel the anticipation of the adventure—to see if my soul could get inspired again by wanting to know what was around the next corner.

Just three weeks before the race, Novak and I officially decided to go for it. We didn't have our dream team assembled, but our alternate athletes were both strong and proven expert expedition racers: Elina Maki-Rautila from Finland and South African Martin Dreyer. I was excited about a team with two women. We also felt strongly that a positive finish to the year would improve morale, keep sponsors interested, and end what had been an incredibly rough season on a high note.

After many dark days of reflection, I had also decided that I didn't want to be labeled as a quitter, no matter the circumstances. None of our peers in the sport would have been surprised if our team had succumbed to all the difficulties of the season and just thrown in the towel. I knew the racing community wouldn't criticize me, but in my heart I would have felt like I hadn't done everything in my power to keep our team together and finish the season. Always my own harshest critic, I would have labeled myself a quitter.

When *Adventure Sports* magazine crowned me the Queen of Pain for my ability to suffer through ultra-endurance exploits despite being cold, hungry, and sometimes lost—thereby putting the hurt on my competition—it was one more thing I could use to keep myself going in tough races or decisions like this. After all, how embarrassing would it be for the Queen of Pain to quit? I had to race again, if for no other reason than to prove to myself that I would finish what I started.

From the moment I stepped onto the plane to San Martin de los Andes and saw friendly, familiar faces smiling at me, I knew I had made the right decision. After months of relative isolation, it felt like a weight off my chest to see racing companions who still loved me, respected me, and were excited to see me despite all that had happened.

The Raid didn't go so well for our persistent team, though it started out smoothly enough. The early part of the race included a trip up the stunning Lanín volcano, and Novak and I were enjoying the thrill of the competition, feeling strong, and looking forward to the journey that lay ahead. I had no expectations of a podium finish, nor did I care at that point. I just wanted to move through the wilderness again and finish honorably. Unfortunately, Elina was suffering from a bronchial infection that was getting worse. Climbing to 12,000 feet in cold, windy conditions had taken its toll on her. She was wracked with endless coughing spells and was struggling to catch her breath with limited lung capacity. I could relate to her pain and suffering from my Tibet experience at high altitude many years before. After hours of nursing her along, resting, and multiple medical evaluations, the race doctors decided that Elina's condition was too serious for her to continue racing. They ordered our team to drop out of the race, and Elina was transported to the hospital.

After they gave us their decision and we officially withdrew, I walked away from the group, plopped down on the ground at the river's edge, and watched other teams embark on a really exciting white-water raft section. Despite my attempts to be a mature leader in the face of adversity, I felt hot tears bubbling to the surface. I was angry, disappointed, and embarrassed to be sitting on the sidelines once again. I also really just wanted to be out on that river, paddling and racing with the other teams. We had worked so hard all season, and here we were with yet another deflating outcome. We'd made very little prize money that year. We'd had very few good race results. We'd had failure and tragedy. We were not intact physically or emotionally. I feared we'd lose our sponsorship and our jobs. Where had I gone wrong as our captain? What could I have done to make things work out better? Why was I working so hard with so little reward? I was used to the equation that hard work equals reward. I had proved this time and time again, even with less ability or skill than others.

As all of these thoughts and questions piled up in my mind, Novak came over, sat down at my side, and put his arm around my shoulder. After so many races and hours together, this may have been the first time he'd ever hugged me except at a celebratory finish line. The tears flowed as I poured out all my frustrations from the year. Like my mother, I tend to be stoic, guarding my frustrations and disappointments. That day, I vented a year's worth of anger, self-doubt, and grievance, and Novak just listened quietly. It was a relief to share it all with someone who had been alongside me for all of these events. I'm always amazed at how much it helps to simply say things out loud. Giving voice to fear and frustration loosens their power over us.

Later Novak commandeered a bottle of red wine from one of the crews and continued my therapy session. All the other crews and the race organization had packed up and moved on to the next transition, so we sat alone in the empty field among our smelly, wet race gear.

Novak opened the bottle and we toasted our lousy season, our great friends, and the hope of a much better year to come.

Over the next few days, as we waited for teams to finish the race, our team and crew drank many more bottles of wine, went on a hike together and got stuck in some bamboo, went shopping for souvenirs, shared meals, stayed up till 6:00 a.m. dancing one night, and overall had a fantastic vacation in one of the most beautiful places on earth. I still harbor disappointment about not finishing that race, mostly because the course seemed so beautiful and I missed being a part of it. Prize money, our reputation, and sponsor obligations were the last things on my mind for the time being. I set my heart on enjoying that wonderful place with my friends. I soaked in what truly mattered in this moment instead of looking back or forward just yet.

THE YEAR FOLLOWING Nigel's death was full of introspection. I questioned who I was and what I was doing with my life. Before that, I'd been jumping from race to race and country to country without considering anything but where the next adventure would be. I came away from Primal Quest a dramatically different person. Something inside me that had burned white hot for many years had died. But Nigel's death also gave me the gift of perspective, and it grounded me once again in what was genuinely important. Every moment with friends in the outdoors is enchanted and something to be cherished. Finish lines are wonderful things, but only if you soak in the grandeur of the scenery and embrace your companions along the way. After the race in Argentina, I had finally worked through the hardest part of the grieving process and was ready to stop dwelling in regret and uncertainty and shift my eyes to the future, to find new and different adventures. I still had growing and living to do.

10

A New Beginning

I have never had a five-year plan, let alone an idea of where I would be in five months. In the fall of 2005, the uncertainty of the life I'd made for myself became very real. Montrail's owner called with news that the company was being purchased by Columbia and come October, just several weeks away, they would be cleaning house and severing most of their sponsorship deals—including the one with my team. Although grateful for the warning that the blade of the guillotine was about to come crashing down, I hung up the phone speechless. Then I relayed the news to all my teammates and support staff.

After 10 years spent building and managing my own adventure racing team with blood, sweat, and tears, it was the end of the line. To some extent, I understood. Eco-Challenge was no longer on TV, and the exposure of the sport was on a downward slide. As luck would have it, I had just bought a condo and had a mortgage for the first time in my life. This was the biggest financial commitment I had ever made, a far cry from being able to just turn the key in the Bronco and drive away.

After a few days of soul-searching, I knew I had to find another job, and fast. I braced myself for the call to Red Bull, my sole remaining paying sponsor. Their response surprised me: "Well, you have another year on your contract. Find something amazing to do."

They say when a door closes, a window opens. It was a glimmer of hope. The Red Bull sponsorship wasn't enough to support an entire adventure racing team or life as I knew it, but it was a small buffer that could delay the inevitable. But what the hell was I going to do? What "amazing" thing would live up to Red Bull's expectations? I've always been durable and multitalented, but never the best at any one thing, which is why adventure racing was so perfect for me. To capitalize on my biggest strength—endurance—I started looking around for the longest things I could find. I considered ultrarunning, but that just seemed painful and lonely. After running in high school and college, there just wasn't much joy left in it for me.

My friend and fellow adventure racer Matthew Weatherley-White suggested I try 24-hour mountain bike racing, where you race around the clock. Even though I'd done a fair share of biking in adventure racing, this seemed like a stupid idea. I'd never learned to love it; in fact, I hated it more than any other sport I'd tried. Bikes were complicated. They always broke. And I wasn't any good on technical terrain, so I'd end up pushing or carrying the damn thing.

But what else was I suited to do? I really couldn't come up with any other ideas. The more I thought about it, the more I thought maybe I could make it work. At this point I had a nice race bike and, since living in Idaho, I had met some other women who rode. I actually had been on some pretty enjoyable rides with them. As an adventure racer, I was well trained to stay awake to race for days on end with no sleep, let alone just one 24-hour period. I could hold a steady pace when it wasn't too technical. The checks in the plus column were adding up. I figured I had one year to dabble in some sort of sport to fulfill my requirements to Red Bull. It was going to be a bit of a celebratory lap at the end of a great athletic career.

In the meantime, I was already laying the groundwork for Plan B and the next phase in my life. In fact, I'd dabbled in Plan B off and on over the years. Back in L.A., most of my outrigger canoe teammates were also firefighters. Confident and powerful, these women used their physical strength and sharp thinking to make a living in a traditionally male career. The job was anything but mundane. For the first time in my life, I thought I might know what I wanted to do when I grew up.

In 2000 I had enrolled in the intensive six-month prep class in L.A., throwing myself into the complexities of fire science, math, and building construction, along with intense physical training: advancing hose lines, hoisting ladders, and hauling dummies up flights of stairs. I was one of only two women in my class of 50, and despite being smaller than most of the students, I was well served by my climbing and paddling strength, my determination, and my ability to work well in teams under pressure. Knowing my way around tools and mechanics from rebuilding my Bronco didn't hurt either.

I was well on my way to a new career path when I decided I couldn't force myself to stay in L.A. Withdrawing my name just prior to the interview process, I drove away, realizing that opportunity could very well remain in my rearview mirror.

When I settled in Ketchum in 2002, I realized that in a small town the hiring process is far less cutthroat because there's a need for part-time employees in addition to the full-time staff. It was the best of all possible worlds because I could actually pursue both of my dream jobs at once: professional firefighter and professional athlete.

Scheduling and travel constraints got in the way and had made it difficult to block out the time for the fire academy training in Ketchum.

But on the heels of what I went through in Primal Quest, I knew I needed to make it happen. I completed fire academy and EMT training and became a proud member of the Ketchum Fire Department. Plan B seemed perfectly logical: I began to research paramedic schools and opportunities to pursue a full-time career in emergency services. I made a plan to begin studying just as soon as my Red Bull sponsorship ran out at the end of the calendar year.

I was still mulling over the cycling thing when I decided to hop into a local 100-mile unsanctioned race in Idaho, a grand tour of the local mountain bike trails. It started in nearby Hailey and made a giant loop through the surrounding mountains and valleys, including Ketchum. There are all kinds of strong riders in this area, many of whom would be on the ride. I figured it would be a pretty good test to see if I could ride 100 miles straight, much of it singletrack. I had no visions of being able to stay with the group, but I wanted to see how I would do on a big ride. I was also excited about exploring unknown territory around my new home, and it's tough to pass up a free event.

I approached the ride as if it was a solo adventure race. I prepared a map with the escape routes highlighted and carried a headlamp, phone, and plenty of food. I wanted to be self-sufficient. Much to my surprise, I did pretty well. Though I bumbled over the technical stuff, I loved the challenge, the exploration, and how far the bike could take me. I was awakened to what there was to love about riding. The Pioneer, Boulder, and Smokey Mountain ranges we rode through went on farther than I could see or fathom. I didn't have to travel to an exotic country to find adventure. It was right outside my back door. I craved to see what was over the next mountain, up the next drainage, and beyond.

Along the ride I met a local rider, Greg Martin, who grew up riding on the technical trails in Virginia and was now racing in 100-mile mountain bike races and 24-hour solo events. With a second opinion that I should try some ultra-endurance mountain biking myself, I probed him with a few questions about how the events worked. More intriguing was this handsome, friendly guy with piercing blue eyes. I knew the bike was the ticket to spending more time with him.

In 2005, I assembled a group of new female riding friends to compete in the women's expert category of the 24 Hours of Moab race. Muffy Ritz, Karoline Droege, Anna Keeling, and I entered as Ketchum If You Can. As an experienced 24-hour racer, Greg agreed to come along as our mechanic and support crew. The road trip sounded like good therapy for the shock I was feeling from having my adventure racing career come to a screeching halt.

We rolled into Moab with the truck piled high with bikes, tools, camping gear, coolers, food, and all the supplies to create a pop-up home and bike pit zone in the desert. I realized what a really incredible guy Greg was to be giving up his riding weekend to crew for us, and it was my first glimpse into how much of a team sport cycling actually is.

After unpacking the mountain of gear and staking out our place in the dirt, the team went out to ride the course. My first thought was, *Holy shit. What have I gotten myself into?* There were gnarly rock ledges, huge drops I could barely walk down, bumpy rock gardens—there was no way I was going to be able to ride everything. But I certainly wasn't the worst rider out there. There were overweight people, riders in jean shorts, athletes on super-junky bikes right alongside the speed racer–looking pros with shaved legs and bikes more expensive than my car. It was a hodgepodge of humanity out there doing their thing in whatever way worked for them.

Because my adventure racing experience had honed my ability to get on and off my bike quickly, I decided that what I couldn't ride, I'd run. Well, during the next 24 hours I ran a lot! Electing not to try to learn to ride technical terrain on the spot, I employed a yo-yo technique to minimize my losses: hustling through the stuff I couldn't ride, then absolutely hammering the places I could to make up for lost time. Riding for 90 minutes at full intensity was very different from the metered, long-distance pacing I knew so well. I was certainly a bit overexcited and probably wasting tons of energy, but each lap felt like a sprint. I also didn't want to let my teammates down.

Our team was cranking as we took turns pulling laps, giving our all, and taking care of each other and our bikes. By noon the next day, we had racked up 17 laps and won the women's expert class race. Even with all of my running, I ended up having the fastest lap time among all of the women, including the pros! My last lap of the race happened to be as fast as my first, which blew Greg's mind. "Nobody does that. Everyone slows down," he said. I figured that maybe I was onto something. This ultra-endurance riding was less about the skill and more about the ability to be efficient and do whatever it took to keep moving.

FOLLOWING 24 HOURS OF MOAB, Greg—who had moved firmly into boyfriend status—encouraged me to race solo. He suggested 24 Hours Round the Clock in Spokane, Washington, the following spring. It was one he had raced himself, so he knew the course and was confident I could do well. Matthew gave his vote of confidence too. "You've got the right physiology and temperament for these events," he told me. "All you need to do is learn how to actually ride a bike!"

I was well aware that I was a "masher," pushing down hard on the pedals rather than developing a smooth spin by pushing down and pulling up evenly. There were so many things I didn't really know how to do in this new discipline. Crazy as it sounds, ever since high school I hadn't formally trained for anything. I'd just go out and do stuff, like paddle for a couple of hours in the morning and then run in the afternoon. The training ethos in adventure racing is all about volume, piling on as much as you can without any real process. You'd go out for six hours a day or more, if you could. Now that I had just one discipline to prepare for, I was even less sure how to approach it. Was I simply supposed to ride as many hours as humanly possible?

Matthew offered to coach me, seeing my potential as a cyclist long before I did. Having competed as a pro cyclist himself, Matthew's passion for sports and education transformed my mind-set about training. He was of the opinion that being a champion endurance athlete required three components: favorable genes, high-functioning OCD (obsessive-compulsive disorder), and a reasonable, intelligent, patient, long-term training program. If you're missing any one component, you can kiss it goodbye. He believed I had the mental profile to succeed and the genetic profile to be competitive. I just needed to tune my body to become an elite-level cyclist. Simple, right?

Sun Valley turned out some great skiing conditions that winter, but I was relegated to an hour and a half each day on the trainer doing single-leg pedaling and boring-ass drills with high cadence and low resistance. To develop the neuromuscular memory needed to efficiently pedal a bicycle, I needed plenty of repetition.

In addition to the technique work, Matthew mixed short, hard days with long, easy ones so I could adapt to the training load and get faster and stronger. To him, interval training and form were elementary training concepts, but they were new to me. As much as they hurt, I could see I was actually getting faster while spending less time training. I would need every bit of that speed and fitness because the clock doesn't stop in a 24-hour race. Pit stops are limited to just seconds or maybe a couple of minutes. To be competitive, you must cover the most mileage possible, so any time you're not moving forward is wasted. The length of the race did not faze me one bit; it was the pace and the actual bike riding part I was afraid of.

Come May, I headed north to Spokane with my one-man crew, Greg. I was nervous about all the logistics and worried about all that uninterrupted saddle time. Greg was my rock once again, and his 24-hour solo experience and calm demeanor eased my nerves. I know he was surprised by my intensity and singular focus, or maybe he would call it obsessiveness, during the event. He had not really seen this competitive side of me. Once the gun goes off and my job is clearly laid out in front of me, I'm fixated on the finish.

The course was about 15 miles long with just over 1,200 feet in total climbing per lap. There were no really big hills or technical obstacles. There were a few rock gardens, but most of the course was fast, open, and flowy. In other words, it was perfectly suited to my strengths. Greg and I reviewed our race plan to deal with food, water, and mechanicals. His job was to handle all of those things for me so I could just keep riding in circles.

Twenty-four hour racing is a mix of team and solo competitors all starting together, so it's confusing to decipher who is in your category and who is in the lead. The lap format also means the field gets jumbled quickly, and you may not know if you are riding the same lap or a lap ahead or behind another rider. Because of this, I didn't really know where I stood in the race field. Greg was in charge of keeping track of the other female solo riders, and he would try to write down race numbers and time splits—the distance between me and the next closest competitor—as they passed our pit area. With hundreds of racers flying by, it was nearly impossible to figure out, especially at night. From his calculations, I took the women's solo lead after a couple of laps and continued to increase the gap as the race went on. I wasn't sure this was accurate, so I didn't think about my placing.

As I'd roll into our pit area, Greg would be ready for me with a paper plate with some pretzels and a quarter of a sandwich, some banana, and a Red Bull. I'd refuel, switch water bottles, and be off. Fast transitions can make all the difference. Over the course of a day, a few minutes here and there can add up to a big lead or a big deficit that's hard to erase on the trail. As dawn came up and with just a few hours remaining in the race, Greg told me that I was very close to passing the men's solo leader and that people in the race camp were taking bets on who would win the entire race. It would likely come down to the last lap or two in a battle between the top male and female. I had memorized each section of the course by now, every turn, every hill, every stone. So even though I was completely spent, I felt like I was riding smoother and smoother with each lap. I don't remember passing him because I was charging like a horse to the barn.

I ended up racking up 18 laps and taking first place overall. I was in a state of exhausted shock. As we celebrated, I realized this performance sealed the deal for this cycling thing. I would spend my last year of sponsorship competing in this race format. Despite my technical riding weaknesses, mentally and physically I was well suited for this. And after adventure racing, certain aspects of mountain bike racing seemed easy or relatively luxurious: There's someone at an aid station with a whole bunch of food waiting for me, I pretty much always know where I'm going, and relatively soon I will get a hot shower and warm bed. Both sports are extremely hard, but the adventure racing background was paying dividends and applied even more than I'd thought it would.

I called up Specialized, my equipment sponsor for our adventure racing team, and told them about my win. They agreed to continue their support. And of course Red Bull was still on board. I was set to embark on a career as a mountain bike racer at age 38.

TWO MONTHS LATER, I was bound for the 2006 24-Hour Mountain Bike National Championships held in Nine Mile County Forest near Wausau, Wisconsin. The national championships would be my second 24-hour solo race. The boldness of this was not lost on me. Greg would also be racing in the men's solo single-speed division, so we could race alongside each other on the same course. Knowing he would be out there was reassuring.

Even though this was a solo event, I knew I needed a strong team around me to keep me fueled, motivated, and rolling. Once again, my adventure racing planning and team experience was coming in handy. The race was in the Midwest, so that meant I could recruit family members like Mom and Uncle Doug to crew for us. I also flew out my good friend, our adventure racing crew chief and master mechanic Jason, from Idaho. Jason had been with me around the world taking care of our adventure racing team, and I knew him like a brother. His experience as a mechanic was essential, and his knowledge of me as an athlete was also key. He had seen me at my best and my worst and knew how to handle that. Like Greg, Jason was calm and unflappable. This is just the contrast I need to temper the stress and intensity that can get the best of me.

As we rolled into the race venue late Thursday night, we noticed motor homes with riders' names on them, house-sized tents, and lots of logos. This was not shaping up to be the same scene as 24 Hours of Moab, and it was a far cry from the small-town feel of 24 Hours Round the Clock. As an underdog and complete unknown in the cycling world, I found it very intimidating. I elected to set up camp away from the melee of the timing tent and all of the logos. I wanted to have our own little cocoon so the team and I could focus and work without distraction. We staked out our homely camp made up of Uncle Doug's borrowed tent, a rental car, a few fold-up chairs, and plastic tarps tied down with rope. Then we went back to the hotel to watch The Weather Channel. There were severe thunderstorm warnings for the weekend. The red radar blob was directly over us, and the newscasters were warning the public to stay inside for the weekend. We knew we'd get rained on; it was just a question of how much and when.

As the solo riders were called up to the line the next day, I looked around at the competition and recognized names I'd read in cycling magazines. The main competition in the women's field was defending champion Monique "Pua" Sawicki. The race director paraded the national championship jersey in front of the crowd asking, "Who wants to win this?" I glanced at the jersey but then looked away, not wanting to psych myself out or get too nervous. The plan was to just go out and ride as consistently as possible and execute fast transition times. This was no different than any other event. I squeezed Greg's hand for reassurance, and then the gun went off.

The first couple of laps were crazy, with the crowd of bicyclists muscling for position on all of the narrow singletrack sections. I never considered mountain biking a contact sport until then. I was intimidated by the aggressiveness. The course was about 14 miles long, with over half of it technical and narrow. Much of the riding was fast, with lots of cornering in very tight trees peppered with slippery, technical rocky sections. It was like a fast-moving video game. Before diving into the singletrack, the first 3 miles were very fast doubletrack with some small climbs, so I tried to use that section of the trail to pedal hard each lap. Once in the singletrack, it was a fine line between riding fast, staying on the bike, and not getting in anyone's way.

I was in second place for the first two laps, with Pua just a couple minutes ahead. The crowds had dispersed a little, and I was riding more comfortably by this time. It felt good to know that her lap times weren't in another galaxy. I figured it would take a while, but I'd try to slowly reel her in over the course of the day and night. I somehow caught up to her on the third lap at the top of a small climb. Seeing her this soon in the race gave me a jolt of adrenaline. On the approach, I tried to relax my breathing so she wouldn't know how hard I was trying. I just wanted to pass quickly and attempt to get out of sight, out of mind. "Hello," I said as I passed, making every effort to appear smooth and low-key. Inside I was reeling, and my heart was jumping out of my chest. I passed and then got really excited as I heard her labored breathing. I was taking the lead from the reigning national champion! I gave an enthusiastic push on the pedals, lost focus, and then crashed unceremoniously right in front of her. My eagerness had gotten the best of me, and my lack of skill was now splayed out on the trail. No doubt she was annoyed and unimpressed.

I sprung up, remounted in a huff, and stayed in front, but my ego was badly bruised. My technical skills had failed me once again, this time right in front of my competition. I set my sights on trying to open up a bit of a gap, riding as hard as I possibly could on the less technical parts, but trying to keep from getting too amped. It was a fine balance, but I put 5 minutes on her in that third lap, then consistently rode 3–4 minutes faster per lap for the remainder of the race.

Sometime late at night, I lapped the third-place female, but my competitive spirit would not allow me to let up. The body's clock tries to wind down with the sun, but being consistent through the wee hours of the night when other riders start to slow down and flail was my strong suit. Determined to remain steady and sharp, I continued to open my lead overnight. I created my own little game to maintain focus and break the riding into smaller goals and chunks, timing certain sections and then challenging myself to get to these points on schedule. Just this lap, just this climb, and finally the sum of those parts would add up to a good race time.

As the night wore on, I grew more wobbly with each lap. I crashed about six different times, but the only witnesses were the trees I was running into. My technique still sucked, and the fatigue only accentuated my weakness. This trail was tight and twisty, with space between the trees barely wide enough for the handlebars to fit through. An error of a few inches in either direction meant clipping a bar and your body stopping all forward momentum by crashing into a tree. I was learning the finer points of cycling finesse the hard way, and I had a throbbing shoulder to show for it.

At about 4 a.m. the wind started howling, the air turned cool, and it was apparent that, as predicted, we were about to get absolutely hammered by a storm. The downpour was torrential. Even in the jungles of Borneo or South America, I had never experienced a deluge like that. It was as if buckets of water were being poured directly on top of my head. The thick forest absorbed any bit of light that was in the sky, and the lack of visibility slowed my pace to a crawl. I was just beginning to find my groove again when race officials waved me down and forced me to stop at an aid station. About 30 of us huddled together under a tent, wearing trash bags that the officials had distributed. As the sky lightened at dawn, an ominous chain of thunder and lightning cracked and flashed around us. Shivering inside my trash bag, I tried to relax the muscles seizing up in my legs. I just wanted to keep moving to stay warm and protect my lead, but we were forbidden to leave. I envisioned my competitors rolling up to the soggy aid station and all of us having to restart the event together. All of that hard work would be for nothing. I worried about Greg out there too. I hadn't seen him in hours. I wanted to get back to our camp to regroup, get warm, and check on the team. I knew they would be concerned about me too.

It felt like the longest 45 minutes of my life. The intensity of the situation could be felt over the radio as organizers tried to preserve the race but keep everyone safe. Finally, they set us free, restarting the race from where we were. It took forever to chase away the chills and to coax my numb, cramping muscles back into race mode. My trash bag kept getting caught on my saddle, flapping in the wind, and snagging on trees, but it kept me warm. When I was reunited with my crew, I ditched the bag and headed out for another lap. The timing was all screwed up, so the only thing I could do was race my heart out and assume that someone was nipping on my heels, trying to steal my lead in the final moments. I would not go down without a fight. I went back to timing myself on little sections of the course and racing full tilt.

At 9 a.m., with just one hour to go in the scheduled race time, I charged up to our transition area like a woman possessed. I was ready to swap bikes and crush my final lap. My trusty crew was just standing around with stupid grins on their faces. I glared at them. Where the hell was my bike? I had to go. They shook me out of my confused state by jumping up and down in excitement. The officials had stopped the race again due to another approaching storm. Everyone would receive an official finishing time from the first rain stop at 5:30 a.m. That meant I'd ridden an extra two hours I didn't get credit for, but I didn't care. In less than one season of bike racing and my second 24-hour solo race, I was officially the new national champion! The coveted jersey was now mine.

As the adrenaline subsided, the pain set in. I could not lift my right arm. I'd separated my shoulder in one of the crashes during the night. My legs were beginning to swell, and I felt my body and mind shutting down. I needed help changing my clothes and had to be directed where to go and what to do. I was too tired to take that shower I'd been fantasizing about. As the awards ceremony got under way, I fell asleep in a folding chair near the stage and woke to the booming voice of the announcer calling my name. The stars-and-stripes jersey was like a healing salve for my injured shoulder. As I stood on the very top step of the podium at my first national championships, all the pain, doubt, and fatigue subsided and I raised my good arm high above my head. Paramedic school would have to wait for a little while longer.

TWO MONTHS AFTER grabbing the stars and stripes in Wisconsin, my 24-hour championship tour continued with the World 24-Hour Mountain Bike Championships in Conyers, Georgia, the site of mountain biking's debut as an Olympic sport.

The race would be held on the very same course, at the Georgia International Horse Park, that the first Olympians had ridden 10 years prior. As promoted, it was not a course for the faint of heart. With more than 1,000 feet of elevation gain in just over 8 miles, there were large granite outcroppings, plenty of climbing, and tight switchbacks that nearly doubled back onto themselves. There were roots and rocks and ruts and everything that makes a world-class mountain bike course world class. I was in over my head. This time around I couldn't just run my way through the hard stuff. There was no faking it at the world championships—this was the real deal.

As I practiced the course with Greg, I felt anything but world class. There were sections I couldn't ride at all and countless places I bumped and bobbled through like a pinball. Reduced to tears, I questioned why I was there, pretending to be a bike racer. The race pitted me against a famous world-class pro, Sue Haywood. Being from the slippery, rooty, rocky hills of West Virginia, she would be at home on this East Coast terrain. Sue was also the current national short track and Super D champion (a race format that focuses on technical downhills), so I knew she was a formidable opponent. My only advantage over Sue was that she hadn't done much 24-hour solo racing. Like me, this was just her third solo event.

Twenty-four hour specialist Louise Kobin was also there, along with Australian endurance rider Katrin van der Spiegel and the race favorite, Pua Sawicki, whom I'd just beaten at nationals. This was another league, and I could only hope not to embarrass myself. My bull-in-a-china-shop technique could be a liability on such a technical course. I planned to stay within striking distance of the front of the field for the first third of the race, and then rely on my opponents fading at 10 or 12 hours.

In fact, Sue led the race from the get-go, with Pua hot on her heels. My adrenaline settled as I learned the lines and racked up a few laps. I caught up and we all rode together for a stretch before Pua faded and Sue began to pull away.

Racing with Sue was like taking a clinic on how to ride a mountain bike. She seemed to float over the technical terrain yet used every ounce of muscle to keep the bike upright. No matter how much stamina and staying power I had, I was wasting precious energy by battling the technical terrain. Over the long haul it would cost me. My fear of falling made me ride tense, which made the bike harder to handle, which ironically made it more likely that I would fall. Fear was slowing me down, just as it did in my rock climbing days. I wanted time to calculate the next move, but cycling demands you let go of the brakes and roll through.

Unfortunately, I wasn't the only one aware of my struggle. Halfway through the race one of the photographers was overheard saying, "There's this girl out there who is so stiff and uncoordinated, it's actually painful to watch . . . I can tell this girl is not a cyclist. Who is she? What is she even doing here?" The feature article published in *Mountain Bike Magazine* several months later was titled "Winning Ugly." I was finding a way to win in mountain biking, but only because I was stubborn, certainly not because I was skilled.

After 24 very intense hours of racing, I came in second. I was absolutely thrilled to be able to hang tough against such a seasoned, expert mountain biker. Sue later admitted that she suffered "an emotional breakdown from exhaustion" in order to stay in front of me. As I proudly climbed up on that second-place podium spot, I vowed to work on my technical skills in the year ahead.

Over the course of the next year, I did just that. I dedicated myself to training on my mountain bike with an intensity I had not tapped before. With Matthew's help, I worked until I was in the best shape of my life, and Greg showed me how to be a better bike handler. I also got some tips from mountain bike legend and Specialized teammate Ned Overend. He didn't hesitate to tell me everything I was doing wrong within 30 seconds of riding with me. "You're too stiff. You brake too much on the downhills. You're not flexing your knees and elbows to float over bumps . . ." It was hard to hear the laundry list of everything I was doing wrong, but if I was going to live down my reputation for "winning ugly," I had to make some changes.

Even as training ramped up, I held on to my part-time firefighting gig. I'd worked too hard for that spot to give it up. Truthfully, my work with the fire department compromises my training at times. If I'm exhausted from a demanding emergency call, I can't expect to jump on my bike and bang out the best ride of my life. Fitting in training for both requires some give and take, but they complement each other far more than they conflict. My cycling fitness certainly carries over to the physical nature of firefighting, and vice versa. To be successful, both jobs require pacing, hydration, physical and mental endurance, and, if I want to avoid injury, sharp focus. Though there have been difficult times, I think being a firefighter has made me more resilient as an athlete.

AFTER A FULL SEASON with more than 15 mountain bike races under my belt, it was time for another showdown in the World 24-Hour Mountain Bike Championships, this time in Monterey, California. When Greg and I pulled into the dusty northern California venue to set up camp on the blacktop parking lot, it was a sweltering 100 degrees. Our practice ride revealed that the physical demands of the course would be as hard to manage as the heat. There was nearly double the amount of climbing as there'd been on the Georgia course, 2,500 feet in just 13.7 miles. Aside from a set of stairs to ride down, the course was mostly smooth singletrack. The technique was all about how fast you could corner on the loose, sandy dirt without sliding into the poison oak or shouldering a tree.

I was lining up with renowned endurance mountain biking coach Lynda Wallenfels, an Ironman triathlete, 100-mile mountain bike champion, and a fierce, smart competitor. Once again I planned to be conservative in the first six hours, then hit it harder when night fell and the temperatures dropped.

Though I quickly memorized the course, it never really got any easier. There were super-high-speed downhills—I clocked 41 mph on one—and ridiculously steep climbs that had me crawling along at 3 mph. The twisting singletrack, sand pits, and stairs left little room for letting up, save for a small stretch of flat trail coming in and out of the transition pits. Lynda and I volleyed for the lead for the first five laps. I could get a slight advantage on the climbs, but then she'd come right back on the descents. I cringed at the possibility of going on like this all day and night. I watched as she took off her jacket while riding with no hands. She had spent so much time on a bike that it was an extension of her body. Although I'd made good progress in the past year, riding was not second nature to me. Back at home, I had been practicing riding with no hands just in case I happened to cross a finish line first and had the opportunity to put my hands up. Lynda's skills swirled around in my head, but I scolded myself, determined to stay focused on my own strengths, like consistency and fast transitions. As the race wore on, my strategy started to work.

I began to pull ahead on the climbs, and as night fell I kept the pressure on and slowly lengthened my lead by riding just a fraction faster and keeping my pit stops lightning fast. I had brought a posse along with me to form a world-class pit crew. Jason Bauer was our mechanic and crew chief from adventure racing days. Donna, my best friend from my Chicago days, lent us her boyfriend and bike fanatic, Charles Kurre. Specialized even sent over a couple of staff members to lend a hand. Everyone had a specific job, from mechanic to nutritionist to timekeeper. We worked in perfect synchronization with no wasted effort, on par with the best of my adventure racing exploits.

By daybreak, I thought I spied Lynda in the distance. By this hour of the race, math is difficult and your mind plays tricks on you. Even though one of my crew members was telling me time splits, I couldn't trust what he was saying. When he told me the extent of my lead, I unceremoniously poked a finger into his chest. "Don't fuck this up!" In my debilitated state I was reliant on my crew to be my brain, but it was hard to let go. Not until I was right behind Lynda did I allow myself to acknowledge the reality at hand. Then in the final six hours I lapped her once again.

Now it was time to celebrate. In a little over one season of being a full-time mountain bike racer, I'd pulled down a national championship and now a world championship in 24-hour solos. Despite my own disbelief, I embraced endurance mountain bike racing as my new calling.

IN 2008, I followed a similar recipe: training with Matthew, working on my technical skills, and racing various 100-milers and 24-hour races with the intent of once again peaking for the World 24-Hour Mountain Bike Championships, to be held that summer in Canmore, Alberta, Canada, site of the first-ever championship event in 1999. We now had a well-oiled 24-hour racing machine with Greg and me racing solo, Charles as our head pit crew, and Jason as the head mechanic. We were a team, and I loved traveling with them and sharing the planning, racing, success, and failures with my best friends. Solo endurance bike racing is certainly not solo, and the camaraderie of my crew kept alive what I had loved most about adventure racing.

The Canmore course and conditions were brutal: sheets of rain, high winds, greasy mud, slick roots and rocks, and endless climbing. The Canadian Rockies have a reputation for rough terrain and brutal weather. I thought the worlds course in Atlanta was technical. Even if the conditions had been dry, this course would put me at the limit of my skills. I practiced the course with Greg and Jason, rehearsing tough sections, watching them ride it first and doing my best to find the easiest lines in the braided tangle of roots on the course. It was as if all of the tree roots were piled above ground. There were riders from Italy, Canada, Australia . . . I didn't know all of the international riders, but I was sufficiently intimidated by their strong legs and serious faces. Just as I was sizing them up, they were doing the same with me. I tried to let the stares roll off me. Suddenly, I was the one to watch. I didn't like the notoriety. Canmore required just one minor change to my strategy: Try not to get seriously injured on this course.

The race started smoothly, with our team sustaining some variation of autopilot. While 24-hour solo racing is dreadfully difficult and tiring, continual motion is the key. That means eating, drinking, and dressing on the bike, and doing rolling transitions whenever possible. If I sit down in a chair to relax, I might as well tie an anchor to my ass; it's impossible to shake off rest. If there is an issue with my bike, I roll into the pit crew and jump straight onto a second clean bike while Jason takes the dirty bike and works furiously to have it ready for the next lap. I see my crew for only seconds at a time, but those few precious moments are fundamental to my success. We write out a race plan of how many calories I burn per hour, what food I need, what bottles I'll snatch and what jacket I might want. Everything is labeled and ready for a fast grab. By the time the race starts, I rarely have to speak to tell them what I need. I rely heavily on their support, and it's also crucial for me to see the faces of my friends each lap. It's what keeps me going through the long, lonely hours of pain and suffering. I want to do my very best not only for myself but for them, because they are working just as hard as I am.

However, I can't always rely on my team. If something happens out in the course, it's up to me to figure it out on my own and get myself back around to the pit zone under my own power. There is no support allowed on the course unless it's through the generosity of another racer. Thanks to the rain, the webs of tree roots were becoming increasingly slimy. I initially got over them using momentum to my advantage, but as the race progressed, momentum only guaranteed a speedy impact. Elsewhere, on the high-speed descents and corners, deep ruts were forming.

In the middle of the night in Canmore I had the worst crash I've ever experienced on a mountain bike. At 25 mph, I was flying down one of the easier descents when my front wheel hit a deep rut. In an instant, I was face down in a streambed 10 feet off the trail. I had been torpedoed off my bike headfirst into a log. I slowly rolled onto my back, took a deep breath, and wiggled my hands and toes. It was pitch black and I was alone. I felt the vertebrae in my neck, blinked my eyes, and slowly got back on my feet to collect my bike.

There are times when my EMT knowledge is a bit of a double-edged sword. On one hand, it makes me sort of paranoid. I'm more educated about the damage I am doing to my body during a really long race, the fluid collecting in my lungs from my asthma, the edema (swelling) that causes cankles after races, the blurry tunnel vision that develops when I'm really fatigued. But on the flip side, I feel more prepared to help myself or others. After a quick self-evaluation, I had no other option but to get on my bike and finish the lap. Shaken, I wondered if my neck would feel injured when the adrenaline wore off.

I didn't mention the crash to Greg or my crew until much later. I just switched out my bike and continued to chase down what I set out to do. There was no hiding the extent of the crash from Jason, but the others didn't find out until the race was over. The inside of my helmet was entirely shattered.

The rain, the international destination, my luck at surviving the crash, and racing with Greg added to the magnitude of this event. The sweet sensation of a second world championship title was topped only by Greg's world championship title in the single-speed men's category. Our tight-knit team celebrated the double win, and all I could think about was how far I'd come from that first bike ride with Greg in Idaho. How far we had come together. He had taught me the technical skills of mountain biking, and I had taught him the pacing, nutritional, logistical, and racing skills I brought to the table from adventure racing. It was extraordinary to share a double world championship win with him, the person who brought me into mountain bike racing in the first place.

Even before the sweat and grime were washed off, I was floored to get a personal call from the director of marketing at Specialized congratulating me on the title. It seemed people were taking note that I was a decent bike racer. At the awards dinner, Greg and I struggled to stay awake until our names were called. We had absolutely left it all out there on the muddy trails in Canmore. Our crew worked overtime to keep us awake long enough to receive our rewards and then shepherded us back to the hotel and tucked us into bed.

Early in my pro cycling career, I arrived at Sea Otter to see my name emblazoned on the team trailer next to some really heavy hitters, including Ned Overend! I was also issued my brand-new global athlete cycling uniform. The only problem was, it was fucking pink. I've always hated pink. It was a breakout year; if I was going to look silly, I might as well be fast.

Successful 24-hour solo racing takes a small village and, in this case, Jason Bauer as my world-class mechanic. He and my A team supported me for well over 24 hours to make sure I had nothing to worry about but turning the pedals. By 2009 we had it down to a science.

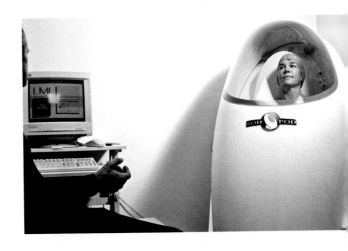

The Red Bull Performance Division offers athletes a host of tools, including the Bod Pod—a space-age tool that measures body composition. Knowledge is power, and this is where you literally learn what you're made of.

My coach, Dean Golich, says that my gift is maximizing my numbers. I may have a four-cylinder engine, but I can keep it on the edge the whole time.

Project Endurance studies the factors that affect human performance— heart function, brain-wave measurements, muscle mapping, oxygen saturation, blood lactate levels, sleep patterns, and whatever else the scientists can dream up.

I lined up less than prepared for my first Leadville in 2009. Never having ridden the course, I taped this hand-drawn course map to my top tube and hoped for the best.

My partner, Greg Martin, is an athlete, and he knows what it takes to win. He's my essential support system in so many ways, and my victories are his victories.

A lot of people walk the Powerline climb, and so did I for my first three years. In 2013, I finally had the legs and experience to ride up that monster. While it didn't feel good at the time, it helped seal the deal for my fourth straight win.

The commitment and intense training it takes to turn out a winning performance in a 103-mile race at elevation is staggering. Over the years, win or lose, Leadville has taken on new meaning for me.

Despite the fact that there is no prize money for winning Leadville, it still draws in the world's best pros from all disciplines of cycling for a chance to walk away with the coveted Leadville Trail 100 MTB ore-cart trophy. It's so heavy that many of the roadies, including Levi Leipheimer, have trouble lifting the thing.

Firefighting was my plan B if this pro athlete thing didn't pan out. With Ketchum Fire Department, I get the best of both worlds. Greg ranks higher than I do, but I don't mind answering to him—at least not in this arena.

Rebecca's Private Idaho and the SRAM Gold Rusch Tour are two of my proudest achievements. I love the fact that I can share the beauty of my hometown and my passion for sports with other people.

My record-breaking ride in Kokopelli was a reminder that I need to keep exploring and covering new territory. Personal goal setting will always be part of my life.

11

A Big Year

Twenty-four-hour mountain bike racing thrashes you. The preparation itself is intense. There's all the training and logistics and making sure you have perfectly functioning lighting systems, backup bikes, and gear. There's ensuring that your nutrition is 100 percent dialed in and that you have the support you need to keep your pit stops as efficient as in Formula 1 racing. And then there's the race itself, which is crushing. Cramps; digestive issues; bruised hands, feet, and ass; blurred vision; and crashing are the norm when you ask your body to race nonstop at a fast past for an entire day. After it's all said and done, it takes a month, sometimes more, before you're fully recovered from the beat down.

Personally, I was coming to terms with the fact that 24-hour solo racing was exacerbating my asthma and breathing issues. The pace was much higher than in multiday adventure racing, so the increased respiration rates put more wear and tear on my lungs. My mind and my muscles were absolutely built for this style of racing, but my respiratory system was not.

In most of my athletic endeavors, I've always had something working against me, such as excessively active sweat glands in my hands (rock climbing), a primal fear of water (paddling), or being a late bloomer (mountain biking). I've always had to work hard to minimize my weaknesses and maximize my strengths. But this was different. No matter how much research or experimentation with medications I did, I could not find a workable solution. Following my second 24-hour solo worlds win, I had to sleep sitting up for a few days because lying down led to severe coughing fits that made me nearly choke on my mucous. I'd hack up thick green phlegm for about 10 days as my lungs struggled to heal. Although I wanted to continue my winning streak and make history with a world championship three-peat the following year, I was questioning how much longer I could hang on and, more important, what sort of permanent damage I might be doing to my body.

But the body's memory of pain fades if given enough time, and soon enough I had buried the memories of the awful coughing fits and how deeply it hurt to do 24-hour solo racing at the highest level. Matthew was amped and had complete faith in my ability to return for another world championship and stamp my name in the record books for endurance mountain bike racing. In 2009, all of my training and racing was focused entirely on peaking for this one race. I still had a demanding race schedule, but the strategy was to train right through these events with my eyes on the bigger goal of the three-peat. This was the first time in my life I'd put all of my stock and planning into a single event. As the race neared, the pressure of everyone's expectations, including my own, became increasingly heavy. What if I crashed? What if I was just plain beaten? What if I got sick? What if I didn't get validation for myself and my sponsors?

The race would again be held in Canmore. After the previous year's experience, Greg likened the race to operating a jackhammer for 24 hours. Once again, I stacked the odds in my favor by putting together the best crew friendship can buy: Charles and Jason, in addition to my best friend, Donna, and Karoline, my riding partner from Idaho. I also packed two tricked-out Specialized Era race bikes, a mountain of spare bike parts, and a duffel bag stuffed full of race food. Nothing was left to chance organizationally. We even stayed in the same house we rented the previous year.

We rolled into town early so I could give myself a few days to ride the course and sort out the technical sections, figure out where I could eat and drink, and try to decipher how to race the course to my best advantage. I already knew how hard it was, but I wanted to see if I was actually any better a year later. There were no sections where you could rest, and although the lap was only about 10 miles, it was jam-packed with intensity. You got your money's worth in every mile of this course. In contrast to the previous year, it was screaming hot, so I knew staying on top of hydration, electrolytes, and nutrition would be more important than ever. I took numerous icy soaks in the nearby lake to aid recovery and keep my core body temperature down leading up to the race.

The women's field was mostly unknown to me, but I could see that I would be put to the test by the Australian 24-hour national champ, Jessica Douglas, some Canadian women, and the U.S. national 24-hour champ, Jari Kirkland. Like me, Jari had an adventure racing background and was the type of athlete who would be strong and consistent over the long haul. Normally my ability to be strong right up to the end of the race was my advantage over the other athletes; in this case, Jari's presence leveled the field.

Race day morning, I strapped my number plate—#1, signify-ing that I was the defending champion—to my bike and tried to stay focused and relaxed. I had never put the #1 number plate on my bike in my life. Greg, as the single-speed defending champ, had race plate #2. We were the 24-hour power couple that year. The unspoken pressure was thick, and anything less than a three-peat would have been a disappointment for me, my team, my friends, and my sponsors. I replayed my race strategy in my head: focus on my own pacing, my own nutrition, and riding the course in my style without trying to target my competitors, especially in the early hours of the race.

The instant the gun went off, I exploded off the start line. I was so amped after a year of focusing on this one day that I threw my tried-and-true strategy completely out the window. That primal instinct that is hardwired into every racer's brain took control, and I rode like I was being chased. I flew through the loop at cross-country pace and as I pulled through the start/finish line after my first lap, I saw the clock and heard the announcer call out, "Rebecca Rusch comes in at 1 hour 40 seconds!" I had beaten most of the men and was up 7 minutes on the rest of the women's field. As I ticked off the laps, my lead steadily expanded by over 5 minutes per lap. I made a mental pact with myself to keep the pressure on until midnight or until I lapped the second-place pro woman. Then and only then would I relax a little. I'm the type to like a huge buffer—at least enough of a gap to allow for a flat tire, major mechanical issue, or physical breakdown like cramping, vomiting, or heat stroke. This cynicism is what provides the motivation for me to keep pushing just a little harder and get just a little more space. It's never over until it's over, and I'll never, ever celebrate a win until I cross the finish line.

The course was relentless, with very little opportunity to spin and recover. I had to maintain nonstop focus and intensity for the whole lap. It was true mountain biking, and I was riding it like a mountain biker! Even the descending sections required nimble reflexes and upper-body strength. Because of the nature of the course, fueling on the bike was a big challenge, so I was taking a little longer in the pits than usual to get a break, take a pee, and try to down some food, often simultaneously. My crew was keeping a sharp eye on the competition and reported that the other women were also stopping for a few minutes each lap, so I felt comfortable matching their downtimes. Before dark, I lapped Jessica and shortly after that Jari. About 12 hours into the race, I had a 90-minute lead and everything was unfolding as planned. I was switching bikes every few laps, and Jason, my pit mechanic, was keeping them silky smooth. He would meticulously perform a full tune-up each time and check tires, brakes, bearings, the works. My crew was working nonstop, and I was pushing hard to do my part and stay strong on the climbs and relaxed in the singletrack. Jason, a really good technical rider, had told me, "Smooth is fast" and "Ride like water over rocks." These became my mantras and visual inspiration as I focused on flowing over the technical sections instead of battling with them. I thought about my first 24-hour worlds and riding behind Sue Haywood. I imagined riding like her.

As always, the power of the mind can be a positive or negative tool. When my mind is strong, it can take me places I never thought possible. When it's weak and self-doubting, I fumble and fall in places that I shouldn't. So when I get tired enough that I just can't mentally fight the terrain anymore, or when the darkness is shrouding the peripheral distractions, I'm a better rider.

As midnight approached, I settled into the darkness and my favorite part of these ultralong races: the witching hours. Night riding adds a whole different dimension to the riding experience: A calm settles over the race. But even though I had a lead, there were still 12 hours more to ride and plenty of time for crashes, mechanical problems, and errors. The body also starts to break down after 12 hours on the bike, reflexes are numb, and the burden of all that time in the saddle begins to take its toll. There were multiple crashes and medical evacuations from the course that night. I could hear sirens and saw the emergency crews multiple times, so staying safe and protecting my lead were high priorities.

I rode on and kept a healthy buffer between me and second place. However, by sunrise my stomach was not cooperating. I had pushed too hard early on, and now my body was revolting against me. As the sun came up, so did most of the food and fluid I had been diligently consuming. My nutrition plan was the same as usual, but it seemed that the intensity of the course was not allowing any blood flow to my stomach to aid digestion. Instead of food and liquid providing energy, they were just piling up in my stomach until there was no more room.

I had set a blistering pace in the first half of the race to send a strong message and now, 18 hours later, that strategy was biting me in the ass. It was a tough morning as I struggled to keep any sort of food down and suffered some debilitating asthma attacks. The biggest scare came when Jari blew by me on an uphill section at around 8 a.m. I was still a lap ahead of her, but she had unexpectedly gained time on me while I was stopped in my pit trying to force-feed myself. She looked fresh and spunky, and even her white uniform was sparkling clean. Had she not been in the same race as me, riding all night long? How was it possible that I looked like I'd been through a war, with snot and dirt all over me, while she looked like a model doing a bike photo shoot? She was on the rise as I was spiraling down. My tired brain began calculating the worst-case scenario, trying to do the math on how many laps I had remaining and what I needed to do to protect my lead despite her fourth-quarter push. Was it possible that she could erase my lead in the time that was left? I couldn't keep the numbers straight. I just knew I had to ride and keep riding. I was now in panic mode, looking over my shoulder like a hunted animal and begging my body to hang on just a little longer.

I managed to keep it together enough to pedal a slow but steady pace for the next three hours. Each small hill was a mountain, and I was willing my legs to turn the cranks. One mile felt like 10, and one hour felt like an eternity. Then, at 11:15 a.m., there it was . . . the world championship finish line. It was mine to cross with no one else in sight. All season, at the end of every single training ride, I had visualized this exact place and this outcome. This precise scene was etched in my mind, my singular motivation for a year. I had ridden 180 miles with 30,000 feet of climbing in approximately 23 hours. I'd completed 18 laps and achieved a goal that I had not dreamed possible: three consecutive 24-hour solo world championship titles. I soaked in the cheering and elation as Jason, Charles, and Donna kept me upright on my wobbly legs. I fell into Greg's arms. He had also defended his title and earned a second consecutive 24-hour single-speed world championship win, so we were the 24-hour power couple for another year.

It was a banner moment in an amazing year, and I was determined to relish that moment as long as I could. After events like 24-hour worlds, where it all comes together precisely as planned on the right day, it's impossible not to be seduced by that feeling of being on form, at the peak of your fitness. It's intoxicating—you want to experience it over and over again at every race. But this elusive state is not sustainable, and after the excitement died down, I knew it was time to move on. Not only were the rigors of 24-hour racing wearing me down, I felt I had nothing more that I wanted to accomplish or prove in this arena.

People often say to me, "Oh, well you knew you were going to win. We all knew you would." Racing certainly would be dull if the outcome was always known ahead of time. I never, ever enter a race knowing I will win. The nature of racing is unpredictable. Bikes and bodies break. People show up in top shape. Not knowing what will happen is what makes racing exciting and keeps people coming back for more. I did not line up at worlds in 2009 knowing I would win. I was very confident in my preparation, which is more than I can say about what came next.

ALTHOUGH MY SEASON was focused on 24-hour racing and securing my third world championship win, I went into it knowing that this year would also be my initiation into 100-milers and stage races to start rounding out my palate. Earlier in the year, I had gotten into stage racing, diving into the deep end with the ABSA Cape Epic in South Africa, one of the longest, hardest stage races in the world. Though the race didn't go as well as planned—my teammate broke her collarbone in a crash on Day 4 and I continued on my own unofficially for the remaining four days of the race—it was an eye-opening experience for me. Stage racing is hard, sometimes brutally so. But it is more like adventure racing and less just a relentless beat down of the senses, like 24-hour solo racing is. You travel to beautiful places and actually catch more than a glimpse of them, immersing yourself in your surroundings and experiencing them on two wheels for days on end. Plus, the riding is point-to-point instead of going in circles. Like adventure racing, mountain bike stage races are multiday events, but the big difference is sleep. The race clock stops every night and begins again the next morning. This format allows civilized recovery and avoids the dramatic physical deterioration that nonstop racing dishes out. This format was going to utilize my endurance, be easier on my lungs, and allow me to put more stamps in my passport.

My new journey would take me around the globe once more, to far-flung places such as Ecuador, Patagonia, Chile, and Australia, as well as every challenging venue the States could serve up, including the slippery slopes of Fayetteville, Tennessee; the rocky, oppressively humid hillsides of central Pennsylvania; the lush forests of Spokane, Washington; and of course, the legendary thin air of Leadville, Colorado.

I rarely pull the pro card and weasel my way into races. But I'll admit straight up that I did just that for my first attempt at Leadville, mostly as a result of my lack of planning and my procrastination. It had been four years since I'd made the switch to professional mountain biking, but as of June 2009, I didn't realize that the next level was going to be Leadville just a couple of months later.

Today you can earn a spot at Leadville by doing well in a qualifying race or by entering a lottery. But at that point in time, the Leadville entry was purely a lottery system. You paid your money early in the year and threw your name in the hat. It was still a mail-in application. You sent your check and a one-page registration form that included a space for you to handwrite why you wanted to race Leadville. It felt like a job application or an appeal for membership into a really exclusive club. Ketchum locals have long been crazy about this race, and each year the chatter in the bike shop was all about who was going to submit their names into the lottery.

The Ketchum kingpin in all of the pre-Leadville hoopla was Roger Mankus, a mechanic at our local bike shop. Roger did the very first Leadville and has raced it every single year since, except the one when he had a broken hip. Roger was going for his 15th buckle. Local pro roadie Richard Feldman had won the men's race twice in the 1990s; my good friend, training partner, and Race Across America (RAAM) regular Muffy Ritz had also raced it a few times and had been on the women's podium every time. Greg had raced it. Now that I was part of the bike scene in Idaho, I wanted in. There must be something special about this race if all of my friends had raced it and kept going back for more, I thought.

I've never been a really good planner, and January in Idaho is cold; it's also the time of year when I'm thinking more about cross-country skiing than mountain biking, so trying to plot the races on my calendar for the summer is not always at the forefront in my mind. Roger had collected a group of applications from locals and sent them in together in hopes of helping their odds for a spot. Since he was going for his 15th time and was basically a fixture at the event, he would surely get an entry. (Even though it's a lottery, there were many exceptions made for returning riders, multi-time participants, and riders with a compelling story that tugged on Ken Chlouber's and Merilee Maupin's—the race directors'—heartstrings. Race staff tell stories of applications arriving by the thousands, being spread all over the LT100 office, each one personally read, and then each filed into boxes labeled "in" and "not in.")

I missed the application deadline. Kicking myself, I made a few calls to see if I could grovel a bit. They couldn't say yes if I didn't even ask. I first asked Roger to call the office to see if they'd make an exception for me. He got nowhere. Next, I called Gretchen Reeves, the previous year's women's winner and an adventure racing friend and teammate. She also got nowhere. I called six-time winner and Leadville legend Dave Wiens, whom I knew from his brief foray into adventure racing. No luck, although I think Dave's superstar influence did help grease the wheels. I called Ken myself, more than once, and spoke about why I wanted to race there and how grateful I would be if he'd let me in. He finally relented. My status as a professional athlete meant absolutely nothing to Ken; in the end, he said he'd let me in because everyone who called and went to bat for me said I was simply a nice person. They consider Leadville participants family, and Ken had every right to fill up his family tree however he saw fit. Plus they were working on growing the women's field, which worked in my favor.

All of this back-and-forth took months. By the time I found out I was definitely headed to Leadville, it was August and the race was less than a week away. Even though I pulled some strings for my entry, I paid full price (as I still do) and made sure to send good old-fashioned thank-you cards to Ken and Merilee for opening the door to me.

As a major bucket list event, this race is months or years in the making for most people. Because I wasn't sure my application would be accepted and the World 24-Hour Mountain Bike Championships were my primary focus, it was quite another story for me. I was completely hammered physically and mentally from the logistics, training, and execution of my three-peat.

Normally I would need at least four weeks to recover from an effort like worlds and feel spunky again. Leadville would fall exactly three weeks after that 24-hour win. I was riding a fine line between recovering, healing my battered body, and trying to milk the season's peak to last a bit longer than originally planned. But Matthew thought it could be done. Even though we didn't get the official word until just before the race, he had me rest and train as if I would be going. If I got in, I'd be ready and rested. The weeks, months, and years leading up to a peak are nothing but suffering, hard work, and insecurity about your fitness. And sadly, those fitness peaks don't last long. What goes up must come down so that it can go back up again. My hope was that I could push off the inevitable slide down the other side for just one more big—really big—race.

The plan was simple. First I got some rest, because, frankly, it's hard to even walk or stand after a solo event that long and arduous. I also had to give my lungs a chance to heal. Slowly, I got moving again with active recovery, including easy, fun rides and a few short, hard efforts to keep reminding my legs that they weren't done for the season yet. I needed to be rested enough from worlds but not too lethargic from taking some rest. Bound for Colorado's high country, I felt fit but knew there were plenty of challenges ahead. In hindsight, it's probably good that I was going into Leadville with very little knowledge of the race. If I had known the magnitude of the event, I might have been enticed to just rest on my laurels and shut it down for the season. Instead I had a few short weeks to get my bike, body, and travel sorted out.

Everyone I knew had already booked their travel and lodging. I put my name on a waiting list at the Super 8, crossed my fingers, and got the lucky call three days before leaving that someone had canceled.

I mooched a ride from the Denver airport with friends from Ketchum. We arrived the Thursday prior to the race with barely enough time to settle in. I met up with Mike Sinyard, the founder of Specialized. Since we were all Leadville virgins, Mike had arranged a lunch meeting with eight-time Leadville veteran Nate Whitman.

Nate has the kind of brain that remembers every turn, every hill, and all the minutia of a course. He meticulously went through every section of the race with us, where the aid stations where, tips on the notorious parts of the course, and time estimates. He was throwing out names for infamous sections of the route like Columbine, Powerline, and Carter Summit. I had no idea where these places were or what they held in store for me. I just nodded and listened intently as he went through the course mile by mile. I was pretty sure I'd forget everything he said come race day. To help me out, Nate sketched the course profile from memory on a piece of notebook paper, complete with estimated split times for an eight-hour race. I hadn't a clue what sort of time I could ride, but I knew Gretchen had done an 8:05:29 the year she won, so that would be a target for me. She was a much more experienced bike racer than I was, but I had done an adventure race with her and had been able to keep up with her on the bike section of that course. I harbored no illusion of matching her time, but I did use it as a general gauge.

I taped Nate's hand-drawn profile and time chart to my top tube and mentally prepared to ride the course cold turkey, completely sight unseen. I was used to being able to practice bike courses before the race, but this course was too long and it was too close to the event start, so I had no choice. I was told the course was not very technical and that it takes place mostly on fire roads. After jackhammering on the roots in Canmore, a race that was more fitness than finesse sounded like a welcome break.

Given the circumstances, I was as prepared as I could possibly be, but I was definitely a bit freaked out. The race has a sensational reputation, and I had no course preparation, no crew, no drop bags arranged, and only the slightest idea of what I would encounter in those 103 miles. The distance was not daunting, but the crowds and tactics required were. I was worried about the pace in this "short" race, the logistics of getting food and water at the crowded aid stations, and, especially, riding with so many people. I love an adventure and heading into the unknown. However, my bike racing success to this point had been more about solid preparation, good logistics, course knowledge, and being able to stick it out for 24 hours straight. As a Virgo, I like that kind of control, especially when I wasn't confident in this new territory. I'd just have to roll with it and stay flexible.

My 4:15 a.m. wake-up call on race day was painful—it was a frigid and particularly dismal morning, with a cold drizzle falling from the cloud-darkened sky. It would have been really easy to roll back under the Super 8's threadbare covers and put the flat pillow back over my head, but I told myself that by letting me into the race, Ken had personally invited me to his family get-together, and he'd be disappointed if I didn't show. I dragged myself up, slowly geared up, and rolled alone in the frigid morning to the start line.

The scene at the start was even more chaotic than I'd imagined. I had heard anecdotes about how many racers lined up here, but I had underestimated the spectacle. At the front of the throng was Lance Armstrong, back for another try at the win after getting bested by local hero Dave Wiens the year prior. This time Lance wasn't messing around. Fresh off his Tour de France comeback, he brought his A game and what seemed like a million fans, along with a camera crew that would film the documentary *Race Across the Sky*. I had never seen so many people gathered at a bike race in my life. I felt like a very small fish in a very big pond.

By 6:15 a.m. there were 1,500 shivering, nervous people lined up for what might be the most monumental challenge of their cycling lives. I was invited to line up in the front with all of the big-name athletes and past winners of the race. I sheepishly slotted in next to the big dogs and made myself as narrow as possible in the tangle of bikes and handlebars. I had not seen a start list for the women's field, so I was fully unaware of the athletes I was racing against. Frankly, it didn't matter at that moment. I had my own plan, which was to survive the infamous chaos of the start without being taken out and stampeded by the anxious wheels behind me.

Riding in a huge, fast-moving amoeba-like pack of antsy athletes was entirely foreign to me. Especially given that most of my sporting career was spent alone or with a few people in the middle of nowhere. I wasn't apprehensive about finishing the course, I was apprehensive about surviving the first 30 minutes. After the pavement roll out, I planned to use Nate's trusty profile and tick off one big hill at a time, breaking the course into smaller goals until I crossed the finish line. I was treating it more like a solo expedition than a gigantic bike race. I would eat, drink, carry a rain jacket, and be as self-sufficient as I would be on any really long adventure.

The shotgun start was fairly civilized, with a neutral roll out for a few miles until we hit the dirt road and started climbing. At that point, the race was *on*. I felt the mass of 1,500 people pulsing behind me, so I just concentrated on staying upright as the throng jockeyed for position and pressed the pace. I rode as steadily as I could, with elbows out and an eye on the crazies who were pushing and shoving and often crashing. I knew I was facing five major climbs that day, all of them over 10,000 feet above sea level, so getting angry, sprinting ahead, and exhibiting trail rage this early on seemed like a waste of energy. The altitude would be a major contributing factor to the pacing for this event.

I remember reading that Michael Phelps used to perform swimming sets with a snorkel that had the mouthpiece duct-taped over and pinholes punched into it to strengthen his lungs. That's kind of what it feels like racing up a mountain at 10,000 to 12,000 feet of altitude. And similar to how I feel just before an asthma attack hits. Because the air is so thin, you breathe harder and your heart pounds just to pull enough oxygen into your system to keep you pedaling at efforts that might normally feel almost easy. You can forget about generating your normal power (not that I was training with a power meter at that time). At elevation levels this high, the maximum power you can sustain plummets by about 20 to 30 percent of what it would be below 5,000 feet. Most important, you have to be *really* careful about how hard you push yourself. When you push past your lactate threshold (the kind of effort that makes your legs burn), you need lots of oxygen to recover. At altitude, the oxygen just isn't there . . . and neither is recovery. Dig too deep and go into the red zone too many times and you might find yourself in a hole you can't climb out of. So although I was wearing my heart rate monitor, I wouldn't use it for pacing, but would instead rely on perceived exertion and the internal pacing experience I had honed through a decade of adventure racing.

I led the women's race from the start. Unlike many races, where Greg or some other support person will give me time splits, I was getting no race status that day. Even riding among 1,500 people, I felt pretty much alone. So I had no idea how close the other women were to me. As usual, I assumed that someone was probably right on my tail and kept the pressure as high as I could sustain, imagining that every guy in front of me was a woman as I tried to keep catching people. No matter what category I am in, having someone to chase motivates me to find that extra 1 percent.

The first half of the race was bitterly cold, with freezing rain pelting what little bits of skin I had left exposed to the elements. Within the first hour, my fingers began to stiffen up and ache so badly I could barely shift or hold on to the handlebars. I had no choice but to stop for a second and pull on a pair of waterproof shell gloves I had stuffed in my pocket. I would have done this while riding, but I just didn't trust my cold fingers to have enough dexterity to pull out the gloves and hang onto the handlebar, so I simply stopped and took care of business as a bunch of riders whizzed by.

I was so thankful I had brought gloves, wool arm warmers, and a jacket. At this early stage in the race, I was already wearing every stitch of clothing I had with me. Many, many top racers were going light and fast and suffered badly because they had no extra clothing. They paid the price by shivering and burning precious calories. It had not occurred to me to leave my jacket and gloves behind given the gloomy weather and high mountain terrain. Those extra ounces of clothing in my pocket were my insurance policy and were unlikely to slow me down.

I rode in a bit of a daze, pushing down harder on the pedals in a somewhat vain attempt to stay warm. Soon I caught up to Matt Luhn, fellow Ketchum athlete and multi-time LT100 racer. I knew that he'd turned in some good race times and that he knew what we were up against. I was happy to see a familiar face at the top of St. Kevin's and ride with him for a while. It made me feel warmer and less alone in the vast sea of riders. As we rolled into the first aid station at Pipeline, I was worrying that perhaps I shouldn't be up this far in the pack with Matt. He was a fast rider with many years of experience. Just as my mind began to spiral in the dismal conditions, I pedaled through a crowd of spectators who went absolutely *insane*, cheering wildly when they saw I was the first female riding by. It made for an extra bit of warmth to combat the stinging chill of the rain. No one knew my name yet, but it was clear they were cheering for me.

The midpoint of the race is Columbine Mine, which sits at nearly 12,500 feet. The distance from Twin Lakes aid station to the summit is 11 miles with more than 3,000 feet of elevation gain. It's the longest and most feared climb on the course. My hometown ski resort, Sun Valley, has 3,300 feet of vertical gain, so despite having no time to practice on the course, I was well aware of what a climb of this magnitude would require. It was a reassuring mental tactic to focus on a known quantity as I made the long, slow climb up to the high point.

I metered my efforts, slowly pulled away from Matt, and started catching and passing more guys. As I got closer to the tree line and the track got sketchier and more rutted, I got to see the top men come down toward me at Mach speed. I saw a blur that was Lance, then Dave. It was exhilarating to see their speed, even though I still had a long way to go in my upward toil. Dave let out a shout of encouragement that was nearly lost on the wind, but it made me crack a smile. He was one of the few people I knew out there. I couldn't wait to be on the down side of this big hill, letting gravity pull me closer to the finish. This was the biggest obstacle in the entire race. As I reached the barren, windy high point, the cold rain turned to stinging sleet. The conditions were absolutely horrendous, so there wasn't time to enjoy the view or celebrate having half of the course behind me.

I never planned to stop at the Columbine aid station, and the sideways sleet made the choice that much easier. As I blew through, once again I was so grateful for the warm gloves. A 3,000-foot descent in freezing rain with two-way traffic would be death defying if I couldn't feel my hands. Squinting into the sleet, I took my first opportunity to get a visual on how close the next women were.

Unfortunately, spotting female competitors was going to be trickier than I'd hoped. I looked at my watch at the top of the climb and then immediately hit the first steep pitch of loose rocks and rain ruts, which demanded complete attention. By now hundreds of riders were facing two-way traffic on the mountain pass, on one side shivering, hypoxic riders plodding up, and on the other side a blur of riders ripping down the hill. I was freezing, exhausted, and focused on going fast downhill but not crashing, but I managed to catch a quick glimpse of Amanda Carey, the second-place female rider. I had hoped to read the look in her eyes and her body posture to evaluate her fatigue, but the moment was gone too soon. At that point, she was probably 15 minutes behind me, but I still had 50 miles to go and plenty more opportunities for flat tires or other problems. I made it down Columbine safely, though it wasn't the relaxing descent I had anticipated. I was relieved to be off that mountain with just two more big climbs remaining.

I was feeling okay, but the cold weather and the lack of pedaling on the descent were making my legs cramp. I needed to get them moving again. I took some electrolyte capsules and made an effort to finish my water, though I wasn't motivated to drink in the freezing cold rain. Swallowing the cold water just seemed to chill me from the inside out. The aid stations definitely helped keep me going. Not just because I could get more food and water there, but because of the thousands of people cheering and ringing cowbells. It was like Mardi Gras but for bikes. People were in costume, playing music, celebrating, blowing up balloons, dancing. This was by far the biggest, craziest turnout I'd ever seen for a mountain bike race, and I felt like I was in the Tour de France as I rode through lines of people crowding the course. I couldn't wipe the smile off my face as I pedaled through the wall of sound. Just then, the sun came out and began to warm my hands as the cheering crowds warmed my soul.

The hardest climb of the course, Powerline, started around Mile 80. Powerline is deeply rutted, very loose, and ridiculously steep, with a 25 percent grade or more in spots. I had fallen in with a small group of men holding about the same pace. So we tackled it together, mostly in silence, except for the sound of our heavy breathing and the few words of encouragement we could manage to utter along the way. I lost traction a couple of times and had to walk the steepest pitches. The guys around me were riding, but I was still keeping up with them on foot.

The crowd of riders had thinned dramatically by this far into the race. Misery loves company, so it was nice to have a little moral support out there on one of the hardest parts of the course.

At this point, the film crew finally caught on that I was winning the women's race and figured they'd better nab a bit of footage of me. As luck would have it, both times they were around me I was walking my bike. Would this turn out to me my only cameo in the movie? I tried to put on a smile and take even bigger steps to get up the climb more quickly. The crazy spectators lining the climb were running alongside us, offering snacks, encouragement, and even a push.

We sailed down the back side of Powerline and made our way back up Turquoise Lake Road for the final big climb. The moments of downhill felt so fleeting in this race, but they helped recharge me every time. At this point, I smelled the barn and the numbers on my odometer were nearing triple digits, so I shifted into the biggest gear I could push and left my little group of guys as I motored toward the finish. I wasn't going to beat Gretchen's winning time, but I didn't care. The last few miles ticked by very slowly. Although I knew it was unlikely that Amanda was going to catch me, my head started messing with me as I hit the final road stretch into Leadville.

I had ridden the final mile the day before to visualize myself finishing the race. There is a road sign on the crest of the last hill that says Slow. I remembered seeing that the day before the event and thinking, *No way would you go slowly at this point in the race when the finish is in sight and the red carpet is pulling you in like a giant magnet.* You can see the finish for about a half mile, and it's the sweetest site: the finish banner, the only stoplight in Leadville, and hordes of screaming fans lining the streets. A wave of relief washed over me. I felt as if I'd been away from Sixth Street and Harrison Avenue much longer than 8 hours and 15 minutes. The magnitude of the journey seemed to fill up more than what could have happened in that amount of time.

As I crested the very last hill and passed the slow sign with an exhausted sigh of relief, my worst nightmare materialized. I saw someone in front of me with curly blonde hair and a pink jersey. Fuck! How had a woman gotten in front of me? Was it a woman? Who was she? My oxygen-deprived brain raced, unable to tell for sure if it was a male or female rider. My mental celebration was short-circuited with self-doubt and anger. All those spectators had told me the wrong information, and I had foolishly believed them. I had pushed my hardest, but if I had known another female was just out of sight, perhaps I could have found another gear. Now it was too late, and I couldn't catch her in time.

As I was charging toward the finish, still making no progress in closing the gap, I shouted breathlessly to one of the bystanders, "Is the person [pant, pant] in front of me [pant, pant] a man or a woman?" "It's a man!" he yelled back enthusiastically. I had just a few moments to let the relief wash over me before I rolled over the red carpet at the finish line with my arms up and a huge sense of accomplishment in my heart. I finished with a time of 8:14, 30th place overall. Amanda finished 25 minutes behind me. For the record, Lance Armstrong pulled off the win and smashed the course record, with Wiens coming in second. The sound of the crowd was deafening and exhilarating. Immediately flowers were thrust into my arms, Merilee draped a medal around my neck, strangers were hugging me, and I was whisked off to the media room for an interview. I was still in a state of shock as I tried to relive the highlights of the race in my disoriented, dirt-covered state. I had no friends with me, but I was far from alone. I now felt and understood what it meant to be part of the Leadville family.

I was reluctant to leave the finish line because I didn't want to break the spell. But I was filthy, covered in sweat and splattered mud. After a quick shower, I went back out onto Sixth Street to watch my friends finish and take part in the crazy scene. At this point I was basking in the warm afternoon sun, and the freezing rain from Columbine was a distant memory. I milled around as strangers congratulated me. It was amazing and heartwarming to watch the steady stream of finishers as they rolled across the finish line and were embraced by friends and family, elated that they'd accomplished what they'd set out to achieve.

It would be weeks before I fully registered what I'd done that day. That red carpet symbolizes so much more than the finish of a bike race. It's the start of a bigger story. And that year, it was a *really* big story. Love him or hate him, Lance Armstrong was by far the biggest name in cycling, so sharing a podium with him catapulted my profile outside the niche realm of ultra-endurance sports. The launch of the film *Race Across the Sky* meant a movie premiere, another kind of red carpet appearance, and additional exposure around the world. I was still the same athlete I'd been for years, but now people were hearing my name, getting inspired, and latching on. Suddenly I was launched into a whole new role as a public figure as well as a professional athlete. Even Mike Sinyard, my longtime sponsor, sat up and took notice of how many men I'd beaten on the course. It would take years for me to fully appreciate the ramifications of this win. But I knew one thing was certain: I would return to Leadville. There was just something indescribably special about that race.

12

Gaining Momentum

As you squeeze into the starting corral and find your place among more than 1,500 wide-eyed, shivering cyclists at the corner of Sixth and Harrison streets in downtown Leadville, Colorado, you are effectively standing on the rooftop of the nation. At 10,152 feet, it's the highest incorporated city in the United States. The often snowcapped mountains you are nervously eyeing require more than 11,000 feet of climbing by day's end, including a trip up to the infamous Columbine Mine, which almost takes your breath away at 12,424 feet.

Rich in silver and other precious metals, Leadville was a boomtown in the late 1800s and early 1900s, when prospectors poured in by the tens of thousands. It suffered the same fate as other mining towns, however, with several periods of boom and bust before almost all of the mines shuttered, including the largest in 1983, leaving half the townspeople suddenly unemployed. The displaced moved on in search of greener pastures—all except former miner and marathoner Ken Chlouber.

The year the mine closed—about the time I laced up my first pair of running shoes as a high school freshman on the Downers Grove North track team—Chlouber hatched a plan to put Leadville back on the map and revive his struggling community. He would create a 100-mile ultrarunning event that would push competitors to their limit as they tackled the big mountains at high altitude. Legend has it that when he told the local hospital administrator about his idea, the man responded, "You're crazy! You'll kill someone!" Ken's reply: "Well, then we'll be famous, won't we?"

He was right . . . about the putting Leadville on the map part, anyway. The running race became wildly popular. So popular that they added five more events to make it a series. Then, in 1994, they added the Leadville Trail 100 MTB race, now just reverently called "Leadville." It parallels the running course, sharing a few sections in common. The course is generally referred to as a 50-mile out-and-back, but it actually runs over 103 miles; the difference between 100 and 103 miles looks miniscule on paper, but when you're pedaling those final 3 very challenging miles back through town and up the section affectionately known as "The Boulevard," they seem like an eternity.

Back in 1994, when the race first started, mountain biking, let alone Leadville, wasn't even on my radar, but the race quickly became the ultimate endurance challenge for mountain bikers who want to test their mettle. Finishers who cross the line within the event's 12-hour time limit get a shiny silver belt buckle. Those who break the 9-hour mark are awarded the "La Plata Grande," a gigantic gold-and-silver belt buckle that is so large, it's actually hard to wear. Outside of the cycling community, it looks a little funny and draws odd glances. But among the endurance cycling crowd, it is worn with extreme pride as a badge of honor. Lots of riders really want those buckles.

LEADVILLE'S SIXTH STREET is the Champs-Élysées of mountain biking. It's the closest thing we mountain bikers have to the magnitude of celebratory mayhem that Tour de France racers bask in as they roll through the streets of Paris on the final day of the grand tour. And like the Tour de France, there are racers who plan their entire season around that singular event. In 2010, I joined the crazed masses and put all of my attention toward Leadville too.

After the Lance-driven documentary *Race Across the Sky*, Leadville—already on many mountain bikers' bucket list—became a must-do for serious endurance cyclists and was easily the biggest, most well-known mountain bike race on the planet. Adding to the growing hype, Chlouber sold the race series to the then title sponsor, Life Time Fitness, a Minnesota-based company that operates more than 100 fitness, family recreation, and spa centers across the United States. With a corporate powerhouse to back it, Leadville was poised to gain unprecedented exposure. On the practical side, for a professional athlete like me that meant an opportunity to be seen by many more potential sponsors. It also meant stiffer competition, since more athletes followed the same train of thought and showed up to take a shot at grabbing a piece of the pie.

Because the 2010 Leadville would be my A race for the year, I approached it differently. Matthew made significant adjustments to my training to allow me to race fast for eight hours instead of the more metered-out 24 that I was used to. I realize that for most people eight hours sounds like a long race, but for me it is short, fast, and furious. I had to work on speed, learn how to go harder, and enter into a different realm of pain—short-lived and sharp.

In preparation I packed in four multiday stage races, Trans Andes Challenge, Tour de la Patagonia, Red Centre MTB Enduro in Australia, and Trans-Sylvania Epic, even before summer rolled around. I even raced short cross-country races. Then I pulled the equivalent of a fitness cram session by stacking multiple 50- and 100-milers in the six weeks leading up to Leadville. It was an aggressive, ambitious schedule. Matthew worked me hard with extended sessions of elevated fatigue, and there were many bleak moments when I struggled to keep my confidence and sanity. Effective training must strip an athlete down almost to the breaking point, then pull back in order to build them back up. It's a process that feels really demoralizing when you're in the middle of it and can't see the light at the end of the tunnel. I was about to succumb to the strain and pressure right before Leadville and I called Matthew in the middle of a meltdown. The conversation pretty much went like this: "I suck. What is wrong with me? I feel fat and slow and awful. I should consider a career change." His enthusiastic reply: "Excellent. We're right on track." I was freaking out, but there was nothing I could do at that point but go with what I had and hope that he was right, that I actually had the talent and fitness it would take to win and that his training regime had been effective for me. All that was left to do now was rest, wait, and absorb the training.

Unlike 2009, when I basically stopped, dropped, and rolled to the start line with barely a clue about which way I was going, in 2010 I committed to being in Leadville 10 days early so I could ride the course and acclimatize properly. I was there alone in town, riding and simply hanging out, breathing the thin air. Without the distractions of home, TV, and other work, I had plenty of time to think about the race, my nutrition, my bike setup, what to wear, the weather, and all the myriad variables that go into Leadville. Some days, frankly, there was too much time to think, and I'd nearly make myself crazy with minutia. But mostly it was a rare respite from my normally chaotic work, training, and travel schedule.

By the time the big red Specialized truck rolled into town, I was like a racehorse kicking in the stall. Specialized had jumped on as the official bike sponsor of the race. Company owner Mike Sinyard was back to better his time on the course. Also on the team roster was newly crowned cross-country and short track national champion Todd Wells, and mountain bike legend Ned Overend, as well as a host of other Specialized employees and dealers. It was really great to see so many Specialized uniforms on the course. We were all part of the Leadville family, and now I had some of my Specialized family there with me too.

Greg was my official crew for feeds, time splits, and moral support. He was an efficient one-man show and all that I needed out there. He'd brought his motorcycle and had scoped the aid stations, and we made a plan where we would meet on course. We even practiced with musette bags—cloth bags with a long handle that you can grab and sling across your shoulder, making it easy to dig out your nutrition on the fly. I had never used this tactic before, but after watching *Race Across the Sky*, I could see that the top guys were saving precious moments by keeping the feeds fast and rolling. I had also seen videos of riders getting tangled in their musette bags and crashing. Grabbing a swinging musette filled with water bottles at race pace required practice. I know I was being laughed at the day before the race as I rolled up and down the street practicing the handoff with Greg. Although I tried to find as many little tricks as possible to shave time, I also needed to rely on what I knew, and that was pacing.

I was armed with support this time around, but my competition would be gunning for me. In particular, Amanda Carey had targeted this race as well, unsatisfied with her race the previous year and back with a vengeance. With new sponsor expectations, media interviews, and a target on my back, it was just about impossible not to get caught up in the hype. The exposure is a form of flattery and job security but also a distraction that can be overwhelming. I set my mind to focus on racing my race and the things I had control of instead of reacting to the other athletes.

After the gun went off, we were soon climbing the first hill up to St. Kevin's. Amanda stuck to me like glue. I tried to shake her a few times going up that hill with no success. It was the two of us and about five guys pushing together in a group until the next big climb at Hagerman Pass. At that point, I surged again, and one by one, Amanda and I dropped the guys. I did not want to pull her around the course, so I was trying to get away early, if possible. I created a small gap, but she clawed right back up before the descent down Powerline. I wanted a clear path on the dangerous descent, so I surged again to keep her from coming around. She didn't pass me before the descent, but I also didn't shake her. "I'm relieved that's over," I told her after we got down safely. Back to business. We played cat and mouse, chasing and pursuing, each of us looking for a chink in the other's armor, through the Pipeline aid station and all the way to the Twin Lakes aid station. On the bike, I ate, drank, tried not to panic, and mentally prepared myself for the 3,200-foot Columbine ascent. At Mile 40, Amanda and I were still together, pushing each other to what was sure to be a record-breaking time. I didn't know our pace or our splits. I was 100 percent focused on our two-person race and nothing else.

In many ways Leadville is a mountain bike race with road racing tactics mixed in. This year, I was experiencing that firsthand by sitting in a group of riders for the first 40 miles and grabbing musette feeds through the aid stations. I found myself really enjoying the strategy and tactics. I was ready to hit the big climb hard to see if I could open a gap there. Greg and I had done a lightning-fast rolling feed, and I was able to pass Amanda while she was stopped with her crew.

I punched hard at the bottom of Columbine and did not look back. Okay, I'm lying. I probably looked back within two minutes of heading uphill, but I couldn't see her through the tree-lined switchbacks. I set my eyes forward and kept pushing, focusing on maintaining an efficient spin with my legs, just like I'd practiced on that hateful indoor bike all winter long. I felt if I could stay out of sight during this forested section, perhaps she'd let her guard down just a little bit. For 5 miles, the Columbine climb is thickly treed with many 180-degree turns and straightaways stacked up like a layer cake. As I made each turn, I would sneak a glance behind me. No one was catching me, and now I started passing some of the faster guys and moving up farther in the field. This felt like the decisive point of the race, so I decided to treat it as a time trial and just go for it. If I blew up on the climb, perhaps I would still have time to recover on the descent. If I didn't blow up on the climb, I might be able to gain an insurmountable lead. My plan was working until I reached tree line.

I started to cramp at the steepest part of Columbine, just as the crest was within reach. The air was thin and the terrain was so steep that I could barely keep the pedals turning over. I stayed on my bike, trying to force down electrolytes and fluids without falling over. I wanted to keep pushing hard to make it to the top so I could rest on the huge descent, but I remembered that the top of the climb was also just the halfway point of the race. I was walking that line between pushing myself to the limit and pushing myself too far past the point of no return. I knew it was risky. I was either headed for an awesome finish or a spectacular failure.

At the turnaround on the top of the world, I looked at my watch for the first time. I was eight minutes ahead of a record-breaking pace. I had to look a second time to be sure I was seeing clearly and not hallucinating. In an instant, the numbers flew out of my brain and I got back to work. I began the descent and darted my eyes from the loose surface underneath me to the uphill traffic next to me. I spotted Amanda and calculated that I'd put about five or six minutes into her on the climb. That worked out to be a gain of about 45 seconds per mile. It was really good given the short distance, but the gap between us was much smaller than the previous year. I set that thought aside and returned my focus to the descent. Between the thousands of oxygen-deficient riders teetering as they pushed up the hill and the fatigue settling deep into my muscles, the descent was treacherous and far from relaxing.

As I came into the Twin Lakes aid station, I saw Greg there, waiting in our usual spot, and I caught the excitement in his eyes. I had finally shaken Amanda. And I had opened a 10-minute lead. His demeanor is always calming for me. He's never frantic. As I grabbed my musette bag he said, "Just do what you do best." In that fleeting moment, it was precisely what I needed to hear. I would not settle for a 10-minute gap. I wanted this, and the fierce competitor in me was prepared to work harder than ever. The risk I took on Columbine had been worth it so far and it was time to protect the lead I'd gained.

Leaving Twin Lakes, you're abruptly greeted with silence and solitude, save for another rider here and there, for the 40 miles back to town. After the mass start with thousands of fans and riders, the pack riding to Columbine, the throng of humanity riding uphill as you're bombing downhill, and the deafening din of the spectators at Twin Lakes, the contrast is enough to make you feel almost lonely. But for me, being in my own world, just riding as fast as I can without distractions is the type of riding I find most familiar. However that section of the race delivers another challenge: It's the windiest part of the course. Naturally, today there was a headwind.

I could pick out a rider in the distance. I set him as my target and crouched as low as I could on my bike for aerodynamics. I had to push harder than I wanted to for about 20 minutes to finally catch him—another strategic individual time trial. Once I caught him, we rode together for about 20 minutes. I desperately needed some shelter from the wind, which he provided. And while few words were exchanged, having another human being to suffer with was somewhat comforting too.

The reprieve didn't last long. As I hit the back side of Powerline at Mile 80, I plummeted deep into the pain cave. I had been flirting with cramps since Columbine and was digging really, really deep, just as the Leadville tagline tells us to do. Powerline is wickedly steep at the bottom, and as I tried to put power into the pedals I felt the cramps coming again. I didn't want to end up seizing and writhing on the side of the trail, so I set my ego aside and put my adventure racing skills to work. I walked up Powerline, but I walked intentionally and took long strides in order to keep a decent pace and stretch out my legs. Fans yelled for me to get back on my bike. In my mind, I was thinking, *You try riding this hill*, but mostly I was too numb to waste the breath. My ultimate goal was the finish line, not this 1-mile section of the course. And my strategy was working. My cramps stayed at bay, and I was able to push fluids down as I walked.

Once at the top, I snuck a look down the hill, but I couldn't make out the riders at the base. I swung my leg back over the bike, took a big mouthful of air and readied myself for the homestretch. I couldn't for the life of me figure out how much time I had left in the race or if I was going to break the course record at my current pace. I finally gave up on the math and fixated on the burdensome task of turning the pedals over faster and faster. *Don't let up, even for a second. No coasting; pedal harder.* This was my mantra.

I was alone at the top of the last big climb. I couldn't see anyone in front of me or behind me. Where were all those people who started the race? I was utterly depleted and running on fumes. I needed water badly. Thankfully, Carter Summit neutral aid station was coming up. I wouldn't see Greg here, but I knew they had some supplies and I was desperate. I had to unclip and step off my bike to fill my bottle, and as soon as I put my foot on the ground, my calf muscle fully seized and I fell over in the dirt with my bike on top of me. The aid station volunteers stared at me in disbelief as I frantically rubbed my cramp away and untangled myself from my bike. Between gasps for air, I begged for electrolytes. I was panicked that the calf cramp could turn into a full leg cramp and prevent me from pedaling the 10 miles home. The eager volunteers shuffled through their supplies and proudly offered me a saltshaker. Not exactly what I was looking for, but it couldn't hurt. I cocked my head back and took a few big shakes straight into my mouth. I swished the salt around with some water, swallowed, and headed off. I probably should have tossed a bit over my shoulder for good luck too.

The final descent down St. Kevin's is the last really high-consequence obstacle on the course. This is the place where many bone-weary riders get complacent and end up flatting or crashing on the rocky trail. It felt great to stop pedaling for a bit, but all of your energy is spent hopping rocks, navigating ruts, and willing yourself not to touch the brakes. In *Race Across the Sky* Lance Armstrong flatted at the base of this descent. Whether it was lack of skill or lack of tools, he was unable to change the tire himself and was forced to ride the final few miles to the finish on his rim with an eye over his shoulder. When I finished this stretch with my tires still inflated and firm, I let out a celebratory shout into the woods.

All that remained was the mind-numbing Boulevard section back into town. I stole another backward glance before turning onto the final grinder hill. No one in sight. I was so close, yet it felt so far away. The film crew moto was with me at this point, but I couldn't manage a smile, comment, or even a glance at the camera. Head down, I was slumped over my handlebars, staring at the ground. My top tube was covered in snot. I was breathing like a horse and pedaling squares— every single stroke hurt like hell. It wasn't pretty, but I wanted to beat that long-standing women's course record. I stared at my odometer and kept glancing at my watch to check the race time. I knew it was within reach, if only this stupid Boulevard would end.

As I crested the very last hill and finally turned onto the smooth pavement of Sixth Street, a group of girls started running next to me screaming and yelling, "It's the first female!" It was a local Colorado high school cross-country team, and they were going crazy for me. I wanted to say something back, but the words wouldn't come. I did, however, muster up a smile as my heart filled with joy. I thought about my high school running team and my introduction to sports so many years before. I hope they realized how their energy and enthusiasm pushed me over that last hill. I could finally see it, Sixth and Harrison, with the red carpet and the finish banner. But it stretched out before me like the ever-expanding hallway in *The Shining*. Was I hallucinating? Was it really getting farther away?

The film guy on the motorcycle must have sensed my struggle and noticed my lethargic cadence because he said, "Come on, Rebecca, only six more blocks." His words broke my trance. I put my head down, shifted into a bigger gear, and went. I had ridden this finishing stretch multiple times visualizing this moment. I could feel the crowd and the time ticking in my head. At last the red carpet was under my tires and the clock finally stopped. I had the win and the record, but I was so depleted I could not even raise my arms in victory.

Crossing the line at 7:47:35, I took first in the women's field and 22nd overall. I'd improved my time from the previous year by 27 minutes, with an average speed of 12.8 mph. I broke Laurie Brandt's course record, which had stood for 10 years, by 11 minutes. I was 1 hour and 30 minutes behind Levi Leipheimer's record-breaking men's time. It was one of the best races of my life. Greg was the first to approach me and give me a hug as I slumped over my handlebars, too fatigued to fully process it all, yet soaking in the relief and joy of those precious moments right after a hard effort.

I attribute the record and the win to great preparation, a little bit of luck, and a whole lot of suffering. In my first attempt at Leadville I went as hard as I could have, but I didn't know the course and my training in the run-up to the race was focused on the 24-hour format. I felt like my focused cycling training was now actually making a difference, and it came together for me on the right day. But all the preparation in the world doesn't take into account the preparation other athletes do, the mechanical problems that can happen, the crashes, the wind, the getting sick, and everything else that can send a race sideways. It was the most painful day I've ever had on a bike . . . but also one of the most rewarding.

I'VE NEVER BEEN ONE to rest on my laurels. As a pro athlete, I wouldn't have that luxury anyway. But I do like to have a day or two to appreciate an achievement and kick back after a season of arduous, all-encompassing training. There is no such luck in professional sports. It's a culture steeped in demands that all ask essentially the same thing: "What's next?" Moments after I crossed over the red carpet in 2010, I was already getting peppered with questions about my 2011 schedule and whether I would be back to defend my title and attempt the first-ever woman's three-peat in Leadville. A friend even prodded me to keep coming back and winning so I could become "the female version of Dave Wiens." Dumbfounded, I responded with a question of my own, "Can't I just enjoy this win for a little while before having to focus on 2011?" The answer, loud and clear, was a big, fat no. In fact, I still had some big plans to see through in the next month, much less the next year.

As a professional athlete, much of your security is pinned to the podium spots you currently have and your potential to garner more in the future. Sponsors like winners, and you are only as good as your most recent result. Performing well over and over and over again is what's expected and rewarded. After just five years of bike racing, I had four national championships, three 24-hour world championships, and back-to-back wins and a course record at Leadville, but my bike sponsor didn't recognize me as a true world champion because I hadn't won a UCI-sanctioned race. At Matthew's suggestion, I decided to go after a bona fide UCI world championship—the 2010 UCI Mountain Bike Masters World Championships in Brazil—and fill that hole on my resume once and for all.

The Union Cycliste Internationale (UCI) is the world governing body for the sport of cycling. It issues cycling licenses, sanctions races, and oversees world championships. When you win a UCI-sanctioned world championship, you get a specially issued team uniform with the coveted UCI rainbow stripes on it, designating you as a world champ. These simple, colorful stripes are known worldwide, and once you earn them, you have the right to wear them on your sleeve for the rest of your life. They can never be taken away. Though the competition was fierce at the 24-hour solo worlds, those events were never sanctioned or officially recognized by the UCI. If I wanted to wear those stripes, I was going to have to step out of my comfort zone and do an exponentially shorter world championship event. Given the rules of physiology, my training regime would have to undergo some big changes in a short amount of time.

13

Riding for the Record Books

The science of sport is pretty clear. Athletes typically hit their peak at age 26. That's when you're in your prime for strength, oxygen uptake (which is especially relevant for aerobic sports like cycling), and other important factors including reaction time and the ability to recover from hard efforts. If you're really well-conditioned, you can hang onto that peak for a few years, maybe into your 30s, but then the top end starts coming down: You simply aren't quite as strong or fast, and you recover more slowly.

Now the great equalizer in sports like cycling and running is distance or duration. Seasoned athletes spend decades building a massive aerobic engine. We also have a boatload of experience, so we know how to fuel, hydrate, pace, and take care of ourselves when the going gets rough. That plays in our favor for long events like marathons, ultras, 100-milers, stage races, and the like. As the level of endurance increases, so does the age at which athletes will peak. A Swiss study of more than 19,000 Ironman competitors found that the age of peak performance was 31 for men and 36 for women. (The Ironman triathlon comprises a 2.4-mile swim, a 112-mile bike ride, and a 26.2-mile run.) So you can see that it's not unreasonable to plan on being competitive in ultra-endurance events into your late 30s and early 40s. It was good news, because this was *exactly* my plan. I hadn't discovered mountain biking until well into my 30s, and I just wasn't ready to let age prevent me from pursuing my new passion—one that was working out pretty well for me so far.

There was just one problem with my plan to win a UCI-sanctioned world championship: The race would be 90 minutes max. I was effectively attempting to go back in time and challenge all of the physiological evidence of diminishing returns as we age. Granted, I would be racing in the masters category (ages 35–44); but at 41 I was on the older side of that range, and short, fast cross-country racing had never been my forte. My body is like a diesel engine: the longer the event, the better I do. Even in my high school and college running days, I was pathetic at the short events like the quarter mile. I excelled in the 2-mile and cross-country events. A short, fast bike race played out on the world stage would challenge my physiology, my talent, and expose one of my biggest weaknesses.

Matthew fully believed I could do it, or maybe he just really wanted a coaching challenge. When he first suggested it, I simply responded, "Bullshit! I'm not at all competitive in cross-country races." But he was convinced that we could retune my physiology output for a short race, so we went for it. Why not? I couldn't win if I didn't show up, and if I lost, no one would be the least bit surprised. Chasing a UCI world championship title was just another way to see what I could do. If it worked, I'd take pleasure in proving the naysayers wrong once again.

After winning Leadville, I had only a month to prepare for Brazil. I started by resting, to let that 103-mile effort sink in. Then I began focusing on extremely short, hard efforts in training. I also did a few local cross-country and short track races, forcing myself to go into the red from the moment the start gun fired. There was no time to wait out my attack like I had in the past. My task was to turn myself inside out in these practice races.

It hurt like hell and it was embarrassing. Working on your weaknesses is demoralizing. My sprint workouts seemed like a joke. I felt like I was spinning my wheels and going nowhere fast. I had no gauge on what the international competition would be like; all I knew was that I wasn't a good cross-country racer. But I faithfully did the workouts Matthew dictated. After some calls to friends in Brazil who helped me with travel logistics, it was time to go. Mostly I was just relieved to be done with the hideous speed training and on to the event.

The trip started with a smack in the face. While we were handling the race registration details, the car with my bike, luggage, and backpack was broken into right in broad daylight. My entire pack was taken, along with my computer, cell phone, and a few personal items such as my beloved lucky traveling gnome named Timmy.

Fortunately, I could still race. The thieves must have been stupid, because my very expensive bike was untouched. I had my passport and credit cards with me at registration, but this unplanned detour was still going to cost me. After days of traveling just to get to the race, I burned precious time sitting in the police station, wrangling with Brazilian law enforcement and attempting to fill out paperwork written in Portuguese. I had no confidence I'd be reunited with my gear, but I needed the police reports to file an insurance claim when I got home.

Eventually I escaped the police station and got onto my bike to review the course. Just as expected, the course had some of the steepest climbs and descents I'd ever seen. It was a short, slippery loop that we'd do multiple times, and of course there were technical sections I couldn't ride. I spent the better part of a day watching riders roll down the sharpest descent as I wrung my sweaty hands and trying to muster the courage to drop in myself. There was a crowd gathered at the base, and I was embarrassed to be standing there as a representative of my country, too chicken to ride the thing.

Most of the riders had left as dusk was settling in. This was it—my last chance to practice before race day. I swallowed the lump in my throat, got so far back on the bike that my saddle was in my stomach, and forced myself to roll over the edge and let go of the brakes. It wasn't pretty, but I slid down the muddy chute on two wheels and now I knew I could ride it during the race. The crowds or other riders could affect my decision on race day, but at least I had a successful example in my brain to draw from.

My race group started 30 seconds back from the age 30–34 women. The course started straight uphill with about a five-minute climb. This was the longest climb on the course, and it was nontechnical. This would be only one of two places where I could use my strengths to pass or get ahead. My strategy was to absolutely pin it at the start and get in front of as many women as I could before the singletrack. So I turned myself inside out in the first few minutes of the race. I wasn't sure how I'd recover from this massive effort, but this was precisely what Matthew had been training me to do over the last six weeks, so at least the torture was familiar. This strategy went entirely against everything I knew from my endurance experience, but this was a different beast that required a different tactic.

By the time I reached the top of the climb to drop into the single-track—just five minutes into the race—I was absolutely gassed and dizzy, but I had caught and passed all the women in the previous age group except for one from Argentina. I didn't look back. There wasn't time. As I dropped into the singletrack, I gasped for air and kept the Argentine woman in sight. I wanted the gap to be big enough that I could hit the descents and focus on being smooth without taking any crazy chances. I didn't want to be distracted by someone on my tail or to have the descent lines blocked by someone right in front of me. Since the descending was really hard for me, I wanted no distractions to fluster me.

Throughout the race, I followed the same protocol. I buried myself on the short, sharp climbs and then held on for dear life on the descents, focusing on recovery and being smooth. The Brazilian mud was like a Slip-'N-Slide in some parts of the course. I rode all of the descents with no crashes, and that was a big victory for me. I had to walk one uphill that was a ludicrously steep 29 percent grade. It just seemed faster to run. I took some heckling from the spectators for getting off my bike, but I just smiled and kept running. They were on the sidelines and I was there on the course competing for a world championship title, running or not.

This race was completely different from my 24-hour world championship experience. It hurt, but the suffering was over so fast. Soon after crossing the finish line, my heart moved out of my throat and I forgot about the pain. There were no lingering effects such as falling asleep in my dinner plate or limping to the awards podium or the awful hacking from my asthma. I'd finished this world championship course in about 1:18 and was 11 minutes ahead of the next woman: an eternity in cross-country bike racing.

It was surreal to stand on that podium with the American flag being raised and the national anthem roaring over the loudspeakers. Regardless of age, I could still improve my weaknesses, leave my comfort zone, and bring home a set of rainbow stripes. I was so proud and a little surprised to add another world title to my three 24-hour solo worlds titles, one adventure racing worlds title, and one masters cross-country skiing world title. Those official rainbow stripes were now mine. Even with these accomplishments, I still laugh a little when citing my profession as professional athlete.

WINNING IS ADDICTIVE, but it's not the only definition of success. Civil rights leader and women's rights advocate Mary Church Terrell lived by the motto "Lift while you climb." It wasn't enough to succeed for yourself, you had to bring others with you, forge a path so they could succeed too and make the world a better place for more people. As a woman who has worked her way through many a predominantly male sport—including my current one—those are words I try to live by, especially since I've seen the power and empowerment sports can provide firsthand. From my first athletic endeavor on my high school running team to my current work with my coach Dean Golich, there have always been mentors and more experienced people along the way who ushered me along, gave me a push when I needed it, and opened my eyes to things I never thought were possible.

After the 2010 Leadville, I was officially climbing, and I wanted to make sure I was doing some lifting too. It was my turn to share, provide opportunity, and give nudges that bring out the best in other people. As I lined up at races around the world, I kept wondering where all the women were and why I was in such a minority. I'm very familiar with the barriers that keep people from riding, because I've struggled with them too, things like intimidation with the equipment, a lack of technical skill, a shortage of other women to ride with, or uncertainty regarding where to ride. But if I could learn to ride, become a pro cyclist at 38, and improve my skill to the world champion level, then anyone could eliminate the barriers for entry. I wanted to help facilitate this and erase some of the excuses. SRAM believed in my cause, and together we launched the SRAM Gold Rusch Tour, a series of unique events focused on getting more women and girls riding bikes.

We've held events in Monterey, California; Raystown Lake, Pennsylvania; Whistler, British Columbia; and soon we'll be heading to Europe. One thing is always consistent, everywhere we go: The events are packed and never short on enthusiasm. I bring in other female pros, female media, and plenty of regular riders to assist with the mission of getting more women on bikes. I love to see older women reborn, finally doing something for themselves now that the kids are out of the house and they have the time to be a little "selfish" with their lives. The best part of these events is that each participant returns to her community with new knowledge and passion—and the net gets cast wider with each individual connection.

The Wheel Girls is the other club I started following my Leadville success. This one is more focused on younger girls, namely teenagers in my hometown. My own experience is proof that the teenage years are a great time for girls to change the trajectory of their lives. Sports can direct that change, provide a sense of purpose, and set girls in a positive direction for life. It's a very simple formula that just happens to take place on a bike. We focus on health, fitness, and fun and throw in some education on changing a flat tire, nutrition, and trail etiquette. The real magic happens on the trails as they gain confidence, develop friendships, and experience success. We only have three rules: Try, Laugh, and Cheer (TLC). Seeing how willing these girls are to try, how fast they learn, and the huge smiles on their faces from little victories all give me a renewed sense of excitement and achievement, and inspire me to try new things as well. They don't realize it, but I'm learning and gaining as much from them as they are from me. Some of my favorite moments are when a girl is jumping out of her skin, beaming, and says, "I rode that thing!" Then she comes up at the next meeting and tells me that she got her mom on a bike. And I think, *Wow, I got to be part of that.* It's awesome that I can share what I know to spread excitement and happiness.

Hanging out and teaching girls about bikes reminds me why I love riding and all the amazing benefits I've gotten from the sport. Even though these extra events add to my already maxed-out calendar, I am committed to them. I have so much fun with these women. They give me motivation and inspiration that I carry into my races. To encourage this sort of growth and change in others is far more rewarding than standing on any podium. I believe the lessons we learn from sports can make us better individuals, and in turn the world becomes a better place. If all that happens is that more women become healthy, push their limits, and have a great time in the outdoors, then I'm content with that achievement too.

AFTER BRAZIL, Matthew and I targeted Leadville as my key race for the following year, and the training began almost immediately. I knew that the field would just keep getting bigger and stronger and that the target on my back was growing exponentially with each win. Matthew had crafted a training plan similar to what we'd done the previous year. We had a proven formula, and I was growing as a cyclist and a competitor. I felt like my winter training was better than ever, but my early season races were anything but consistent. I'd do well one week and fall flat the next, and overall my results weren't showing the fitness that I'd been building—or should have been. Why was this getting harder and not easier?

A few weeks out from Leadville, I lined up at the Galena Grinder, a local marathon mountain bike event in my hometown of Ketchum. I was off the back right from the start. I just couldn't pedal any faster as I watched the field ride away. Something was missing. I didn't have my usual killer instincts or motivation. I was so far behind that I never even saw the woman who won—who, incidentally, would also be lining up for Leadville. Throttled in front of my hometown crowd, it was one of the worst races of my life. I walked away feeling slow, unfit, and depressed. I questioned whether I should go to Leadville or even be a bike racer at all. I fully trusted Matthew and the work I'd done with him, but I was suffering some serious self-doubt, yet again. I kept asking myself, *Why am I so flat so close to my key race?* Matthew wasn't at all surprised. He knew why and told me in no uncertain terms that it wasn't what I was doing on the bike that was sapping my power and energy. It was what I was doing off it.

I take recovery very seriously and usually take plenty of rest days. Most of us are ingrained to think that more training equals better performance, but that's not the case for me. I love my forced recovery days and know they pay off. Matthew and I had proven it over the past few seasons. But it's hard to ignore the voice that says taking time off means you're being lazy or losing your edge. Part of the reason I have a coach is because it's a lot easier for me to listen to my body and let myself rest when he says, "The race is won. Get in bed. Rest." It's like being given a hall pass.

I'm also fortunate to have plenty of friends in Idaho I can call on to take a casual ride with me when the emotional stress threatens to boil over or I need a light recovery. I take off the heart rate monitor, and we just roll out and take in the beauty of the mountains. These rides are just as important to my physical and emotional health as the interval-packed full-throttle training days.

But after the previous year's successes, my year had been jammed with sponsor appearances, movie screenings of *Race Across the Sky* that I had organized as a fundraiser for the International Mountain Biking Association, and the demands of the SRAM Gold Rusch Tour. These were all things that I was passionate about, but they were taking time and energy away from my performance. I had worked hard to lay the foundation for a sustainable career, so I had to take on some of these new responsibilities. But pile these commitments on top of trying to maintain an intentional focus for training and you have a recipe for poor recovery and lingering fatigue. I had simply spread myself too thin, and it was catching up with me.

What I needed was a stint of intense recovery. I had to change my surroundings to make that happen. I went to Colorado a couple of weeks early to race one last race and then take some much needed quiet time. Leadville is a sleepy little place with not much going on except the great outdoors. The two-week sabbatical prior to the race proved to be just the focused recovery and rejuvenation that I needed. I slept 8–10 hours a night, trained at altitude, ate really well, tinkered with my bike, and just decompressed. It was the first time in the season when I was 100 percent focused on myself: my rest, my health, and my own race. It felt selfish, but it was a smart and necessary break in the schedule.

A growing women's field was hungry to take me down. But despite that, I was strangely calm in the days leading up to the race. My mental energy was focused not on my competitors but on bettering my own time from the previous year. I knew that if I went faster than I had before or close to it, I would feel good about that performance, regardless of my placing. It was one of those rare times where I felt I had done absolutely everything I could have to prepare properly, so really there was nothing to be nervous about. A deep well of experience was also now part of my bag of tools, and I had the confidence that only comes with age.

Everywhere I went, people asked how I felt about the stiff competition. Without hesitation I would tell them, "It's awesome!" And I meant it. It's great to have deep men's and women's pro fields at an endurance race. It's good for everyone—the sport, the event, the fans, the competitors. It means the sport is growing. It adds credibility to the event and keeps it exciting. If you knew who was going to win a race every time, it wouldn't be very fun or inspiring to watch.

Race day arrived clear and warm. I lined up on the front line next to Specialized teammate Todd Wells. Greg was back as my one-man support staff, his motorcycle stocked with spare wheels, a cooler, and everything I needed or might need. I felt strangely calm and happy on the start line. Greg later told me this made him nervous because it was out of character for me. I looked around at my friends, who today were also my competitors—Gretchen Reeves, Jenny Smith, Kelli Emmett, and Pua Mata (formerly Sawicki)—and gave them a genuine smile. I was glad they were there and proud to be on the line with them. I knew these girls were gunning for me, but I sincerely wished them all a safe and good race (though of course I silently hoped not *that* good). A few minutes later, the race was on. As we rolled into the very first climb at St. Kevin's, I was feeling okay but just couldn't respond as all four of them steadily rode away from me.

The race had barely begun and I was already getting dropped. I wasn't happy, but I wasn't panicked, either. I just put my head down and reminded myself that I had lots of time to just stick to my strategy and race my own race. I was fit, I knew the course inside and out and had more experience there than any other woman in the race. I was giving myself this internal pep talk when right around Mile 20, as we rolled through a group of spectators, a man leaned in close enough that I could feel his breath in my ear and said, "You've got A LOT of work to do, Rebecca." I snapped a feisty glance his way and a fire stirred in my belly. I was pissed. I thought, *Well, you just wait. This race is far from over, and I'm not out of it yet.* But confidence is elusive and fickle. My determination gave way to self-doubt and negative thoughts.

I was sitting in fifth place and a few minutes off the lead as I rolled into the first aid station at Mile 30. Greg was there. With a concerned look, he asked me how I was doing. He could see in my body language that I didn't have the usual eye of the tiger. I told him I was fine, just a little flat. By the time I reached the second aid station, I got reports that I was just two minutes off the lead and was now sitting in third place going into the Columbine Mine climb. I was so confused. How had I jumped to third without passing anyone? Apparently both Kelli and Pua had mechanical issues and had fallen back, but I never saw them. The news that I was that close to the lead got me amped, and my confidence started to return. Two minutes was miniscule, and this was where I typically pulled away for the win.

I went to work to chip away at my deficit on the climb. I was catching some of the faster men, so I knew I was moving the bike better now and finding my rhythm. Even though I had no visual through the trees, a few of the guys told me that Jenny and Gretchen were just ahead. I finally caught both of them right where the climb really kicks up, above tree line. These girls are both great friends of mine and have been teammates in the past. Seeing them meant I was riding well. I knew they could beat me easily in a shorter event but that I might have an upper hand in a race this long. Gretchen had also won in Leadville before, so she knew how to perform here. I steadily went around them both and said a few genuine words of encouragement.

At over 12,000 feet, there is not enough oxygen for aggressive maneuvers, so passing happens in slow motion. Gradually, I opened up some space on Gretchen, but Jenny stuck to me like a terrier for the remainder of the climb. She was still right on my tail at the turnaround. Gretchen and Jenny are great descenders, so I was forced to really hang it out past my comfort zone on the way down. I managed to stay in front of them and even open a small gap. I had the lead, but only by a fraction of a margin. It was mine to keep if I didn't make any mistakes at all—a tall order with many hours of racing still left.

Coming down Columbine and hearing all the uphill riders scream my name was invigorating. The trees flew by like a meteor shower, so there was no way to react to anything except the riding. When I rolled into Twin Lakes aid station, thousands of crew members were screaming, giving me a second (or third or fourth at this point) wind. With 40 miles to go, it was time to finish the job.

I made it to the Powerline climb and still could not see any female riders behind me. I had gotten a split time of around three minutes at the Pipeline aid station, but that was dangerously close. I was cramping and at my limit. This is always the moment of truth. There is no faking it as you try to get up this climb. If you've gone too deep, you may not be able to claw your way back out. If you've exerted yourself just the right amount, you'll find yourself dancing close to the edge but not quite falling off.

I decided to get off my bike and walk the lower section of the Powerline climb for fear of pushing my cramps into a full-blown spasm. I slammed a Red Bull energy shot and walked/ran while hoping that it wasn't a mistake to be conservative in this spot. When I felt like my legs were settled and the pitch mellowed slightly, I got back on, took a quick glance down the hill, and finished the climb.

Fifteen miles stretched between me and victory. For me, these final miles are the most mentally challenging. Town feels so near, but is still impossibly far, and your tank is completely empty. I did my best to sink into the zone of one pedal stroke, one breath, one moment at a time. I was running scared and knew I must not make even the slightest error. I focused on keeping up with my nutrition and being very light on the descents. A flat tire at this point would surely mean losing the lead and likely the race.

Once off the St. Kevin's descent and onto the roads to town, I relaxed about flat tires and stole a look at my watch for the first time in the race: 7:10. I blinked, wiped the dirt and sweat droplets off my Garmin and looked again. 7:10. I knew I was only about 20 minutes from the finish. I couldn't believe the time I was seeing. Could I really be more than 15 minutes ahead of my own course record? I thought the clock on my odometer had malfunctioned and stopped earlier in the race. I stared at it for a few seconds to make sure the numbers were still ticking. The seconds kept counting up. I was blown away. Holy crap, we were flying. I knew the other girls must still be nipping at my heels, just a few minutes back, but this was the first point I actually thought that I might have it in the bag. There just weren't many miles left for them to close the gap. I snuck looks behind me whenever I had a stretch of visibility, but I didn't relax until I turned onto Sixth Street and could physically see the red carpet and the famous finish line, surrounded by historic brick buildings.

Despite visualizing that finish for more than a year, particularly on the most rigorous training days, I was never certain that I would be the first woman to roll across it, and I never dreamed I'd break my own record by over 15 minutes. Having been ready to quit this bike racing thing just a few weeks earlier made my third win all the more sweet, because I truly had to work for it and rise to the occasion. Perseverance, race experience, and staying calm paid off. Not only did I break my own course record, but so did the top four women in the race—another giant leap forward for women's cycling. The third time was a charm, for sure.

I stood there soaking in the fanfare, thinking it was probably the last time I'd stand on top of that podium straining to hold that super-heavy ore cart trophy. My mind drifted back. I'd shared the LT100 podium with Lance Armstrong, Levi Leipheimer, and now Todd Wells. I had just squeaked out a hard-fought win and had to break my own record by 16 minutes just to fend off a charging field of women—three of whom also broke my old record. I knew the trajectory of the women's race had forever changed. So when within moments someone asked the inevitable "Coming back next year?" I nodded. But inside, I honestly didn't know how I could ever top this.

AFTER MY THREE-PEAT in Leadville, I wasn't planning to do the race again. Three is a nice round number, a nice bookend to my three 24-hour world championship titles. My race calendar was full, and there were other races I wanted to do and more places I wanted to explore on a bike. I now knew exactly what it took for me to win a race like Leadville, and the idea of again summoning that level of dedication and sacrifice was daunting. I was tired, busy, and supremely satisfied with my performance in 2011. There was no way I could top what I had achieved there. But try as I did to weasel my way out of it, the pull was too great. There's nothing like Leadville for full value: You get 100 percent hard-core racing on the biggest stage in endurance mountain biking, along with the best community and people you'll ever meet. I thought about the hordes of racers, fans, and friends I've made over the years at the event and what it would be like not to stand at 10,200 feet on Sixth and Harrison along with them. The Leadville mystique is hard to explain, but it's got me hooked, so I decided to not fight the gravitational pull and committed to line up once again in 2012.

I had a new coach this time around, Dean Golich. After five years with Matthew, other job responsibilities and a new baby had pulled him in other directions, and we'd agreed it was time I find a new coach. I did my research on Dean and talked to many of his former athletes and other people in the industry. On paper, I could find no one better. Dean has a stellar reputation, having successfully trained a laundry list of Olympians and world champions in mountain biking, cycling, triathlon, and even NASCAR, hockey, and motocross. He was touted as a pioneer when it came to applying strategies to improve athletic performance. Still, I had developed a deep friendship with Matthew and was reluctant to work with anyone else, regardless of their impressive resume. How could another coach get to know me and really squeeze the most out of me and my complicated psyche? I just wasn't sure I wanted to commit to the long process of building a relationship again.

My first conversation with Dean had made me even more nervous. He'd looked at my previous training and began to slash and change things—things that had earned me world champ titles and three Leadville wins. But Dean felt I could still achieve more, and he plainly said so. Dean does not sugarcoat anything. He's a hard-core, no-nonsense numbers guy with a mind like a steel trap. But he also has a great sense of humor, and I felt that beneath the surface he was a really good guy. And he couldn't have had so many successes without being exceptional at his job. Tentatively, I agreed to give his method a trial run. If it worked, the results would speak for themselves. Really, I had no other choice. I had to set aside what had worked for me in the past and acknowledge there could still be room for improvement.

Matthew taught me how to ride smoothly and efficiently and showed me what structure can do for performance. Now Dean was teaching me about power, about monitoring the wattage you can put out to get better and stronger on your bike. At first I was reluctant to buy in. After all, we are humans, not machines, so I wanted to be sure I used my own experience to dictate the training. I had achieved everything in my career this far without using a power meter, so clearly it wasn't essential. But he insisted, so I added a power meter to all of my bikes.

Some of my training was similar to 2011's program. I did a couple of long stage races in the spring, a 24-hour duo, some 50-milers, and the usual hill intervals and long days on the bike. Some of my training was different. For one, I was learning to look at power numbers and train specifically based on wattage. And my training was more focused on time in the saddle. I was spending way less time in the gym or cross-training. Dean wanted me doing my interval workouts on my mountain bike rather than my road bike. He had me doing much shorter workouts with more intensity, saying I already had plenty of endurance under my belt and I didn't need all those long miles since I was no longer doing 24-hour solo racing. I was relieved that I didn't have to hit the gym so much and squeeze in other aspects of training. Dean's rationale was that whatever time I had to train should be specific to the event I was training for: mountain biking.

Unfortunately, the months and weeks leading into my fourth Leadville were not what either of us would have liked. I was far from

100 percent focused on this race and my training. Instead, I was juggling growing business obligations, women's events, sponsor commitments, and advocacy work. The growth of my business was a positive thing, but competing at the top level and building a business for the future were vying for my time and energy. In mountain biking, podium finishes are not enough. You need them to keep your job, stay relevant, and build for the future, but you also need to think about life after racing, even while you're still on the top of the podium. It's a tricky balancing act.

Under the weight of it all, I really didn't think I could win again. I doubted my abilities not only as a result of how my season was going and the demands of my business, but also because I'd been checking out the competition. The women's field at the Leadville had become the best group of endurance pros assembled anywhere, drawing international pros from road, mountain bike, and triathlon. It had become a feather in a pro athlete's cap to race and finish well in Leadville. I was pretty happy to already have three of those feathers of my own.

I know that before a race like Leadville you're supposed to have your feet up with compression socks on and go to bed early, but that just wasn't an option for me this time around. I spent the week prior to the race riding in Leadville with friends, hosting group rides, giving a nutrition talk with my sponsor GU, signing posters with Specialized teammates, and just being way more social and active in Leadville than I'd ever been. The good news was that all the extra work I was doing took my mind off the stress and pressure of racing. I went into the race feeling relaxed and excited. Podium wins are part of the formula, but so is being available and visible off the racecourse. It's a part of being a pro that I really enjoy, interacting with the other riders, fans, sponsors, and race organizers.

Specialized-Lululemon road cycling world champion and German national champion Ina-Yoko Teutenberg also turned up at Leadville straight after the Olympics to take part in her first mountain bike race. We were sharing a team house together, and it was really nice to be there with another female racer who wasn't in Leadville to take me down. I knew she'd ride well, but since this was not her discipline, she wasn't flipping the switch and turning on her fighting form for this event. So often I'm alone at races and not traveling with a team, so this felt a little bit like having a teammate who had my back and could share the experience with me.

I know it often seems like pro athletes have an entourage of support and hand-holding, but really Greg was all I needed or wanted for this event. He had the timing and the aid stations so dialed in that he could get to every single point on course, and we always hand off in precisely the same way. Knowing a course and my plan down to the smallest detail took a ton of the pressure off and really just left me to worry about pedaling and nothing else. It was a far cry from my first Leadville, when I had nothing but a laminated course profile taped to my bike.

Greg makes me want to work harder. He knows precisely how I'm feeling by the look in my eyes and knows exactly what I need in order to stay focused and fueled. Few words are exchanged in the fleeting moments that we see each other at the aid stations, but just seeing him there and knowing he's as invested in the race as I am gives me extra motivation. Greg is my ultimate teammate for Leadville and the first person I want to see at the finish line. We had matured into a world-class team for this event.

THE START LINE of Leadville is special. It's so early, so cold, so dark, and there are so many people. The excitement is thick, and the air is thin. In 2012, I had been secretly hoping for some nasty weather to give me an edge against some of the really fast competition. If the skies above Colorado unleashed like they had in the past, I felt the race could turn from an all-out horse race into a race of survival and persistence. My adventure racing experience could shine, and maybe my course record could stand another year. But the morning was cold, crisp, and clear, and it looked to be another perfect record-setting type of day.

I was strangely calm on the start line again. I looked across the line at my competition and felt that if I could simply make the podium, it would be a really great accomplishment. I vowed to just ride my own race and give it all I had. No matter what placing, I would be happy if I was anywhere near my record time.

As usual, the race started out with a fast, twitchy, amped-up peloton. My strategy for the first 10 minutes before we hit the dirt is always just to survive and not get knocked over. Ina was in her element, darting through the field and up to the front with the top men. As we hit dirt and started to climb St. Kevin's, one of my competitors passed me and slowly rode away. I've always taken a while to warm up in this race and have never been in the lead heading up St. Kevin's. It always bums me out a little, but I also know that I will be consistent and will likely see many of those riders again. I was sitting in fifth place just 30 minutes into the race. Ina was just enough ahead of me to be a rabbit to chase. I really wanted to catch up to her so we could ride together on the flat road sections.

I caught her just as we began the Powerline descent, and she hopped on my wheel to follow my lines. Despite being a roadie, that girl can handle a bike. Once out on the pavement, we made an awesome two-person female train that many of the guys were trying to latch onto. As I tucked in behind Ina, I laughed out loud at the audacity that I was now sitting on (and barely hanging onto) the wheel of a real live Olympian.

Endurance mountain biking is such a solitary sport, I'm not at all used to having someone to ride with and work with who is not trying to beat me. Ina was absolutely on fire, and I was amazed at her power on the flats. As the course turned up again, Ina began to slow, and she yelled to me in her thick German accent, "You go NOW!" I call Ina the German Honey Badger. If she tells you to do something, you do it, no questions asked.

I thanked her profusely and obeyed, giving her a mental hug as I rode off alone. I missed her right away, but I had a renewed purpose to make sure her help was not in vain. I did a quick tally and figured I was now sitting in third place. As I rolled into the chaos of Twin Lakes, I snatched my musette from Greg, and he ran alongside me, telling me that first place was just 2.5 minutes up. Wait! How did I go from third to second without passing anyone? Turns out some of the riders at the front of the race missed a turn just before Pipeline aid station, but I'd rolled through so fast he hadn't been able to tell me before. I was now in second.

Heading into Columbine, the biggest climb of the course, I was on my way to the halfway point and I felt good. I love that climb, and I knew I was riding well. I was elated to be just a couple of minutes off the lead and in the mix for the podium. Until that point, I hadn't been thinking about placement or time. I hadn't even looked at my Garmin. Now, on the climb, I would use it to monitor my speed and try to pedal just 0.10 mph faster and maintain a consistent average speed. Historically, this race is often decided on the slopes of Columbine, and it is also the place in the course where I finally feel warmed up and start picking off people who rocketed by me in the start. People often ask me why I start so slowly and then go faster at the end. Actually, I'm not going faster, I'm riding a consistent pace for the entire race. It's just what works for me.

I was picking off more and more men going up the climb. As I crested the very top and approached the turnaround and the breathtaking scenery there, I also spied Pua Mata, the current first-place woman, making the turn just about one minute ahead of me. Then, as I turned, I could see Sally Bigham chasing me down as she approached the turn on the other side. At the 50-mile point, with 53 more miles to go, the top three women were all within a couple of minutes of each other. It was exhilarating and a display of endurance racing at its very best. No room for errors in fueling, concentration, pacing, or even one bad line choice.

As I approached Twin Lakes aid station for the second and last time, the roar of the crowd was deafening. There was Greg, running full speed with my musette bag of fuel, making the hand off and looking at my eyes, my riding position, the salt on my jersey, assessing what I needed, how much fluid I'd taken, giving me splits and a boost of motivation all within about 30 seconds. He told me first place was just a minute ahead. Without speaking, I knew he was saying to me, "You have a shot at this. You are always strongest in the last third of the race. You're riding great. I believe you can do this." I rode away from the deafening chaos and headed off alone with an empty stretch of rolling flats ahead and the image of Greg running along beside me in my head.

I focused on round pedal strokes, momentum, aerodynamics, and a big gear for the flatter sections. I focused on eating and drinking while the terrain was less technical. I tried to calm my adrenalized mind and just ride, reminding myself that I was gaining time just riding my own race. *Don't change a thing.* Then I saw Pua alone on the road ahead.

I kept doing the same things while trying to contain my excitement. She is a rock-solid competitor I have gone head to head with so many times. She's beaten me, and I've beaten her. She is an amazing endurance athlete, and I knew that this would be a hard fight to the finish. I took the final few moments before I caught her to calm my mind and gather energy and focus for the battle ahead. I reminisced about the first time I passed her at my first 24-hour solo nationals. I had gotten so excited and amped about catching her that I crashed. This time, many years later, I was determined to use all of my experience from my previous three wins to play this chess game exactly right.

I caught Pua just as the pavement turned to dirt, and we dove into a really fun singletrack climb, one of my favorite places on the course. In the moment I passed her, we were alone except for a course official waving a flag for the turn and three spectators. This pivotal lead change and the intensity of the race at the top end were being witnessed by just the six of us. The singletrack climb would only last about 15 minutes, and then we'd hit a rolling, fast gravel road section. I did not want to provide a draft for her and pull her all the way back to town just so she could pass me in a sprint. I cannot sprint, nor did I want to after this gargantuan effort. The turning point of the race was right at that moment, at Mile 65.

I knew I had to go right then or I wouldn't get another opening, so I geared a little harder, focused on my leg spin, and attempted to relax my upper body. I didn't want the extreme effort in my lungs and legs to show in my body language. I treated this hill as an interval within a 100-mile race.

I couldn't hear her, but I forced myself not to look back until the final switchback. When I did, it was a quick glance because I didn't want her to notice and think I was fading. My heart jumped because I was actually pulling away. I couldn't believe that I was pulling away by that much. That glance lit a fire in my belly, and the next goal was to get out of sight and out of mind. I notched my effort up again for the next 10 minutes to get up the hill and around the corner before she crested. I was completely blasted and running on fumes and adrenaline. But I kept the pressure on.

At Mile 75, I flew through the Pipeline aid station and spotted Greg. I knew he had as much adrenaline coursing through his veins as I did when he saw me coming in first. A running refuel and I was gone. He shouted, "Go, baby, go!" as I sped away, and my heart filled with love.

Pipeline was still in front of me. It's the steepest and hardest climb of the race, hitting 26 percent grade in some places and with about four false summits. It takes nearly 45 minutes. I've never been able to ride the whole thing, but this time I vowed to ride it once and for all. I knew my lead was perhaps just a minute, and I didn't want my competitors to see me walking up the hill and get a mental edge. I set my goal, and even though the pedals were barely turning over on the steepest pitches, I clenched my jaw, kept moving and stayed on the bike the entire way up. It was a first for me, and this little victory at the top of the steep pitch was another boost of confidence I needed to carry me to the finish. I had just ridden Powerline for the first time in this race and I was in the lead, but I also knew 20 miles still remained and that they are often the hardest on the course. The potential for flat tires, cramping, and crashing was still very real. A flat tire in a race this close could cost me three places.

I made my descent down the rubbly back side of Powerline without a flat. There was still more climbing and descending, and I knew I wouldn't get any more splits, so I needed to squeeze every last bit of energy out of my body that I could. The last time I saw Greg on the course he said to me, "Leave nothing out there," and that's exactly what I was doing. I was riding harder than I ever have in my life, fully focused on drinking, eating, riding smooth, and pushing a bigger gear. Every pedal stroke, I tried to go harder and harder. I was now in a time trial to the end.

Pavement. Now I just had to cross the tracks and push through the last climb up the Boulevard to the finish. On the Boulevard, I snuck another quick look back. The thought of having to sprint after 99 miles above 10,000 feet is a nightmare, so I really hoped to see no one. I was so relieved to see I was alone. With about 4 miles to go, I looked at the elapsed time on my Garmin for the first time in the race. I couldn't believe what I was seeing. I was going faster than I'd ever gone before. How was this possible? Every single year I have gone as deep as I possibly could and never imagine I can go any faster than what I had previously done. As I crested the last hill, saw the red carpet, and clicked bigger and bigger gears for the last half mile to the finish, my good friend Kathy screamed from the sidelines, "You're going to break your own record!" Those words clicked in my head, and I began my own solitary sprint against the clock. I had the win, but now the excitement of beating my own time was urging me on. I could see the clock. I had no more gears. I was standing, heaving, and screaming as I crossed under the timing banner. No hands up, just head down, full bore ahead to stop the clock.

Greg (who later confessed that he thought there was no way I was winning this one) was there to give me the biggest hug of my life as tears of disbelief and laughter came flooding out. I could not believe I had just earned my fourth Leadville win and broken my own record by more than three minutes. The improvement gaps were getting smaller each year, but somehow I was still going faster.

I had not dreamed of this or planned for it. I had thought it was impossible. The competition out there made me rise to another level that even I didn't know I could reach. I had raced a perfect race and defied my own belief. I was a bona fide bike racer now, and maybe I had laid the groundwork to become Leadville's female Dave Wiens.

The biggest compliment I received was from Dave Wiens himself, when he told me how impressed he was with my consistent performances each year. No one has more respect or collateral at this race, and his words are like a trophy that I save alongside all of those Leadville ore carts.

It was my first really big win with coach Dean. When I called him to share the news with him, he was as happy as I was. His athletes had had a disappointing Olympics, and he said my win was the boost he really needed. It felt good to share the victory with him, since he had laid out the plan and patiently put up with me while I tried to execute and juggle the rest of my commitments. His tolerance and belief in me propped me up numerous times during the long buildup to this day.

It seemed impossible, but each year at Leadville I was getting better and the race was getting more rewarding and meaningful. In four years of this historic race, my race times had followed a progression: 8:14, 7:47, 7:32, and 7:28. I was faster, smarter, stronger, and more personally invested in this 103-mile course than I have ever been with any race. It had bonded me to Greg in ways I never dreamed of, pushed me to a level of cycling I never imagined possible, and forged the kind of friendships that will last a lifetime.

I HAVE ALWAYS believed that endurance events require nearly as much, if not more, mental strength as physical strength. You have to be willing to suffer and to still believe that you are capable of persevering when everything in your body is telling you that you cannot. That's true no matter what physical shape you're in. When your brain strength fades, your physical strength follows. I've hobbled to more than one or two finish lines feeling pretty defeated because my mental game was off. I have also completed races on sheer will alone, and I attribute those successes to mental toughness.

Some people, like Antarctic explorer Ernest Shackleton and Mount Everest legend Sir Edmund Hillary, might have been born with an extra-large dose of mental fortitude, but for the rest of us, this is a skill that can be trained and honed. Athletes who skip this part of training are often left stranded on course or dragging at the back when their bodies have reached their physical limit.

Those who have that mental strength to draw from are often the ones raising their arms across the finish line. I love the mental aspect of endurance racing because it means we are not just automatons who followed a prescribed training program. Instead, our brains, for better or worse, dictate much of our racing and training successes and losses.

Training your brain goes a long way toward overcoming fear of failure. There are studies that show a body goes through a very similar chemical and physical reaction by visualizing a racecourse as it would if you were physically doing it. Now this doesn't mean you don't have to go out and do your hill intervals, but it does mean there is another dimension to training that can give you that extra edge when it's most needed.

The brain is a muscle and will respond to regular training. We all have moments in sport where we've found the zone. It's that effortless moment where skill, concentration, and fitness are all in tune and you feel fast, light, and on fire. It's a fleeting, addictive sensation that we constantly grasp for and so rarely reach. I'm telling you that you can get into that zone more often by doing regular mental calisthenics in addition to your physical training.

Our brains can either be a huge asset that pushes us beyond what we dreamed possible, or they can be the limiting factor. I know this from experience when I've backed off rock climbs or walked technical bike sections because I just didn't believe in myself. I've also ridden those same sections in the middle of a race and even in the dark when my brain has finally given me the mental push to go for it.

I think about and rehearse sections of racecourses in my mind. Oftentimes it is a technical section, a particularly grueling climb, or the finish line. I see myself going through these sections with ease, great form, and a smile on my face. If I lapse into a negative thought during this exercise, such as *I can't ride that part*, then I snap back into seeing myself riding like I want to. After all, it's my visualization. If I know the racecourse, then I put in as many specific details as possible. If I don't know the course details, I can still visualize myself riding fluidly, feeling strong, and celebrating at the finish line. It may seem silly to do this, but having a mental picture in your head is an essential step to actually achieving your goals.

Part of effective visualization is practicing positive talk and relaxation techniques on and off the bike. Being tense and negative has a direct, adverse relationship to performance. This is proven science. On the bike, I tell myself *yes* as I'm riding up to a difficult obstacle, and I take a deep breath. Mentally saying *I can't* and tensing up will guarantee a failed outcome, so just override the negative talk with positive every chance you get. As Henry Ford famously said, "Whether you think you can or think you can't, you're right."

Of course, there is no substitute for experience, nor is there any easy way to acquire it. This is where seasoned racers have an edge. The more rides in the rain, races where you've flatted or bonked, mental challenges you've faced, finish lines you've crossed, the bigger mental toolbox you have to draw from when the going gets tough. If you've seen a challenge before, it's easier to deal with in an effective manner. This may not seem like mental training, but by gathering these experiences, you can then tell yourself, *I've got this. I've been through worse before.*

14

Winning & Losing

In 2012, Red Bull asked me to find an endurance project that would push me into new territory. I welcomed the challenge. The one thing that has kept me motivated and at the top of my game for so long is my ability to adapt in pursuit of my passion. It is sweet to feel the speed of a horse race like Leadville and have what you need waiting for you in aid stations along the way, but more and more I wanted to return to my adventurous roots and explore what results my new cycling fitness could deliver. I researched notorious ultra-endurance trails, Guinness World Records in distance and time, and epic multiday cycling events like the Tour Divide and Race Across America. Unsupported ultra-endurance rides like Iditabike, Colorado Trail Race, and Arizona Trail Race seemed to bring together my adventure racing and cycling experience.

Ultimately, I set my sights on breaking the women's record for the Kokopelli Trail, 142 miles of rocky mountain-bike trail that goes from Moab, Utah, to Fruita, Colorado, climbing 20,000 feet, and ranging in elevation from 4,000 to 8,000 feet. I had read about the route and the records that had been set there, but I never considered attempting the record until Red Bull prompted me to dream big.

Going for a record-breaking individual time trial on the Kokopelli Trail was above all else a personal challenge. Although my effort would be publicized, there would be no prize money, no spectators, no one on the trail except for me. The only cheering would be the voice in my own head, the only tangible reward my name and time recorded on an obscure web site.

The Kokopelli Trail is a mountain biker's theme park. At one point it played host to an unsactioned race that ran the entire length of the trail. That race no longer exists, but riders still make nonstop attempts to set personal bests or break records all the time. Ultra-endurance cycling fanatics are more interested in speed than frivolity, and they take their sport quite seriously. There is a set of rules that must be followed precisely if you want your attempt to be considered legitimate. The more blogs and stories I read about this route, the more my mind was made up.

We labeled my attempt the Red Bull Rusch Hour and put it on the calendar for April 2013. I would handle all of the planning myself, and Red Bull would provide a skeleton film crew to intersect with me at certain sections and document my attempt. Their focus was to produce a short film that would use my ride to illustrate the power of setting and charging after your own goals.

I began researching the equipment I'd need such as a water filter, headlamp, and map data. I also explored route information, including water sources. Everything I would need on the trail—except water—I had to carry with me, including a tracking device and Garmin to prove I completed the correct route and to verify my time. Even with a film crew intersecting with me occasionally, I could receive no support, no directions, absolutely no help at all. I was strict with the crew that I didn't even want them to talk to me when I was on the course. Even though they needed to get footage, I wanted to be certain my attempt was legitimate and no one could say I received support. I also wanted to stay in my own solitary world.

I started at midnight with Greg and four other people cheering as I pulled away from the Slickrock parking lot in Moab and headed up Sand Flats Road. My strategy was to start at night to take advantage of the cooler temperatures for the biggest climbs on the course. The challenge for this ride, besides the sheer distance, was route finding in desert maze, sourcing water, and being totally self-sufficient throughout the journey.

I started the ride with just a Garmin course profile and valuable information from previous riders, but I'd never ridden an inch of the trail. Scheduling my attempt in the spring meant that the trail was inaccessible until just a few days before the ride, when the snow had melted off the high-altitude sections. Also, I had other races, other training, and other work competing for my time. A recon trip just wasn't an option, and if I wanted to make this attempt, this was the only window of opportunity that fit into the rest of my race schedule. I studied the maps, the critical intersections, the descriptions from other riders, but that was the best preparation I could do. I was venturing into the unknown and was really excited about it.

I may have been a little too excited, because I knocked out that first 3,000 feet of climbing and 20 miles in just two hours and was completely in the zone and loving it. I did not need other athletes in front of me to find motivation to push harder. The temperatures were in the 40s, but I'd been working so hard that I was dripping with sweat. Before descending I put on my thin wind jacket and gloves as my heart pounded. This was a race for me, and every precious second counted; those seconds would add up many hours later.

Minutes into the first descent I was flying at top speed and relishing the fact that the biggest climb was now behind me. Suddenly, my front tire caught a rut that was hidden in the shadows. I was flat on the ground before I ever had a chance to brake. My first though was *Is the bike okay?* My next was *Oh, I tore my shorts.* Then came this realization: *My left index finger is in the wrong place.* It was actually pointing straight back at me, taunting me for being careless. Instinctively, I reset my finger, gingerly flexed it to be sure I could still operate my brake lever, and saddled back up to keep going. I was stopped less than a minute. In my mind, it was just a minor hiccup that meant I could no longer reach into my left pocket or use my left hand to filter water or dig into my Camelbak. Otherwise, everything was fine.

I was sailing along, loving the isolation and the intensity and racing my heart out. Around 4 a.m. I reached a short, sharp climb that was full of rocks and required hiking the bike. Previous men's record holder Dave Harris had named this incline Four-Hour Hill based on the time it took him to reach this point on the route. This was the only landmark on the entire course for which I had a split time to shoot for. It was the first reassurance that I was at a really good, record-breaking pace, not only for the women's record but maybe even the men's. The celebration didn't last long.

Just a few minutes later, as I made the turn onto a section called the Rose Garden and some of the most technical trails on the course, my light malfunctioned. It just flickered once and went black. In all my years of adventure racing and 24-hour racing, I'd never had a light malfunction. I had calculated the battery life and had been running the beam on low to save juice. There should have been plenty. All I could think was that in the crash I had damaged the light when my head smacked the ground.

Back in my hotel room as I was packing for this ride, I had laid out all of my gear and selectively edited every bit of food, clothing, tools, and equipment I would carry. I wanted to be as light as possible and have just the essentials. It was a risk, but I had elected not to bring a backup light source. I had stood there with both lights in my hands and made the conscious decision that I trusted my equipment and I would take just one light.

To this point, I was on pace, but now in the dark in the middle of the Utah desert with 2.5 hours until sunrise, I was stopped dead in my tracks. The thought of turning back never entered my mind. If I was going to ride in the dark, at least I could stay on the trail that was marked on my GPS. There was nowhere to go but forward and nothing to do but try to ride by moonlight. Even for the most technical section of the course, this would be my strategy. As hard as this was, the nearly full moon was my savior. I had not planned the timing of my attempt with the moon, so this was just a lucky break. Had it been pitch black, riding any of this trail would have been impossible.

This section of the Kokopelli Trail is littered with softball-sized rocks and hemmed in by rock ledges and drop-offs. My eyes were wide as I tried to decipher the terrain in the moonlight. I kept my body as loose and jello-like as I could to absorb the impact of unseen obstacles as I rode over them. I was bobbling, surfing, and balancing the bike as best as I could to keep moving.

When I couldn't ride in the dark, I'd just run. All I had to do was make it until sunrise without stopping, just keep pedaling and running with the bike, making progress. It was a rough two hours, a full body and mind drain. Just as I was getting out of the most technical terrain and back onto smoother dirt roads, the sun slowly lit up the sky and I was still on my bike in one piece.

I had lost precious time, but could now get back to work. I had finally reached Dewey Bridge at the Colorado River, the approximate halfway point. If I had stayed on my original pace, I would have been there an hour earlier. Greg was there with the film crew, and I could see he was concerned. He knew something had happened out there in the night that caused me to slow down. As I flew past them, I pointed at my light and then gave him a feeble thumbs-up to let him know I was okay.

The next section of the course was high-speed, flat desert riding, so I put in a big effort to make up for lost time and take care of my nutrition. The nighttime debacle had taken all of my focus, so I hadn't eaten or drunk enough water. I was still ahead of the women's record, but not by very much. I wanted to claw some of that time back to provide a buffer for any other potential mishaps such as crashes or getting lost. I had calculated that I needed to stay above an average of 10 miles per hour in order to come in under the record. At this point, I was at a 10.2 miles per hour average. I was on target, but the last 20 miles of the trail are also much slower, with some hiking and technical singletrack, so I needed a bigger cushion.

Although I had a GPS with the course marked and there are tiny signs along the way, the braided network of trails in this part of the desert required me to stop and look at the map more than a few times to verify the route. I only saw the film crew one more time on my ride, just as I descended a huge hill into Rabbit Valley. I let out a celebratory yell as I eased off the brakes and gravity took over. The 500-foot descent to Salt Creek and climb back out the other side was the last major obstacle before I hit the Mary's Loop Trail system, which would take me to the finish.

I had been out of water for about an hour. I knew this was going to happen because I had made a calculated decision to bypass the last available water stop at Westwater Ranger Station, which was a 3-mile detour off course. I didn't want to take the extra time to go there, so I gambled and filtered water at the last possible point on the muddy Colorado River. This meant riding about 70 miles to the finish without another water stop, in the heat of the afternoon. By Salt Creek, I was less than miles from the finish. I could have stopped to filter water there, and I had that in my head as a backup plan, but when I got to the creek, the bridge was high above it and I didn't want to take the time to walk down the banks and push through the willows to get to water.

I was still ahead of schedule, but didn't know how long the last technical trails would take. I gambled again, passed up the water, and started the trudge up the other side of the deep ravine with my bike on my back. Once on the singletrack, I began seeing other day riders. I was still wearing my useless bike light on my helmet, carrying much more than a normal rider would, and had a glazed look in my eyes. Greg had ridden out on the trail to offer me a bit of company for the last miles. I was so grateful to see him, because it meant I was close. He rode just ahead of me, warning the other riders on the trail that there was a zombie coming through.

I was riding like I'd never ridden a bike before—completely spent, dehydrated, and with nothing left in my legs. I had to walk over plenty of the rocky climbs and obstacles. Normally these trails would be a blast, but right now they felt like climbing Everest. When I could, I let off the brakes and allowed momentum to take over. Finally, I was on the last turn off the singletrack, with one more 50-foot climb to the parking lot and the trailhead that marks the end of the route.

Coach Dean was like a mirage standing on the trail in the middle of this hill, cheering for me. "Last hill. You look good," he said as he ran along next to me. As I crested the hill, I saw the film crew waiting, heard music pumping, and a small gathering of Red Bull and Specialized friends came into view. They were clogging up the parking lot and jumping up and down. After 13.5 hours of solitary riding, it was a sensory shock, but a welcome sight.

Before celebrating, I carefully saved the file in my Garmin. I was fearful that in my stupor I'd somehow not stop the timer or erase the file by accident, so I put all my attention into doing that task correctly before anything else. Finally, I could step off the bike, remove the Camelbak that had become part of my body, and take off my bloody glove. The injury hadn't slowed me down more than a minute or two on the ride; ten hours later, when I took off my glove and saw the extent of the damage, the pain finally kicked in. I had dislocated my finger so far back that it had ripped the skin on the underside of my knuckle in a jagged tear. I could see tissue and tendons.

As we posed for pictures, the magnitude of my dehydration, exertion, and the extent of my finger injury sank in. As I started to walk toward a chair, telling Greg I needed to sit down, my body shut down. I passed out and was falling face first onto the gravel parking lot when Greg, who always has my back, made a miraculous catch before I face-planted. When I woke up a few seconds later, I was staring up at Greg, Dean, and the film crew, all of whom were wondering what had happened. All I wanted to do was sit in that parking lot and soak in one of the biggest accomplishments of my life. Instead, I spent the next eight hours in the emergency room, getting to know the hand specialist very well. The finger healed okay, but it'll always look a little screwed up. It actually curves a bit, like the bent figure of the trickster Kokopelli, a permanent souvenir I'll always carry with me.

ONE OF MY FAVORITE books of all time is *The Things They Carried*, a collection of short stories by Tim O'Brien about a platoon of American soldiers in the Vietnam War. His stories weave friendships and hardships with what we choose to carry along with us in our lives—our emotional baggage, our memories, and physical items that often represent something much bigger. In my travels, I've carried Tibetan prayer beads in my truck, my dad's MIA bracelet, photos of friends, and even a little ceramic gnome that Greg gave me when we first met. I carry the scar on my thigh from rebuilding my Bronco and now my new Kokopelli finger. I also have those four big shiny belt buckles from each of my memorable wins in Leadville.

Many people do Leadville for reasons that have nothing to do with belt buckles or race results. The physical challenge is part of a much bigger journey. They are there because they've lost loved ones or a limb or something important deep inside. Some are conquering an illness or challenging themselves to do something that seems impossible. They are there to win something back, to prevail over the altitude and the freezing rain and the big mountains, to show they can stand up to the hardships of life and emerge victorious. And they do this again and again, year after year.

The race had never been about that for me. It was about tapping into my personal best and, honestly, about winning so I can continue doing what I love to do as a paid professional athlete. It's my job. To that end, I'd gone to work once again in 2013, scrutinized my past results, crunched power meter numbers, and painstakingly studied the details of all this data to see if I could squeak out just a little bit more speed. Was it possible at 44 years old? I wasn't sure, but I was going to try.

Coach Dean and I, now headed into our second year together, had developed a fantastic working relationship, and my year of preparation was unfolding well. I'd had success at my early season races, with wins at Trans Andes, Dirty Kanza, Marathon Mountain Bike Nationals, and my record-breaking ride on the Kokopelli Trail. Dean was happy with the improvement of my power numbers. We also both knew that experience pays off in Leadville, and I had more of it than any woman out there. With four consecutive wins to my name, I no longer had to prove myself, and I wasn't feeling the pressure like I had in previous years.

I touched down in Leadville nearly two weeks early again, happy to have the time to acclimate, make some appearances, tweak my bike, enjoy some solitary riding, and generally put the final touches on getting myself race ready. Then, three days before race day, I was on the phone with my assistant and fellow firefighter Emilee and heard her Ketchum Fire Department pager go off in the background. She stopped talking, and we both listened to a page about a female bicyclist with major injuries. It ended with radio traffic from the medics on scene saying the case was a "no transport to the hospital." Emilee and I both knew this meant the cyclist hadn't survived the crash.

We continued our conversation, but it was difficult to concentrate. Ketchum is a small town, and it was likely someone I knew. When I joined the fire department, I knew there would inevitably be calls like this, and friends might be involved.

Later that evening, another friend called and told me the cyclist was my friend Bonni Curran. I could barely process what I was hearing. She'd been hit by a truck in downtown Ketchum, right in front of the local bike shop, as she rode on her townie home from the store and a pedicure. They said something about her wobbling and falling into the truck's path, underneath the rear wheels. She was crushed and killed instantly. I stopped hearing as my brain struggled to wrap itself around what I was being told.

My friend Bonni—Bonni with the huge smile and gigantic heart, the most impressive woman I've ever met—was dead. Whatever the adventure, Bonni was the ringleader. She fished and ran and rode her bike everywhere. With her boundless energy, she seemed to have time and inspiration for anyone and everyone. She was a mother of two who traveled the world and wanted to squeeze every drop of experience out of life. She was a doctor who cared so much about helping others that she helped set up a women's clinic in Cambodia. She served on the boards of the Sun Valley Center for the Arts and the nexStage Theater. She was one of those rare gems who made us all strive to be better, to do more, to give freely, and to openly love life. This amazing woman was dead. I was silent and hung up the phone, too stunned to cry.

I called Greg at home in Ketchum and told him the news. Then, the next day, I called my coach Dean and told him. I called my sister and a few close friends. My shock broke, and the tears finally fell. Suddenly none of this race crap mattered. As I sat there, lost in my grief, trying to ride my bike fast above 10,000 feet seemed like a ridiculous notion. A year of preparation, visualization, and riding in the rain and cold was rendered pointless. Maybe I should have just spent more time riding with Bonni and my other friends—after all, they didn't care if I held the Leadville course record or not. And now neither did I.

I spent the next two days aimlessly spinning around Leadville with a heavy heart. The stormy weather leading up to the race matched my dreary mood. I tried to fall into my usual preparations, but I was just going through the motions, as if I was on autopilot, without any real purpose. Instead of doing hill sprints to prepare, I'd stop at my favorite places along the course, stare out at the mountains and question why I was here and not at home to mourn properly with my community. My motivation was gone. I was empty.

When Greg finally arrived in Leadville on the Thursday before the event, it felt so good to fall into his arms and cry. All of my doubts and questions spilled out, and I confided in him that I didn't think I could ride, let alone race, on Saturday—I was considering going home. "You need to line up," he replied flatly, without hesitation. "No matter what, you need to line up and dig deep and give it 110 percent like you always do. You aren't just here for yourself. You are here to inspire others to do what seems impossible to them. Your presence out there matters to them." The tears silently rolled down my cheeks as he continued, steadfast. "Rebecca, listen. Now you're facing your own challenge. If you quit, what message does that send to everyone who is here facing theirs?"

I braved poster signings at the SRAM and Specialized booths and posed for pictures with fans, a hollow smile plastered on my face. I pretended to be excited for the thousands of racers around me. I felt I had to continue to do my job—not for me, but for them. I carried Greg's words to the athlete meeting, where racers gather to get final details and are served a gigantic dose of motivation by race founders Ken and Merilee. The excitement and tension at these meetings are palpable, and they often end with chanting and cheering. Normally, I sit in the front row, soaking in the explosive energy. This time, I hung back behind the stage, trying to be invisible yet still fulfill my duties to be there.

During the presentation, Dave Wiens and I were called onstage to say a few words as past winners and the only athletes with multiple race wins. Dave is a good friend, and I respect him as much as any athlete I've ever met. I had told him the situation earlier, so he knew I was hurting. He put a supportive arm around me as we stepped onstage. As we were handed the microphone, he quietly asked if I wanted to say anything. I swallowed, took the microphone, and unexpectedly opened up to the sea of strangers.

"I recently lost a good friend and almost went home," I told them, fighting back tears. I went on to explain that the only reason I stayed in Leadville was for all of them, and that I looked forward to sharing a great day on the course with them the next day. It felt good to let everyone know how I felt. A little bit of the heaviness lifted. Dave, the ultimate people's champion, gave me a hug, and we left the stage.

I was met by a line of athletes who came up to me to give me a hug, tell me about their own losses, share notes of inspiration, and thank me for being there with them. It was now crystal clear that my presence at Leadville was bigger than a time on the clock or four wins. Like Bonni, all of these people loved to see me win. But now I could feel that they really appreciated that I was human, and they were now offering their strength and encouragement to inspire me. My new purpose was to show others what is possible when you give it your all and resist the urge to walk away or quit. That's exactly what I had to do— follow my own advice and not give a halfhearted effort. If I didn't go out there and race, I would disappoint myself or anyone else who looks to other riders for inspiration. Exhausted and weak, I was no longer the steely competitor motivating thousands of others. Racing would require every ounce of courage and strength that this extended family of riders was offering me.

Although I had a renewed sense of purpose, I confess I was still struggling to put my grieving, spinning mind into race mode. I had done this race so many times, so I had mastered the pre-race ritual of prepping my bike and my gear. That part was easy. What I really didn't know how to do in this uncharted territory was find race motivation, that extra 1 percent it takes to go as fast as possible and really make yourself hurt on race day. I was already hurting and didn't want to feel more pain. Again, Greg brought me back to reality. "Forget the time splits, the results, the expectations, and just go and do what you know how to do. Race your bike as hard as you can."

I rode for Bonni that day, and I carried her with me the entire way. I was riding because I could. Every inch of that course is burned into my memory, so I instinctively pushed in sections I liked and recovered where I knew I could. I met Greg's supportive gaze as I sailed through the aid stations. I didn't slack off. It physically hurt because I was truly racing. But I was also looking into the clear sky at the top of the world and into the eyes of the other competitors as I rode down Columbine. I was soaking in the strength from people shouting my name at Twin Lakes. As I crested Powerline and let go of the brakes, I looked out across Turquoise Lake and the surrounding snowcapped peaks, the tears flying off my cheeks.

When I reached the Powerline climb it was clear that the race would not be mine this year. I would cross the line in third place, and the women's course record would likely change hands. In the end, both first and second place broke my record—smashed it, really.

Yet even with the burden of my sadness, I rode only six minutes slower than my fastest time. I was genuinely happy with my finish. The sight of the red carpet brought elation and satisfaction because I knew I rode well. I followed Greg's advice and simply raced my bike. It was my most difficult Leadville to date, but also probably my biggest achievement on the course. Dean agreed that it was one of my best performances of the year. At the finish, I broke into tears in Greg's arms, crying for the loss of a dear friend but also shedding tears of joy for the privilege of riding in the Race Across the Sky with the biggest family I could ever dream of having.

On paper, I lost. I fell short of one of my biggest goals for the year. In my own mind, I won. I didn't give up when it would have been easier to do so. By digging deeper than I had before, I won something far more important and learned what Leadville and racing are really all about.

15

Keeping It Real

When I started gathering sponsors for my first adventure racing team, I couldn't have fathomed that I would still be racing as a professional athlete 15 years later. As the end of each year of racing approaches, I find myself again staring into the unknown. My partnerships are negotiated annually, and if I don't prove myself to be a viable investment year after year, I will find myself on the chopping block. The uncertainty of it all is a tremendous weight; winning year after year is the only way out from under it. Paying a mortgage, buying health insurance, and planning for retirement are burdens for everyone, but they can seem exponentially overwhelming given the unpredictability of the career I have chosen. I've gone long stints without insurance, which is risky in a job that requires me to be healthy and mobile at all times. Never in my life have I purchased a brand-new car, because I always need to pay cash up front.

Early in my career, I embraced the uncertainty. When I was living out of my car, I had a Home Is Where the Heart Is magnet from my mom stuck proudly on my dashboard. It was a vaguely reassuring sentiment when I was a nomad, but as the years went on, I was eager to seek out stability, find a place where I could always return. In the past few years I fell in love with Ketchum and settled down. My home is most definitely in Idaho.

I've dug in deeper here than I ever imagined. Greg and I had been living together in my condo for years, but now we were looking at purchasing a house to have more space and build a permanent life together. As I signed the mortgage papers for our house, my hand was sweaty and shaky. My entire life, all I had wanted was freedom: from commitment, from bills, from any strings that threatened to tie me down. When I sold my Bronco a few years earlier, I cried as I watched the new owners drive her away. Betty was a symbol of my independence and freedom, and I worried that my days of adventure were coming to an end. Then I realized that my adventures weren't over; they would just start from a fixed address. When it came time for Greg and me to move into our house, all those special things I had gathered from around the world in my travels suddenly found a home too. There are masks from Fiji, a machete from Borneo, mate cups from Argentina, prayer flags from Tibet, carpets from Kyrgyzstan, and hundreds of other items I gathered and carried with me en route to Idaho.

This professional athlete life can be a bizarre existence. I'm away from home more than half of the time, living out of a suitcase and taking part in intense experiences. The schedule is nonstop, often taking me to far-flung places. Sometimes I'm treated like a rock star: People ask me for photos, autographs, and interviews. When I step off the plane in Idaho, though the mountain air is cleansing and I love coming home to Greg and our dog, Diesel, reentry is tough. It's back to picking up dog poop, doing laundry, and taking out the trash. And, after especially grueling events, it can take several days for me to muster the energy to get back to my normal routine. But coming back to a home and the schedule and predictability of everyday life is what keeps me grounded.

Most surprising to me is that I've become a homebody, embracing the comforting tasks that accompany "normal" life. Despite having a pretty black thumb, digging in my garden is therapeutic. There were many, many meals of canned tuna and ramen noodles when I was living out of my car and hunting down paychecks. Now that I have an actual kitchen, I love making bread and having someone to cook for.

I've always joked that when I have a garage I'll know I've really made it. Now I do, with a place for all my bikes, tools, skis, and my motorcycle. It's one of my favorite rooms in the house. I've amassed an impressive collection of gear over the years, and my garage gives me the space to indulge my inner Virgo and be a little neurotic about how it's organized.

In more than 20 years of traveling, I have developed deep friendships with people in all corners of the world, from Australia to Kansas. Although I might not see some of them for years at a time, the friendships were forged in the sweat of many miles racing together. Being able to open my home and offer a haven to my adventure racing, climbing, paddling, and cycling friends as well as my family is one of the most satisfying feelings I've ever experienced. Seeing as how I crashed at so many friends' homes during my nomadic years, it's nice to be able to offer a crash pad to others.

Outside of being able to buy a home in Ketchum and make a living here, I've been able to take part in building a community. Getting involved in the local fire department and hosting my own event in Idaho have helped ground me and pave a path to the future for myself and my community. I sit in city council meetings, take part on advisory boards, and offer my opinion when asked by local business owners and policy makers. It's gratifying to be able to give back to the community that welcomed me with open arms.

As a professional racer, I ride in some of the most sublime places on the planet. It's a privilege to do this as my 9–5 job. But honestly, there's no place I'd rather be than nestled in the mountains in my own backyard.

For so many, Idaho is a state to fly over or pass through on their way to another, more-well-marketed destination. When I tell people where I'm from, they often look at me with blank stares. Sometimes they pause and ask, "Iowa?" Everyone seems to associate Idaho with potatoes, but it's also a land of jagged mountains and wildflowers blooming as far as the eye can see. There are endless miles of single-track and distant dirt roads leading to ancient glacial basins—the type of high country that epitomizes western landscape. Best of all, you don't have to share it with hordes of tourists or thrill seekers. The ano-nymity of this corner of the world is one of its greatest traits.

Instead of trying to describe Idaho to people I meet in my trav-els, in 2013 I created my own destination ride, Rebecca's Private Idaho, so I can simply bring people here and show them firsthand why it's heaven on earth. The idea sprouted after taking part in a couple of unlikely events, the first of which I only agreed to do out of obligation to a sponsor. The Dirty Kanza 200, as the name suggests, is a 200-mile gravel-road race through the Flint Hills of Kansas. With 12 hours being the fastest time and not a mountain or singletrack trail in sight, I was convinced this event represented death by boredom. I loaded up my iPod with the best playlist I had in hopes of staying awake and some-what motivated without the usual external stimulus.

I was wrong about gravel racing. The thousands of other people who line up every year obviously feel the same way. It was a superb event, and those little shards of stone really added a challenging and interesting aspect to the ride. After riding my first gravel-road event, I was convinced that gravel is the great equalizer for roadies and moun-tain bikers. It's a middle ground that's technical, challenging, and exhil-arating no matter what bike you ride. After my maiden gravel voyage, I realized gravel-road riding was also the ticket to get more people on their bikes and to showcase the maximum amount of stellar terrain. Since there is more gravel than pavement around Ketchum, this format was a no-brainer.

The other event that inspired me was Levi's GranFondo. This is another popular event that draws cyclists to Santa Rosa, California, by the thousands for a massive ride that somehow retains the feel of a small-town community event despite the numbers. I wanted my event to include the best of Dirty Kanza and GranFondo: miles of gravel trail traversing Idaho's remote terrain with Ketchum's hometown vibe. Rebecca's Private Idaho was born.

I began the laborious process of building a brand, gathering partners, and rallying a mountain of volunteers and local business support. My goal was simple: to ride with cyclists on my very own training ground, putting on display what I see every day from my front porch. I also wanted to use my reach as a professional athlete to support cycling in a more meaningful way. I've never had much disposable income to donate to worthy causes, but I do have a public name and image that I can use to bring support to the causes I believe make the world a better place.

With the idea formulated in my head and friends and sponsors holding my hand, I announced the event to the public and held my breath to see if anyone would actually show up. A great idea doesn't necessarily mean a great event. Hosting an event for hundreds of people with my name attached to it was both all-consuming and ter-rifying. If I failed, it would be a very public and expensive flop. Like anything I've ever done, I was not alone, and I didn't want to disap-point my supporters. This idea would not have taken off if it weren't for some key personal and industry friends who gave me the collective push to go for it.

Heading into the event, I endured the most challenging two months of my life to date. I was still reeling from the heavy emotional blow of my friend Bonni's death. On top of this, the risk and workload involved in launching a new event was grinding me down. And then there was the fact that I had just purchased my first home. Never mind the financial stress of committing to the biggest purchase of my life, it was the sawdust and disruption of moving and remodeling that really wore on me. Greg and I were gutting the place with our own bare hands. For a month, I didn't have a moment to ride my bike, but at least all of the moving demolition was giving me a great strength workout. I was juggling like never before. But there were 250 riders registered for Rebecca's Private Idaho, and all of the pieces were fitting nicely into place.

Just 16 days out from race day, lightning struck near Ketchum, beginning a horrific domino effect that would lead to the biggest forest fire the Rocky Mountains would see that year. I was in Canada at a SRAM Gold Rusch event when I heard the news: The fire was moving toward Ketchum, and mandatory evacuations were under way. Just 24 hours and a few hundred dollars in airline change fees later, I was on my way home to go to work with the fire department.

By the time I got there, the blaze was completely overwhelming the Wood River Valley. The airport and most local businesses were closed, the air was heavy with smoke, and nearly all of the residents were being evacuated. In their place, an operational camp city had sprung up with 2,000 firefighters, hundreds of rigs, and a complete command structure to deal with the 126,000-acre fire. I headed into the black cloud, the sole vehicle driving north in a sea of people fleeing the scene.

The next five days were spent working 17-hour shifts on structure protection and watching the skies turn orange. My event coordinator and course director are also members of the fire department, so all work on Rebecca's Private Idaho came to a screeching halt during the fire. Our singular focus was protecting our community as the fire was quickly upgraded to a Type 1 (the highest level) incident. The stress of my dream being crushed and my hometown in turmoil was overwhelming, without even considering my professional and personal responsibilities. I was near the limits of my endurance.

Ten days from event day, I had to decide whether or not the event would go on. I jumped rank, going directly to the Operations Branch Director on the fire. Captain John Kennedy from the Reno Fire Department happened to be an avid cyclist, and he'd heard I lived here and was on scene. He was more than willing to consult with me on the decision. We pored over maps to make educated guesses on fire and smoke movement and containment. Captain Kennedy also consulted with the head meteorologist. His input was somewhat reassuring, but there were no guarantees. We were trying to predict how the fire would behave. By now the blaze had burned over 100,000 acres, and only 20 percent was contained. I made the risky decision to host the event as planned, thinking the fire would be brought under control in the nick of time. Incredibly, it was. Over the next few days the fire containment numbers continued to grow and crews were slowly sent home. The tide had turned, and the air was clearing.

Ketchum came back to life, and Rebecca's Private Idaho was a much-needed celebration for a community back from the brink. As RPI visitors rolled into town, Thank You, Firefighter signs could be seen in windows of local businesses and all throughout the residential neighborhoods. The sense of relief and joy among the locals returning to their homes was palpable. There were street parties nearly every day, with firefighters treated as honorary guests. I proudly wore my Ketchum Fire Dept. T-shirt , not just for the free beer, but out of pride for being able to do my small part to protect my community. As the riders arrived for the event, community leaders and shop owners thanked me for bringing tourists back to town following the big losses they had endured during peak season because of the fire.

On September 1, 2013, my dream became a reality. Standing on the start line the sky was free of smoke and a banner with my name in bold letters stretched overhead, bringing tears to my eyes. People came, sponsors rallied behind me, and everyone pitched in. Riders were smiling and ready to roll 100 miles through my beloved training grounds. I felt light as a feather. Our announcer called out the race start: "Three. Two. One. Giddyup!" and I crossed my personal finish line and settled in for what would be my favorite ride of the year and one of my biggest accomplishments.

I took my place in the middle of the peloton. Flanked by my former coach, my sponsors, and my friends, I couldn't wipe the smile from my face. I rode with different people throughout day, chatting, fixing flats, snapping photos, offering motivation, socializing at aid stations, and eventually rolling across the finish in the middle of the pack. It was the best ride I've ever done. I closed out the day by celebrating with live music and plenty of beer sliding my way in a grand display of Gelande Quaffing. It was the perfect end to a fantastic ride.

I have high hopes that this event will become my legacy. I want even more people to know about the scenery, the hospitality, and the sheer perfection that my Idaho home offers cyclists. More than that, though, after so many years living as a nomad and laying my head down in so many different towns, Ketchum welcomed me with open arms. I knew I was home the first week I arrived. There was no pretense, no cliques, just small-town hospitality and jaw-droppingly beautiful terrain. The mountains sell themselves.

When they come to Rebecca's Private Idaho I want people to feel like they're Idaho locals, if only for a few days. That it takes place from the seat of a bike is just a convenience, something we all share that helps us reach a bigger, better understanding of what's important in the world around us.

I'M PASSIONATE ABOUT preserving wild places like my Idaho home, but for a long time, I just cruised along, oblivious, taking it all for granted. I hiked, climbed, rode, and paddled around the world without giving much thought to what happened before or after I moved through a place. I was truly living in the moment with the friends and teammates who were with me, all of us soaking up one adventure and then charging on to the next. I had no savings or assurances for my own future, so I wasn't protecting the future of the outdoor places where I spent most of my time.

In the '90s, the Access Fund was formed to help keep climbing areas open, and I remember throwing a few bucks toward the cause, mainly because I didn't have more than a few bucks to offer. With cycling, it wasn't until some of my favorite local trails in the Boulder-White Cloud Mountains were threatened to become a designated wilderness area closed to bikes that I sat up and took notice. The idea was not to get all conveyances off the trail; they'd still allow hikers and horses (even though horses do more damage to trails than bikes), but by using the word *mechanical* instead of *motorized*, the designation lumped bikes into the same category as a motorcycle or ATV. I honestly believe the designation is antiquated, so I decided I should try to do something about it. I'm just one voice, but if I don't speak up, who else will? International businesswoman and activist Anita Roddick said it best: "If you think you are too small to make an impact, try going to bed with a mosquito in the room."

I started talking about trail advocacy and helped start the Wood River Bike Coalition in Idaho. This began as a small group of passionate local cyclists, spearheaded by Greg. There were plenty of meetings over beers and screenings of bike movies with a jar put out for donations before we eventually grew to have our own official International Mountain Bicycling Association (IMBA) chapter with members, trail work days, and a strong, collective voice. Now the coalition is involved in a groundbreaking multiuser group collaboration to protect recreation and conservation in the Boulder-White Cloud Mountains near my home. Swinging a Pulaski and moving rocks on our local trail work days is an excellent strength-training workout that feels so much more rewarding than moving weights around in a gym. There is also nothing better than riding a switchback that I've personally worked on or hearing other riders getting stoked about a new trail that I was part of creating.

There remains a bigger job that extends beyond Idaho: to rally for federal recreation funding and the development and protection of riding areas worldwide. I paid my IMBA dues and accepted a position as the chair of its honorary board, alongside cycling industry greats like Mike Sinyard and mountain bike legends Juliana Furtado, Hans Rey, Ned Overend, and Dave Wiens. I joined them because I felt I had to. I believe cyclists are the new generation of conservationists. Our human-powered vehicle of choice for exploration is a fast growing part of the recreation economy, and it's important for us to be at the table when access issues are discussed. Mountain bike racers are the most active cycling user group out on the mountain bike trails, but the lowest user group when it comes in advocacy. I don't mean to sound preachy, but if you ride a lot, you must give back just a little in whatever way you can. Don't wait until it's too late and your favorite place to ride lands on the chopping block. You might regret it.

As I've matured as an athlete, I've come to take pride in protecting and sharing what I know and love with others. Whether that's through Rebecca's Private Idaho, advocacy, or the SRAM Rusch to Glory events, it's grounded me and enriched my life in a new way. It's made me a little less terrified of what life will look like after the sponsors walk away. Because when the finish line celebration is a distant memory and the scars and muscle soreness have faded away, what you have left is the life you've woven together, the people in it, and the home you've built.

The Outer Limits

'm 45 years old and still racing faster than I ever have, beating men and women much younger than me, but my accomplishments can't be chalked up to pure talent or great genetics. In fact, I have surprised myself over and over again by doing things that were seemingly impossible, things that didn't come naturally to me. The human body is an incredibly adaptable machine, and this has played to my advantage when I've given myself permission to indulge in what-ifs and put in the hard work.

All my life I've been focused on what lies beyond what I know—whether it be outside the neighborhood I grew up in or over the next mountain pass. I've always pushed my potential, asking myself, *How far can I go? How fast can I go? What's around the next corner, and can I get there?* This openness and drive has defined my notion of what is within my grasp as an athlete.

Two decades of climbing, paddling, adventure racing, cross-country skiing, and mountain biking have made me a more resilient athlete, both physically and mentally. Along the way, I've received some coaching and plenty of advice—some of it good, some terrible. Through experimentation and exploring every opportunity, I've cobbled together my own education in how to become a better athlete than I ever thought possible. I've dedicated my career to self-study. What worked for me early on doesn't necessarily work for me now. For example, interval training overhauled my engine so I am more race car than diesel truck, and it's allowed me to train smarter instead of longer. I have ditched Swedish Fish and Cheetos as race fuel and bought into the nutritional theory of "garbage in equals garbage out." The impact of these changes is reflected in my test results from the Red Bull High Performance Team. As I have aged, my physiology has consistently improved. Every year, I experience gains in my VO_2max, a measurement of the body's ability to use oxygen. The higher the number, the better you can expect to train and race. My VO_2max is not off the charts in comparison to other professional athletes, but VO_2max is supposed to *decline* with age. It goes to show two simple truths: There's more to performance and winning than genetics, and physiology can be positively influenced by the choices we make and the time we invest.

Every year I've lined up in Leadville against much faster riders who have beaten me in the past and appear poised to beat me once again. Beyond my refined nutrition and training regime, my biggest advantage is that I know how to suffer and persevere. Mentally, I'm as tough as anyone. I don't quit. I break down and feel pain like everyone else, but I just don't quit. The shame of walking off the cross-country course so many years ago changed me. At first I balked at being called the Queen of Pain—I don't love suffering. But I'm not afraid to suffer. I'm not afraid to keep going. To me, going longer and farther means I'm en route to a new discovery. I like what I learn about myself and who I am when I push through to the other side.

Some people are born with tenacity, some hone it with experience, and others miss out on it altogether. In my case, I believe my tenacity was born out of the circumstances of my childhood: My sister and I learned to fend for ourselves as our single mom worked overtime to made ends meet. Sharon and I adapted to the daily challenges because that was the only option. We lived with the daily example of Mom's perseverance and absorbed the stories of Dad's commitment to the things he believed in. Our endurance and grit were born by circumstance and cultivated by the people around us.

The nontraditional sports I've pursued as an athlete only furthered my education in mental toughness. Whether it's climbing, paddling, adventure racing, or mountain biking, there's no team bus, no directeur sportif, and there's certainly not an organized development system to shepherd you through the ranks from amateur to professional. Hell, there aren't even really ranks, per se. It's simply win or lose most days of the week. You have to be hardened; you have to scrap for the wins. You have to make your own way.

The only thing harder than making a living in these sports is doing it as a woman. Apart from my experiences in paddling, I've spent the better part of my career surrounded by men. At the time I stumbled into these sports, the endurance sports scene was dominated by men. They welcomed me and taught me the ropes. Fortunately, I was completely oblivious to the idea that "girls didn't do these types of things." Throughout my career, I've been committed to passing on the same exposure and know-how that was given to me, and in recent years I've been thrilled to see more and more women succeed. Mental toughness has served me well in racing and in life.

Although there isn't an easy stat to quantify experience and mental toughness, it factors into the results every time you toe the line. When *Velo* magazine analyzed the power data from my 13.5-hour Kokopelli ride, my Training Stress Score (TSS) totaled 775. For reference, TSS is a value that indicates how hard and how long you worked out. An all-out 60-minute effort can earn you 100 TSS points, though it's difficult to get that many points in a single hour because it's rare to go full throttle for so long. But a score of 775 is off the charts. *Velo* described it as the "equivalent of doing nearly eight 40K time trials back to back at 100 percent effort." My TSS score was nearly double that of a typical "big day" for Tour de France riders, who average in the range of 250–400 TSS per stage. It's just a number, but I believe it's the difference that mental toughness makes.

Personally, I've never spent much time thinking about TSS and wattage. Both reinforce the effectiveness of my training; however, I'm more interested in what I can overcome—in the case of the Kokopelli ride, crashing, dislocating my finger, and dealing with equipment malfunctions. It's persevering through adversity, not mechanically putting out watts, that makes an epic journey that much more satisfying. Mental toughness is the result of testing and pushing against your limits, whether in a leech-infested jungle or in everyday training. It comes from experiencing harder efforts, heading out when it's raining or dark, and committing to something you've never done before. It changes your perspective on what is truly hard.

Mental toughness and experience are highly coveted, but it's a given that at some point during a race or on a big adventure you are going to feel like shit. The notion that it's somehow easier for pro athletes is a fallacy. As Leadville Trail 100 founder Ken Chlouber is fond of telling amateur athletes, "It hurts the pros just as much as it hurts you. It just doesn't hurt them for as long." All the problems you're likely to face—lack of motivation, burning lungs and legs, difficulty getting food and water down, the desire to quit—are the same ones I encounter. The only difference is that with experience, those issues become familiar and easier to ignore. What you do when you hit that rough patch and how you respond to those feelings are entirely within your control. And that's what separates winners from losers. Each time I persevere, I'm that much more primed to take on bigger and better challenges in life, both on and off the bike. I approach every challenge with the same winning formula: I follow my passion, work hard, and never give up.

I'll always race or put myself on an arbitrary start line, if only for the thrill of finishing. I'm addicted to finish lines, that place and time when my mind and body are simultaneously elated and exhausted. I live for that moment just after a competition or a brutal effort when the sweat is still soaking my clothes and the adrenaline still courses through my veins, but the pain has vanished into thin air. That is my drug of choice, and I need to keep feeling it over and over again. It's why I continue to push myself now and will go on doing so long after I've dropped off the top of the podium. This primal need to feel satisfied, in control, proud of my achievement, and better than I thought possible is insanely powerful. It is what keeps me going through cold training rides, hideous interval sessions, and hours on the indoor trainer.

My two proudest race achievements in 2013 were more personal than public, and neither one landed me on top of the podium. When I rode the Kokopelli Trail through the night, the only cheering to be heard was the voice in my own head. There was no prize money, no trophy to shelve, but the experience fed my addiction. When I finished third in Leadville, it was my lowest finish to date. But it was a race with unexpected challenges, so a finish, any finish, simply not quitting, was a massive victory. I'll keep indulging my competitive spirit as long as my body allows.

My next great adventure will require a combination of every skill I've been honing over my entire career. I'm in the early planning stages with Red Bull to ride the entire length of the Ho Chi Minh Trail that runs between North and South Vietnam, touching into Laos and Cambodia. The 800-mile maze of once-peaceful footpaths was dubbed The Blood Road and became the main artery for the movements of the entire Vietnam War. The bicycle was the essential tool that enabled supplies and weapons to be moved under the radar, hidden by the thick jungle canopy. The Ho Chi Minh Trail is also where my father's plane was shot down in 1972.

This bold expedition encompasses a great deal of history, both cultural and personal, and a tremendous physical challenge. To my knowledge, no one has ridden the length of this historic route. I plan to ride the route adventure-racing-style with a small, elite group of athlete friends. Selecting the team, mapping the course, and handling the logistics will make this expedition a multifaceted challenge. Along the way, route finding, managing the elements, taking care of ourselves, and cycling many miles a day will all be juxtaposed with the beauty and history of this route and our interaction with the locals who live along its edges.

At this stage in my life, I could quietly retire and ease into a role better suited to someone in their "middle years." But I've never had much use for resignation. It didn't enter into my head when I was plunging through the swirling rapids of the Colorado River in Grand Canyon, close to drowning. It had no place in the pitch-dark canyons of Morocco or the peaks of the Andes, shrouded in clouds. I've certainly never felt it in the rarified, lonely air of the mountains outside of Leadville. My next chapter may play out on a grand scale, or it may not, but that's hardly important. I remain eager to find new challenges that push my mind and body to new limits.

The way I see it, every moment is an opportunity to outlast and overcome the odds that threaten to either paralyze us or tether us to fear and doubt. The moments when we endure define us and mold us into the people we want to be, as athletes, leaders, or partners. In these agonizing spaces we learn who we are, and I'm grateful for every last one of them. I've built my career and my life around these moments. And I'm never going to stop chasing them.

RESULTS

Bold indicates career highlight.

2014

1st	Dirty Kanza 200, Female overall
3rd	24 Hours in the Old Pueblo, 4-Person Team, Female Open (w/high school girls team)
1st	Trans Andes Challenge, Solo Open Women

2013

1st	Brasil Ride 2013, Women's Team (w/Selene Yeager)
3rd	Leadville Trail 100 MTB
1st	**USA Cycling Marathon MTB National Championships, Women's Single-Speed**
1st	Trans Andes Challenge, Women's Solo
1st	Dirty Kanza 200
	Kokopelli Trail (Moab–Fruita) course record: 13:32.46
1st	24 Hours in the Old Pueblo, Duo Mixed (w/Nat Ross)

2012

1st	**Leadville Trail 100 MTB, women's course record: 7:28.06**
1st	Dirty Kanza 200, course record
1st	Milenio Titan Desert, Feminina, Morocco
1st	24 Hours of the Old Pueblo, duo team (w/Nat Ross)
3rd	USA Cycling Masters Road National Championships
4th	USA Cycling Masters TT National Championships
	Singletrack.com Mountain Biker of the Year

2011

1st **Leadville Trail 100 MTB (41st overall), women's course record: 7:31**
1st   Tour de la Patagonia, Mixed Category (w/Greg Martin)
1st   24 Hours of Argentina, Mixed Team (w/Cary Smith)
1st **USA Cycling Marathon MTB National Championships,**
      Women's Single-Speed
1st **USA Cycling 24-Hour MTB National Championships,**
      4-person women's team
2nd   La Ruta de Los Conquistadores, Costa Rica

2010

1st **Leadville Trail 100 MTB (22nd overall), women's course record: 7:47**
1st   Trans Andes, Open Women (w/Jennifer Smith)
1st   Tour of Patagonia, Open Women (w/Heidi Volpe)
1st **UCI Masters MTB World Championships, Women's 35–44, Brazil**
3rd   Red Centre Enduro, Australia
3rd   La Ruta de Los Conquistadores, Costa Rica
3rd   Trans-Sylvania Epic Stage Race

2009

6th   Cape Epic, South Africa, Mixed Division
      (w/Matthew Weatherley-White)
1st   Dirt, Sweat & Gears, 12-hour race
1st **World 24-Hour Mountain Bike Championships, Solo Division,**
      Canmore, Canada
1st **Leadville Trail 100 MTB (30th overall)**
1st   24 Hours of Targhee, Solo Division
1st **24 Hours of Moab–USA Cycling MTB National Championships,**
      Women's Duo (w/Gretchen Reeves)
1st   Idaho State Cyclocross Championships
1st   Vuelta al Cotopaxi, Ecuador, Mixed Team (w/ Greg Martin; 11th overall)
      USA Cycling Ultra Endurance Series Winner

2008

1st **USA Cycling 24-Hour MTB National Championships,**
      4-person women's team
1st **World 24-Hour Mountain Bike Championships, Solo Division,**
      Canmore, Canada
4th   USA Cycling Marathon MTB National Championships
1st **Masters World Cup Cross-Country Skiing Champion, 15K skate**

2007

1st   **World 24-Hour Mountain Bike Championships, Solo Division**
2nd   24 Hours of Moab, Women's Solo
1st   Mountain X-Games Adventure Race, Women's Team
       USA Cycling Ultra Endurance Series Winner

2006

1st   24 Hours of Spokane (1st Solo Overall, 1st Female)
1st   XPD Expedition Race, Tasmania (Team AROC/Mountain Designs)
1st   **USA Cycling 24-Hour MTB National Championships, Women's Solo**
6th   Adventure Racing World Championships, Sweden/Norway
       (Team Buff/Coolmax)
DNF   Primal Quest, Utah (Team Buff/Coolmax)
2nd   World 24-Hour MTB Championships, Women's Solo
4th   La Ruta de los Conquistadores MTB stage race, Costa Rica
1st   **24-Hour Orienteering National Championship**
       Idaho Mountain Express Athlete of the Year
       USA Cycling Ultra Endurance Series Winner

2005

4th   Explore Sweden, Sweden (Team Montrail)
DNF   Adventure Racing World Championships, New Zealand
5th   Raid World Championships qualifier, Australia
14th   Raid World Championships, France (Team Montrail/Revo)
1st   Tamarack Bushwhack Adventure Race, Female Solo
2nd   Women's International Adventure Race, Women's Duo, Spain
1st   24 Hours of Moab (4 person women's expert team;
       fastest female lap time)

2004

2nd   Raid World Championships Qualifier, Australia (Team Montrail/Revo)
4th   Bimbache Extreme Adventure Race, Canary Islands (Team Montrail)
DNF   Adventure Racing World Series, Newfoundland (Team Montrail)
DNF   Primal Quest Adventure Race, WA (Team Montrail)
DNF   Raid World Championships, Patagonia (Team Montrail/Revo)
       Adventure Sports Magazine's "Queen of Pain"
       Adventure Sports Magazine's 20 Most Pivotal People in
       Adventure Racing

2003

1st   **Raid Gauloises Adventure Racing World Championships, Kyrgyzstan (Team Montrail)**

3rd   Bimbache Extreme Adventure Race, Canary Islands (Team Montrail)

1st   Expedition Adventure Hidalgo, Mexico (Team Montrail)

1st   Appalachian Extreme, Maine (Team Montrail)

DNF   Primal Quest, California (Team Montrail)

2nd   Balance Bar 24-Hour Adventure Race series

5th   Mild Seven Outdoor Quest, Borneo (Team Montrail)

Sports Illustrated Adventure Racing Team of the Year

Outside Magazine's Top 20 Female Athletes of the Year

Competitor Magazine Endurance Sports Awards Adventure Racer of the Year

2002

5th   Expedition Adventure Hidalgo, Mexico (Team Montrail)

1st   **Raid the North Extreme, Yukon Territory (Team Montrail)**

4th   Raid Gauloises Vietnam (Team Montrail/Parallax)

1st   **U.S. White-water Rafting National Championships, Women's Team, Virginia**

2nd   Subaru Primal Quest, Colorado (Team Montrail)

DNF   Eco-Challenge Fiji (Team Montrail/Parallax)

2001

4th   Eco-Challenge New Zealand (Team Montrail)

3rd   Discovery Channel Adventure Racing World Championships, Switzerland (Team Montrail)

1st   Adventure Xtreme, Colorado

1st   Appalachian Extreme, North Carolina (Team Pearl Izumi)

1st-ever 300-mile self-supported descent of the Grand Canyon (w/Julie Munger and Kelley Kalafatich)

1st   **U.S. National White-water Rafting National Championships, Women's Team, Colorado**

3rd   Four Square Challenge Raft/Adventure Race, India (Team USA)

2000

7th   Raid Gauloises Trans Himalaya Tibet/Nepal
       (Team Tactel Ispira; highest-ranking American team to date)
8th   Eco-Challenge Borneo (Team Oobe; 2nd U.S. team)
       Lunar Ecstasy, 5.10, C2+, Zion, aid climb (1st female ascent)
**1st   Catalina Challenge, U.S. Outrigger Canoe Championships
       (Offshore Canoe Club)**
2nd   Camel White-water Challenge White-water Rafting World
       Championships, Chile (w/U.S. women's white-water rafting team)
DNF   Southern Traverse New Zealand (Team Wigwam/Ultimax—
       3 woman, 1 man)

1999

**4th   Eco-Challenge Argentina (Team Atlas Snowshoes/Rubicon,
       w/Cathy Sassin, Ian Adamson, Robyn Benincasa)**
       Romulan Warbird V, 5.9, C2, Yosemite 1999 (1st female ascent,
       1st solo ascent)

1998

       Eco-Challenge Morocco, finisher, unranked
       (Team Rubicon—3 women, 1 man)
1st   USA Supreme Adventure Race, Montana (Team SCAR)
       Skull Queen V, 5.10, A3, Yosemite, solo aid climb

1997

DNF   Eco-Challenge Australia (Team ROAM)
1st   Eco-Challenge Race Series, Malibu (Team ROAM)
1st   Hamilton International Outrigger Canoe Championships, Australia
       (Offshore Canoe Club)
1st   Survival of the Fittest, Canada
       Spaceshot, IV, 5.7, C2, Zion, solo aid climb

1996

1st   Hamilton International Outrigger Canoe Championships, Australia
       Lunar Ecstasy, Zion, Utah, 3-day aid climb, 1st female ascent
       (Offshore Canoe Club)
       **Bermuda Dunes, VI, 5.11c, A4, El Capitan, Yosemite (2nd ascent,
       1st female ascent)**

CREDITS

Front cover photo by Todd Meier Photography (toddmeier.com)
Back cover photo by Dan Campbell Photography
    (dancampbellphotography.com)
Photo of Rebecca Rusch on p. 279 by Michael Darter (michaeldarter.com)
Photo of Selene Yeager on p. 280 by Jaime Livingood
    (jaimelivingood.com)

First Photo Section

pp. 1–4: photos courtesy of the author
p. 5: Paul Markow (paulmarkow.com)
p. 6: Chris Kalous
p. 7: *above,* International Rafting Federation; *below,* Carr Clifton
    (carrclifton.com)
p. 8: photos by Carr Clifton

Second Photo Section

p. 1: Nate Galpin
p. 2: photos by Dan Campbell
p. 3: *above,* Dan Campbell; *below,* courtesy of the author
p. 4: photos by Corey Rich Productions (coreyrich.com)
p. 5: photos courtesy of the author
p. 6: photos by Dan Campbell
p. 7: *above,* courtesy of the author; *below,* Tim Holmstrom
p. 8: photos by Corey Rich Productions
p. 9: Dan Campbell
p. 10: photos by Marc Roussel (marcroussel.com)
p. 11: *above,* Tim Holmstrom; *below,* courtesy of the author
p. 12: *above,* courtesy of the author; *below,* Monica Dalmasso
    (coyotecity.com)
p. 13: Tony DiZinno
p. 14–16: photos by Dan Campbell

Third Photo Section

p. 1: Nate Galpin

p. 2: photos by John Gibson (gibsonpictures.com)

p. 3: photos by Michael Darter

p. 4: *above,* courtesy of the author; *below left,* Todd Meier; *below right,*
Glen Dellman (glendellman.com)

p. 5: Rocky Arroyo (arroyophotography.com)

p. 6: *above,* Glen Dellman; *below,* Todd Meier

p. 7: *above,* courtesy of the author; *below left,* Tal Roberts (talroberts.com);
below right, Kris Hanning Photography (krishanningphotography.com)

p. 8: photos by Josh Glazebrook (joshglaze.com)

ABOUT THE AUTHORS

REBECCA RUSCH is one of the great endurance athletes of her generation. She has amassed victories and broken records in endurance mountain biking, adventure racing, Nordic skiing, and white-water rafting. Through her SRAM Gold Rusch Tour, female media camps, and an all-girls mountain biking camp in her local community, Rebecca takes pride in sharing her love for cycling with women and girls. She also works as a firefighter in her beloved hometown of Ketchum, Idaho, where she also stages a charity race, Rebecca's Private Idaho, every August.

SELENE YEAGER is a top-selling professional health and fitness writer who lives what she writes as a certified personal trainer, USA Cycling certified coach, elite mountain bike racer with Rare Disease Cycling, and All-American Ironman triathlete. She has authored, coauthored, and contributed to more than two-dozen book titles and dishes out training advice monthly as *Bicycling Magazine's* "Fit Chick." Her work has appeared in numerous magazines and newspapers including *Details, Shape, O Magazine, Fitness, Redbook, Men's Health, Marie Claire, Better Homes & Gardens, Good Housekeeping, Mountain Bike, Runner's World, Better Health and Living, More, Cooking Light, The Bottom Line,* and *Cosmopolitan.* Yeager was nominated for a 2007 National Magazine Award for excellence in service journalism for her work in *Bicycling Magazine.*